Praise for *Effective XML*

"This is an excellent collection of XML best practices: essential reading for any developer using XML. This book will help you avoid common pitfalls and ensure your XML applications remain practical and interoperable for as long as possible."

**—Edd Dumbill, Managing Editor, XML.com
and Program Chair, XML Europe**

"A collection of useful advice about XML and related technologies. Well worth reading both before, during, and after XML application development."

—Sean McGrath, CTO, Propylon

"A book on many best practices for XML that we have been eagerly waiting for."

—Akmal B. Chaudhri, Editor, IBM developerWorks

"The fifty easy-to-read [items] cover many aspects of XML, ranging from how to use markup effectively to what schema language is best for what task. Sometimes controversial, but always relevant, **Elliotte Rusty Harold**'s book provides best practices for working with XML that every user and implementer of XML should be aware of."

**—Michael Rys, Ph.D., Program Manager, SQL Server
XML Technologies, Microsoft Corporation**

"*Effective XML* is an excellent book with perfect timing. Finally, an XML book everyone needs to read! *Effective XML* is a fount of XML best practices and solid advice. Whether you read *Effective XML* cover to cover or randomly one section at a time, its clear writing and insightful recommendations enlighten, entertain, educate, and ultimately improve the effectiveness of even the most expert XML developer. I'll tell you what I tell all my coworkers and customers: You need this book."

**—Michael Brundage, Technical Lead, XML Query Processing,
Microsoft WebData XML Team**

"This book provides great insight for all developers who write XML software, regardless of whether the software is a trivial application-specific XML processor or a full-blown W3C XML Schema Language validator. **Mr. Harold** covers everything from a very important high-level terminology discussion to details about parsed XML nodes. The well-researched comparisons of currently available XML-related software products, as well as the key criteria for selecting between XML technologies, exemplify the thoroughness of this book."

—Cliff Binstock, Author, *The XML Schema Complete Reference*

Effective XML

Effective SOFTWARE DEVELOPMENT SERIES ⋏⋎

Scott Meyers, Consulting Editor

The **Effective Software Development Series** provides expert advice on all aspects of modern software development. Books in the series are well written, technically sound, of lasting value, and tractable length. Each describes the critical things the experts almost always do—or almost always avoid doing—to produce outstanding software.

Scott Meyers (author of the Effective C++ books and CD) conceived of the series and acts as its consulting editor. Authors in the series work with Meyers and with Addison-Wesley Professional's editorial staff to create essential reading for software developers of every stripe.

TITLES IN THE SERIES

For more information on books in this series please see www.awprofessional.com/esds

Effective XML

50 Specific Ways
to Improve Your XML

Elliotte Rusty Harold

✦Addison-Wesley

Boston • San Francisco • New York • Toronto • Montreal
London • Munich • Paris • Madrid
Capetown • Sydney • Tokyo • Singapore • Mexico City

Many of the designations used by manufacturers and sellers to distinguish their products are claimed as trademarks. Where those designations appear in this book, and Addison-Wesley was aware of a trademark claim, the designations have been printed with initial capital letters or in all capitals.

The author and publisher have taken care in the preparation of this book, but make no expressed or implied warranty of any kind and assume no responsibility for errors or omissions. No liability is assumed for incidental or consequential damages in connection with or arising out of the use of the information or programs contained herein.

The publisher offers discounts on this book when ordered in quantity for bulk purchases and special sales. For more information, please contact:

U.S. Corporate and Government Sales
(800) 382-3419
corpsales@pearsontechgroup.com

For sales outside of the United States, please contact:

International Sales
(317) 581-3793
international@pearsontechgroup.com

Visit Addison-Wesley on the Web: www.awprofessional.com

Library of Congress Cataloging-in-Publication Data

Harold, Elliotte Rusty.
    Effective XML : 50 specific ways to improve your XML / Elliotte Rusty Harold.
        p.   cm.
    Includes bibliographical references and index.
    ISBN 0-321-15040-6 (alk. paper)
    1. XML (Document markup language) I. Title.

    QA76.76.H94H334 2003
    005.7'2—dc21   2003056257

ISBN 0-321-15040-6
Text printed on recycled paper
1 2 3 4 5 6 7 8 9 10—CRS—0706050403
First printing, September 2003

Contents

Preface

Learning the fundamentals of XML might take a programmer a week. Learning how to use XML effectively might take a lifetime. While many books have been written that teach developers how to use the basic syntax of XML, this is the first one that really focuses on how to use XML well. This book is not a tutorial. It is not going to teach you what a tag is or how to write a DTD. I assume you know these things. Instead it's going to tell you when, why, where, and how to use such tools effectively (and, perhaps equally importantly, when not to use them).

This book derives directly from my own experiences teaching and writing about XML. Over the last five years, I've written several books and taught numerous courses about XML. Increasingly I'm finding that audiences are already familiar with the basics of XML. They know what a tag is, how to validate a document against a DTD, and how to transform a document with an XSLT stylesheet. The question of what XML is and why to use it has been sufficiently well evangelized. The essential syntax and supporting technologies are reasonably well understood. However, although most developers know what a CDATA section is, they are not sure what to use one for. Although programmers know how to add attribute and child nodes to elements, they are not certain which one to use when. Although programmers know what a schema is, they don't know which schema language to choose.

Since XML has become a fundamental underpinning of new software systems, it becomes important to begin asking new questions—not just about what XML is but also how to use it effectively. Which techniques work and which don't? Less obviously, which techniques appear to work at first but fail to scale as systems are further developed? When I teach programming at my university, one of the first things I tell my students is that it is not enough to write programs that compile and produce the expected results. It is as important (indeed more important) to write code that is extensible, legible, and maintainable. XML can be used to produce robust, extensible, maintainable, comprehensible systems; or it can be used to create masses of unmaintainable, illegible, fragile, closed code. In the immortal words of Eric Clapton, "It's In The Way That You Use It."

XML is not a programming language. It is a markup language, but it is being successfully used by many programmers. There have been markup languages before, but in the developer community XML is far and away the most successful. However, the newness and unfamiliarity of markup languages have meant that many developers are using it less effectively than they could. Many programmers are hacking together systems that work but are not as robust, extensible, or portable as XML promises. This is to be expected. Programmers working with XML are pioneers exploring new territory, opening up new vistas in software, and accomplishing things that could not easily be accomplished just a few years ago. However, more than a few XML pioneers have returned from the frontier with arrows in their backs.

Five years after the initial release of XML into the world, certain patterns and antipatterns for the proper design of XML applications are becoming apparent. All of us in the XML community have made mistakes while exploring this new territory, the author of this book prominently among them. However, we've learned from those mistakes, and we're beginning to develop some principles that may help those who follow in our footsteps to avoid making the same mistakes we did. It is time to put up some caution signs in the road. We may not exactly say "Here there be dragons," but we can at least say, "That road is a lot rockier than it looks at first glance, and you might really want to take this slightly less obvious but much smoother path off to the left."

This book is divided into four parts, beginning with the lowest layer of XML and gradually working up to the highest.

- Part 1 covers XML syntax, those aspects of XML that don't really affect the information content of an XML document but may have large impact on how easy or hard those documents are to edit and process.
- Part 2 looks at XML structures, the general organization and annotation of information in an XML document.
- Part 3 discusses the various techniques and APIs available for processing XML with languages such as C++, C#, Java, Python, and Perl and thus attaching local semantics to the labeled structures of XML.
- Part 4 explores effective techniques for systems built around XML documents, rather than looking at individual documents in isolation.

Although this is how I've organized the book, you should be able to begin reading at essentially any chapter. This book makes an excellent bathroom reader. You may wish to read the introduction first, which defines a number of key terms used throughout the book that are frequently misused or confused. However, after that feel free to pick and choose from the topics as your interest and needs dictate. I've made liberal use of cross-references throughout to direct you along other paths through the book that may be of interest.

I hope this book is a beginning, not an end. It's still early in the life of XML, and much remains to be discovered and invented. You may well develop best practices of your own that are not mentioned here. If you do, I'd love to hear about them. You may also take issue with some of the principles stated here. I'd like to hear about that too. Discussion of many of the guidelines identified here has taken place on the xml-dev mailing list and seems likely to continue in the future. If you're interested in further discussion of the issues raised in this book, I recommend that you subscribe and participate there. Complete details can be found at http://lists.xml.org/. On the other hand, if you find outright mistakes in this book (the ID attribute value is missing a closing quote; the word "cat" is misspelled), you can write me directly at elharo@metalab.unc.edu. I maintain a Web page that lists known errata for this book, as well as any updates, at http://www.cafeconleche.org/books/effectivexml/.

Finally, I hope this book makes your use of XML both more effective and more enjoyable.

Acknowledgments

For me, this book is the culmination of more than five years of debate, argument, and discussion about XML with numerous people. Some of this took place in the hallways at conferences such as Software Development and XMLOne. Some of it took place on mailing lists like xml-dev. Along the way a few names kept popping up. Sometimes I agreed with what those folks said, sometimes I didn't—but their conversations and thoughts were always illuminating and helped clarify my own thinking about XML. These gurus include Tim Berners-Lee, Tim Bray, Claude Len Bullard, Mike Champion, James Clark, John Cowan, Roy Fielding, Rick Jelliffe, Michael Kay, Murata Makoto, Uche Ogbuji, Walter Perry, Paul Prescod, Jonathan Robie, and Simon St. Laurent. I doubt any of them agree with everything I've written here. In fact, I suspect a couple of them may violently disagree with most of it. However, as I look at this book, I see their influences everywhere. If they hadn't written what they've written, I couldn't have written this book.

Many people helped out in more direct ways with comments, corrections, and suggestions. Alex Blewitt, Janek Bogucki, Lars Gregori, Gareth Jenkins, Alexander Rankine, Clint Shank, and Wayne Tanner submitted numerous helpful corrections for the draft of the manuscript I posted at my web site. Mike Blackstone deserves special thanks for his copious notes. Mike Champion, Martin Gudgin, Sean McGrath, and Tim Bray did yeomanlike service as technical reviewers. Scott Meyers both founded the series and helped me keep the focus squarely on track. Their comments all substantially improved the book. As always, the folks at the Studio B literary agency were extremely helpful at all steps of the process. David Rogelberg, Sherry Rogelberg, and Stacey Barone should be called out for particular commendation. On the publisher's side at Addison-Wesley, Mary T. O'Brien shepherded this book from contract to completion. Chrysta Meadowbrooke performed the single most pleasant copy edit I've ever experienced. I would also like to thank the people who worked on the production of the book, Patrick Cash-Peterson for coordinating this book through production, Stratford Publishing Services for layout and design, Sharon Hilgenberg for the index, and Diane Freed for proofing.

Finally, as always, my biggest thanks are due to my wife, Beth, without whose love and understanding this book could never have been completed.

Introduction

As I stated in the preface, this is neither an introductory book nor an XML tutorial. I assume that you're familiar with the basic structure of an XML document as elements that contain text, that you know how to ask a parser to read an XML document in your language of choice, that you can attach a stylesheet to a document as necessary, and so forth.

However, I have noticed over the last few years that certain words and phrases have taken on a diverse set of meanings and are often used inconsistently. Sometimes this just confuses people, but occasionally it has led to serious process failures. Some of this has been caused by authors and trainers (embarrassingly, sometimes including the author of this book) who weren't sufficiently careful with their use of words, such as *element* and *tag*. However, some of the confusion rests with the XML working groups at the W3C who are often not consistent with each other or even within the same specification. Before we proceed with the detailed items, it is worth taking the time to define our terms carefully, making sure we agree about which words mean what as well as recognize those areas where there are genuine disagreements about the meanings of common technical terms.

Toward that end, I've prepared the following list of the most frequently confused XML terms:

- Element versus tag
- Attribute versus attribute value
- Entity versus entity reference
- Entity reference versus character reference
- Children versus child elements versus content
- Text versus character data versus markup
- Namespace versus namespace name versus namespace URI
- XML document versus XML file
- XML application versus XML software
- Well-formed versus valid

- DTD versus DOCTYPE
- XML declaration versus processing instruction
- Character set versus character encoding
- URI versus URI reference versus IRI
- Schema versus the W3C XML Schema Language

Confusing these terms often causes much misunderstanding regarding how various APIs and tools work. For instance, if you think that a character reference is an entity reference, you may find yourself wondering why a SAX parser never invokes the `startEntity` method for character references in your documents. When you ask a question about this on a mailing list, you may not phrase your question in a way that others can understand. You might even spend several hours carefully devising a test case and filing a bug report on a feature that's operating exactly as it should.

The answers to many apparently difficult questions become almost obvious when you're careful to state exactly what you mean. Thus it behooves us to define our terms carefully.

Element versus Tag

An element is not a tag and a tag is not an element. An element begins with a start-tag, includes some content, and then finishes with an end-tag. Tags delimit elements. They are part of elements but not themselves elements, any more than a piece of bread is a sandwich. The tags are like slices of bread. The element is the entire sandwich made up of bread, mustard and mayonnaise, meat and/or cheese. The tags are just the bread. For example, `<Headline>` is a start-tag. `</Headline>` is an end-tag. `<Headline>Crowd Hears Beth Giggle</Headline>` is a complete element. Elements may contain other elements. Tags may not contain other tags.

There is one degenerate case. A single empty-element tag may represent an entire element. For instance, `<Headline/>` is both a headline tag and a headline element. However, this is a special case. Semantically the empty-element tag is completely equivalent to the two-tag version `<Headline></Headline>`, and most APIs will not bother to inform you which of the two forms was actually present in the document.

In brief, the structure of an XML document is formed by nested elements. The individual elements are delimited by tags.

Attribute versus Attribute Value

An attribute is a property of an element. It has a name and a value and is normally a part of the element's start-tag. (It can also be defaulted in from the DTD.) For example, consider this element:

```
<Headline page="10">Crowd Hears Beth Giggle</Headline>
```

The headline element has a page attribute with the value 10. The attribute includes both the name and the value. The attribute value is simply the string 10. Either single or double quotes may surround the attribute value—the type of quote used is not significant. This element is exactly the same as the previous one:

```
<Headline page='10'>Crowd Hears Beth Giggle</Headline>
```

If an element has multiple attributes, their order is not important. These two elements are equivalent:

```
<Headline id="A3" page="10">Crowd Hears Beth Giggle</Headline>
<Headline page="10" id="A3">Crowd Hears Beth Giggle</Headline>
```

Parsers do not tell you which attribute came first. If order matters, you need to use child elements instead of attributes:

```
<Headline>
  <id>A3</id> <page>10</page>
  Crowd Hears Beth Giggle
</Headline>
```

It's not exactly a terminology confusion, but a few technologies (notably the W3C XML Schema Language) have recently dug themselves into deep holes by attempting to treat attributes and child elements as variations of the same thing. They are not. Order is only one of the differences between child elements and attributes. Other important differences include type, normalization, and the ability or inability to express substructure.

Entity versus Entity Reference

An entity is a storage unit that contains a piece of an XML document. This storage unit may be a file, a database record, an object in memory, a stream of bytes returned by a network server, or something else. It may contain an entire XML document or just a few elements or declarations.

Entity references point to these entities. There are two kinds of entity references: general entity references and parameter entity references. A general entity reference begins with an ampersand, for instance, `&amp;` or `&chapter1;`. These normally appear in the instance document. For example, you might define the `chapter1` entity in the DTD like this:

```
<!ENTITY SYSTEM chapter1 "http://www.example.com/chapter1.xml">
```

Then in the document you could reference it like this:

```
<book>
  &chapter1;
...
</book>
```

`&chapter1;` is an entity reference. The actual content of the document found at http://www.example.com/chapter1.xml is an entity. They are related, but they are not the same thing.

Parameter entities and parameter entity references follow the same pattern. The difference is that parameter entities contain DTD fragments instead of instance document fragments, and parameter entity references begin with a percent sign instead of an ampersand. However, the entity reference still stands in for and points to the actual entity.

XML APIs are schizophrenic about whether they report entities, entity references, neither, or both. Some, like XOM, simply replace all entity references with their corresponding entities and don't tell you that anything has happened. Others, like JDOM, only report entities they have not resolved. Still others such as DOM and SAX can report both entities and entity references, although this often depends on user preferences and the abilities of the underlying parser; and normally the five predefined entity references (`&amp;`, `&lt;`, `&gt;`, `&quot;`, and `&apos;`) are not reported.

Entity Reference versus Character Reference

Not everything that begins with an ampersand is an entity reference. Entity references are only used for named entities, including the five predefined entity references such as `&lt;` and any entities defined with ENTITY declarations in the DTD such as `&chapter1;` in the example above.

By contrast, character references use a hexadecimal or decimal Unicode value, not a name, to refer to a particular character. Each always refers to a single character, never to a group of characters. For example, ` ` is a hexadecimal character reference referring to the nonbreaking space character, and ` ` is a decimal character reference referring to that same character. XHTML's ` ` is an entity reference referring to that character.

Almost always, even APIs that faithfully report all entity references do not report character references. Instead, the parser silently merges the referenced characters into the surrounding text. Your code should never depend on whether a character was typed literally or escaped with a character reference. Almost all the time, it shouldn't depend on whether the character was escaped with an entity reference either.

Children versus Child Elements versus Content

An element's content is everything between the element's start-tag and its end-tag. For example, consider this DocBook `para` element.

```
<para>
  As far as we know, the Fibonacci series was first discovered
  by Leonardo of Pisa around 1200 C.E. Leonardo was trying to
  answer the question, <!-- Scritti di Leonardo Piasano. Rome:
  Baldassarre, 1857. Volume I, pages 283 - 284.Fibonacci,
  Leonardo. --> <quote lang="la"><foreignphrase>Quot paria
  coniculorum in uno anno ex uno pario germinatur?</foreign
  phrase></quote>, or, in English, <quote>How many pairs of
  rabbits are born in one year from one pair?</quote> To solve
  Leonardo&rsquo;s problem, first estimate that rabbits have
  a one month gestation period, and can first mate at the age
  of one month, so that each doe has its first litter at two
  months. Then make the simplifying assumption that each litter
  consists of exactly one male and one female.
</para>
```

The content of this `para` element contains some text, including white space, a comment, some more text, a `quote` child element, some more plain text, another `quote` child element, some more plain text, the `&rsquo;` entity reference, and finally some more text. All of that together, including all the content of child elements such as `quote`, is the `para` element's content.

The para element has two child elements, both named quote. However, these are not the only children of the element. This element also contains a comment, lots of character data, and an entity reference. These are considered to be children of the para element as well, although different APIs and systems vary in exactly how they represent these and how many text children there are. At one extreme, each separate character can be a separate child. At the other extreme, each text node contains the maximum contiguous run of text after all entity references are resolved so the para element has exactly four text node children.

On the flip side, the foreignphrase element and other content inside the quote elements are not children of the para element, although they are descendants of it.

The common reason for confusing children with child elements is forgetting about the very real possibility of mixed content. However, even when a document has a more record-like structure, the difference between children and child elements can be important. For example, consider the following presentation element.

```
<presentation>
  <title>DOM</title>
  <date>Thursday, November 21, 2002</date>
  <host>Software Development 2002 East</host>
  <copyright>2000-2002 Elliotte Rusty Harold</copyright>
  <last_modified>November 26, 2002</last_modified>
  <author_name>Elliotte Rusty Harold</author_name>
  <author_url>http://www.elharo.com/</author_url>
  <author_email>elharo@metalab.unc.edu</author_email>
  <abstract>Elliotte Rusty Harold's DOM tutorial</abstract>
</presentation>
```

It may look like this element has only child elements. However, if you're counting child nodes you have to count the white space too. There are at least ten text node children containing only white space. Furthermore, what about the title, date, host, and similar elements? Each of them has a child node containing character data but no child elements. Bottom line: Elements are not the only kind of children.

Text versus Character Data versus Markup

XML documents are composed of text. You'll never find anything in an XML document that is not text. This text is divided into two nonintersecting sets: character data and markup. Markup consists of all the tags, comments, processing instructions, entity references, character references, CDATA section delimiters, XML declarations, text declarations, document type declarations, and white space outside the root element. Everything else is character data. For example, here's the DocBook `para` element with the markup identified by boldface text and the character data in a plain font.

```
<para>
  As far as we know, the Fibonacci series was first discovered
  by Leonardo of Pisa around 1200 C.E. Leonardo was trying to
  answer the question, <!-- Scritti di Leonardo Piasano. Rome:
  Baldassarre, 1857. Volume I, pages 283 - 284.Fibonacci,
  Leonardo. --> <quote lang="la"><foreignphrase>Quot paria
  coniculorum in uno anno ex uno pario germinatur?</foreign
  phrase></quote>, or, in English, <quote>How many pairs of
  rabbits are born in one year from one pair?</quote> To solve
  Leonardo&rsquo;s problem, first estimate that rabbits have
  a one month gestation period, and can first mate at the age
  of one month, so that each doe has its first litter at two
  months. Then make the simplifying assumption that each litter
  consists of exactly one male and one female.
</para>
```

The markup includes the `<para>` and `</para>` tags, the `<quote>` and `</quote>` tags, the `<foreignphrase>` and `</foreignphrase>` tags, the comment, and the `&rsquo;` entity reference. Everything else is character data.

Sometimes the "everything else" part is called *parsed character data* or *PCDATA* after the PCDATA keyword used in DTDs to declare elements like `interfacename`.

```
<!ELEMENT interfacename (#PCDATA)>
```

However, that's not perfectly accurate. Generally speaking, the parsed character data is what's left after the parser has replaced entity and character references by the characters they represent. It contains both character data and markup.

Namespace versus Namespace Name versus Namespace URI

An XML namespace is a collection of names. For example, all the element names defined in XHTML (`html`, `head`, `title`, `body`, `p`, `div`, `table`, `h1`, and so on) form the XHTML namespace. The SVG namespace is the collection of element names used in SVG (`svg`, `rect`, `polygon`, `polyline`, and so on). Only the local parts of prefixed names belong to the namespace. The prefix and the prefixed names are not parts of the namespace.

Each such namespace is identified by a URI reference called the *namespace name*. For example the namespace name for XHTML is http://www.w3.org/1999/xhtml. The namespace name for SVG is http://www.w3.org/2000/svg. The namespace name identifies the namespace, but it is not the namespace.

The namespace name is supposed to be a URI reference, but it's not technically an error if it's not one. For instance, a namespace name may contain characters such as { or the Greek letter λ that are illegal in URIs. However, since in practice almost all actual namespace names are legal URI references, namespace names are often carelessly called *namespace URIs*. Actually, they are namespace URI references, but most developers don't bother to make this distinction.

XML Document versus XML File

Technically, an XML document is any sequence of Unicode characters that is well formed according to the rules laid out in the XML 1.0 specification. Such a document may or may not be stored in a file—it can be stored in a database record, created in memory by a program, read from a network stream, printed in a book, painted on a billboard, or scratched into a subway car window. There is not necessarily a file anywhere in the picture. If the XML document is stored in a file, it may be in a single file or split across multiple files using external entity references. It's even possible for multiple XML documents to be stored in a single file, although this is unusual in practice.

When discussing XML documents it is sometimes useful to distinguish the documents themselves from the DTDs or other forms of schemas. In these cases, the actual document that adheres to the schema is called an *instance document*. Here the document is an instance of a particular schema.

XML Application versus XML Software

An XML application is a class of XML documents defined by a schema, specification, or some group of rules. For example, Scalable Vector Graphics (SVG), XHTML, MathML, GedML, XSL Formatting Objects, and DocBook are all XML applications. The simple language I invented last Thursday to categorize my comic book collection is also an XML application even though it doesn't have a DTD, schema, or even a specification. An XML application is not a piece of application software that somehow processes XML, such as the XMLSPY editor, the Mozilla web browser, or the XEP XSL-FO to PDF converter.

Well-Formed versus Valid

There are two levels of "goodness" for an XML document. Well-formedness refers to mandatory syntactic constraints. Validity refers to optional structural and semantic constraints. There's a tendency to use the word *valid* in its common English usage to describe any correct document. However, in XML it has a much more specific meaning. Documents can be correct and processable yet still not valid.

Well-formedness is the minimum requirement necessary for an XML document. It includes various syntactic constraints, such as every start-tag must have a matching end-tag and the document must have exactly one root element. If a document is not well formed, it is not an XML document. Parsers that encounter a malformed document are required to report the error and stop parsing. They may not attempt to guess what the document author intended. They may not fix the error and continue. They have to drop the document on the floor.

Validity is a stronger constraint than well-formedness, but it's not required in order to process XML documents. Validity determines which elements and attributes are allowed to appear where. It indicates whether a document adheres to the constraints listed in the document type definition (DTD) and the document type declaration (DOCTYPE). Even if a document does not adhere to these constraints, it may still be usefully processed in some cases. The decision of whether and how to reject invalid documents is made by the client application, not by the parser.

The word *valid* is also sometimes used to refer to validity with respect to a schema rather than a DTD. In cases where this seems likely to be confusing, particularly where one is likely to want to validate a document against a DTD and against some other schema, the term *schema-valid* is used. As with DTD validity, whether and how to handle a schema-invalid document is a decision for the client application. A schema-validating parser will inform the client application that a document is invalid but will continue to parse it. The client application gets to decide whether or not to accept the document.

DTD versus DOCTYPE

A document type *definition* is a collection of ELEMENT, ATTLIST, ENTITY, and NOTATION declarations that describes a class of valid documents. A document type *declaration* is placed in the prolog of an XML document. It contains and/or points to the document's document type *definition*. The document type definition and the document type declaration are closely related, but they are not the same thing. The acronym *DTD* refers exclusively to the document type definition, never to the document type declaration. The shorthand form *DOCTYPE* refers exclusively to the document type declaration, never to the document type definition.

For example, this is a document type declaration:

```
<!DOCTYPE chapter PUBLIC "-//OASIS//DTD DocBook XML V4.1.2//EN"
                       "docbook/docbookx.dtd" >
```

It points to the DTD with the public identifier -//OASIS//DTD DocBook XML V4.1.2//EN found at the relative URL docbook/docbookx.dtd.

The following is also a document type declaration.

```
<!DOCTYPE book SYSTEM "http://www.example.com/docbookx.dtd">
```

It points to the DTD at the absolute URL http://www.example.com/docbookx.dtd.

Here is a document type declaration that completely contains the DTD between the square brackets that delimit the internal DTD subset.

```
<!DOCTYPE book [
  <!ELEMENT book (title, chapter+)>
  <!ELEMENT chapter (title, paragraph+)>
  <!ELEMENT title (#PCDATA)>
```

```
   <!ELEMENT paragraph (#PCDATA)>
]>
```

Finally, the next document type declaration both points to an external DTD and contains an internal DTD subset. The full DTD is formed by combining the declarations in the external DTD subset with those in the internal DTD subset.

```
<!DOCTYPE chapter PUBLIC "-//OASIS//DTD DocBook XML V4.1.2//EN"
                  "docbook/docbookx.dtd" [
 <!- add XIncludes ->
 <!ENTITY % local.para.char.mix " | xinclude:include">
 <!ELEMENT xinclude:include EMPTY>
 <!ATTLIST xinclude:include
    xmlns:xinclude CDATA #FIXED "http://www.w3.org/2001/XInclude"
    href           CDATA #REQUIRED
    parse          (text | xml) "xml"
 >
]>
```

Whether the DTD is internal, external, or both, it is never the same thing as the document type declaration. The document type declaration specifies the root element. The DTD does not. The DTD specifies the content models and attribute lists of the elements. The document type declaration does not. Most APIs routinely expose the contents of the document type declaration but not those of the document type definition.

XML Declaration versus Processing Instruction

One of the more needlessly confusing aspects of the XML specification is that for various technical reasons the following construct, which appears at the top of most XML documents, is in fact not a processing instruction:

```
<?xml version="1.0"?>
```

It looks like a processing instruction, but it isn't one—it's an XML declaration. Processing instruction targets are specifically forbidden from being xml, XML, Xml, or any other case combination of the word *XML*.

APIs may or may not expose the information in the XML declaration to the client application; but if one does, it will not use the same mechanism it uses to report processing instructions. For instance, in SAX 2.1 some of this information is optionally available through the `Locator2` interface. However, the parser does not call the `processingInstruction` method in `ContentHandler` when it sees the XML declaration.

Character Set versus Character Encoding

XML is based on the Unicode character set. A character set is a collection of characters assigned to particular numbers called *code points*. Currently Unicode 4.0 defines more than 90,000 individual characters. Each character in the set is mapped to a number, such as 64, 812, or 87,000. These numbers are not ints, shorts, bytes, longs, or any other numeric data type. They are simply numbers. Other character sets, such as Shift-JIS and Latin-1, contain different collections of characters that are assigned to different numbers, although there's often substantial overlap with the Unicode character set. That is, many character sets assign some or all of their characters to the same numbers to which Unicode assigns those characters.

A character encoding represents the members of a character set as bytes in a particular way. There are multiple encodings of Unicode, including UTF-8, UTF-16, UCS-2, UCS-4, UTF-32, and several other more obscure ones. Different encodings may encode the same code point using a different sequence of bytes and/or a different number of bytes. They may use big-endian or little-endian data. They can even use non-twos complement representations. They may use two bytes or four bytes for each character. They may even use different numbers of bytes for different characters.

Changing the character set changes which characters can be represented. For instance, the ISO-8859-7 set includes Greek letters. The ISO-8859-1 set does not. Changing the character encoding does not change which characters can be used—it merely changes how each character is encoded in bytes.

XML parsers always convert characters in other sets to Unicode before reporting them to the client application. In effect, they treat other character sets as different encodings of some subset of Unicode. Thus, XML doesn't ever really let you change the character set. This is always Unicode. XML only lets you adjust how those characters are represented.

URI versus URI Reference versus IRI

A URI identifies a resource. A URI reference identifies a part of a resource. A URI reference may contain a fragment identifier separated from the URI by an octothorp (#); a plain URI may not. For example, http://www.w3.org/TR/REC-xml-names/ is a URI, but http://www.w3.org/TR/REC-xml-names/#Philosophy is a URI reference.

Most XML-related specifications, such as *Namespaces in XML*, are defined in terms of URI references rather than URIs. For example, the W3C XML Schema Language simple type `xsd:anyURI` actually indicates that elements with that type are URI references. In casual conversation and writing, most people don't bother to make the distinction. Nonetheless, it can be important. For example, the system identifier in the document type declaration can be a URI but not a URI reference.

Note *I've heard it claimed that relative URIs are URI references, not true URIs, and the authors of the XML specification seem to have believed this. However, the URI specification, RFC 2396, does not support this belief. It clearly describes both relative URIs and relative URI references. Perhaps the authors intended to require all URIs to be absolute; however, if this is the case, they failed to do so. The only difference between a URI and a URI reference is that the latter allows a fragment identifier while the former does not.*

Currently, the IETF is working on Internationalized Resource Identifiers (IRIs). These are similar to URIs except that they allow non-ASCII characters such as ζ and é that must be escaped with percent symbols in URIs. The specification is not finished yet, but several XML specifications are already referring to this. For instance, the XLink `href` attribute actually contains an IRI, not a URI.

Schemas versus the W3C XML Schema Language

The word *schema* is a generic term for a document that specifies the layout and permissible content of a class of documents. It actually entered computer science in the context of database schemas. For XML, there are multiple different schema languages with their own strengths and weaknesses, including DTDs, RELAX NG, Schematron, and, of course, the W3C XML Schema Language.

There is a tendency among developers to use only the word *schemas,* or perhaps the only slightly less generic *XML Schemas,* when referring to the W3C XML Schema Language. This needs to be resisted because the W3C XML Schema Language is neither the only such language nor, in most people's opinions, the simplest, most powerful, or best designed. It is merely one language promulgated by one group of inventors. It has some good points and some bad points, but we should not implicitly ignore all the other languages (some of which are demonstrably simpler and/or more powerful than the W3C XML Schema Language) by using the generic term to refer to the specific.

Unfortunately, the W3C has not chosen to assign its schema language an appellation less cumbersome than "W3C XML Schema Language." Consequently, to avoid repeating this phrase incessantly, I will occasionally succumb to temptation and use the word *schemas* to mean the W3C XML Schema Language. However, I will only do this in those items that discuss this language exclusively, and I will make it very clear at the outset of the chapter. Think of the word *schema* as more of a pronoun for the schema language currently being discussed than as a proper noun for the W3C's entry into the field.

Words have meanings. XML is a very precisely defined language, so its words have very precise meanings. It pays to use those words correctly. There are indeed some confusing aspects to XML. It doesn't make sense to make the problem worse by adding to the confusion. Using the right words for the right concepts can simplify many unnecessarily complex problems to save brain power for the things that are genuinely difficult.

1 | Syntax

Syntax is the lowest level of XML. To a large extent the contents of this section focus on the microstructure of XML. By investigating different ways to represent the same structures, the items answer the question, how can XML best be authored for maximum interoperability and convenience? Little of what's discussed here affects the information content of an XML document.

However, just as there are better and worse ways to write C code that produces identical machine code when compiled, so too are there better and worse ways to write XML documents. In this section we explore some of the most useful ways to improve the legibility, maintainability, and extensibility of your XML documents and applications.

Item 1   Include an XML Declaration

Although XML declarations are optional, every XML document should have one. An XML declaration helps both human users and automated software identify the document as XML. It identifies the version of XML in use, specifies the character encoding, and can even help optimize the parsing. Most importantly, it's a crucial clue that what you're reading is in fact an XML document in environments where file type information is unavailable or unreliable.

The following are all legal XML declarations.

```
<?xml version="1.0"?>
<?xml version="1.0" encoding="UTF-8"?>
<?xml version="1.0" encoding="ISO-8859-1" standalone="no"?>
<?xml version="1.0" standalone="yes"?>
```

In general the XML declaration must be the first thing in the XML document. It cannot be preceded by any comments, processing instruction, or even white space. The only thing that may sometimes precede it is the optional byte order mark.

The XML declaration is not a processing instruction, even though it looks like one. If you're processing an XML document through APIs like SAX, DOM, or JDOM, the methods invoked to read and write the XML declaration will not be the same methods invoked to read and write processing instructions. In many cases, including SAX2, DOM2, XOM, and JDOM, the information from the XML declaration may not be available at all. The parser will use it to determine how to read a document, but it will not report it to the client application.

Each XML declaration has up to three attributes.

1. `version`: the version of XML in use. Currently this always has the value 1.0, though there may be an XML 1.1 in the future. (See Item 3.)
2. `encoding`: the character set in which the document is written.
3. `standalone`: whether or not the external DTD subset makes important contributions to the document's infoset.

Like other attributes, these may be enclosed in single or double quotes, and any amount of white space may separate them from each other. Unlike other attributes, order matters. The `version` attribute must always come before the `encoding` attribute, which must always come before the `standalone` declaration. The `version` attribute is required. The `encoding` attribute and `standalone` declaration are optional.

The `version` Info

The `version` attribute always has the value 1.0. If XML 1.1 is released in the future (and it may not be), this will probably also be allowed to have the value 1.1. Regardless, you should always use XML 1.0, never version 1.1. XML 1.0 is more compatible and more robust, and it offers all the features XML 1.1 does. Item 3 discusses this in more detail.

The `encoding` Declaration

The `encoding` attribute specifies which character set and encoding the document is written in. Sometimes this identifies an encoding of the Unicode character set such as UTF-8 and UTF-16; other times it identifies a different character set such as ISO-8859-1 or US-ASCII, which for XML's purposes serves mainly as an encoding of a subset of the full Unicode character set.

The default encoding is UTF-8 if no encoding declaration or other metadata is present. UTF-16 can also be used if the document begins with a byte order mark. However, even in cases where the document is written in the UTF-8 or UTF-16 encodings, an `encoding` declaration helps people reading the document recognize the encoding, so it's useful to specify it explicitly.

Try to stick to well-known standard character sets and encodings such as ISO-8859-1, UTF-8, and UTF-16 if possible. You should always use the standard names for these character sets. Table 1–1 lists the names defined by the XML 1.0 specification. All parsers that support these character sets should recognize these names. For character encodings not defined in XML 1.0, choose a name registered with the IANA. You can find a complete list at http://www.iana.org/assignments/character-sets/. However, you should avoid nonstandard names. In particular, watch out for Java names like 8859_1 and UTF16. Relatively few parsers not written in Java recognize these, and even some Java parsers don't recognize them by default. However, all parsers including those written in Java should recognize the IANA standard equivalents such as ISO-8859-1 and UTF-16.

For similar reasons, avoid declaring and using vendor-dependent character sets such as Cp1252 (U.S. Windows) or MacRoman. These are not as interoperable as the standard character sets across the heterogeneous set of platforms that XML supports.

The `standalone` Declaration

The `standalone` attribute has the value yes or no. If no `standalone` declaration is present, then no is the default.

A yes value means that no declarations in the external DTD subset affect the content of the document in any way. Specifically, the following four conditions apply.

1. No default attribute values are specified for elements.
2. No entity references used in the instance document are defined.
3. No attribute values need to be normalized.
4. No elements contain ignorable white space.

Table 1–1 │ Character Set Names Defined in XML

Name	Set
UTF-8	Variable width, byte order independent Unicode
UTF-16	Two-byte Unicode with surrogate pairs
ISO-10646-UCS-2	Two-byte Unicode without surrogate pairs; plane 0 only
ISO-10646-UCS-4	Four-byte Unicode
ISO-8859-1	Latin-1; mostly compatible with the standard U.S. Windows character set
ISO-8859-2	Latin-2
ISO-8859-3	Latin-3
ISO-8859-4	Latin-4
ISO-8859-5	ASCII and Cyrillic
ISO-8859-6	ASCII and Arabic
ISO-8859-7	ASCII and Greek
ISO-8859-8	ASCII and Hebrew
ISO-8859-9	Latin-5
ISO-8859-10	Latin-6
ISO-8859-11	ASCII plus Thai
ISO-8859-13	Latin-7
ISO-8859-14	Latin-8
ISO-8859-15	Latin-9, Latin-0
ISO-8859-16	Latin-10
ISO-2022-JP	A combination of ISO 646 (a slight variant of ASCII) and JIS X0208 that uses escape sequences to switch between the two character sets
Shift_JIS	A combination of JIS X0201:1997 and JIS X0208:1997 that uses escape sequences to switch between the two character sets
EUC-JP	A combination of four code sets (ASCII, JIS X0208-1990, half width Katakana, and JIS X0212-1990) that uses escape sequences to switch between the character sets

If these conditions hold, the parser may choose not to read the external DTD subset, which can save a significant amount of time when the DTD is at a remote and slow web site.

A nonvalidating parser will not actually check that these conditions hold. For example, it will not report an error if an element does not have an attribute for which a default value is provided in the external DTD subset. Obviously the parser can't find mistakes that are apparent only when it reads the external DTD subset if it doesn't read the external DTD subset.

A validating parser is supposed to report a validity error if `standalone` has the value yes and any of these four conditions are not true.

It is always acceptable to set `standalone` to no, even if the document could technically stand alone. If you don't want to be bothered figuring out whether all of the above four conditions apply, just set `standalone="no"` (or leave it unspecified because the default is no). This is always correct.

The `standalone` declaration only applies to content read from the external DTD subset. It has nothing to do with other means of merging in content from remote documents such as schemas, XIncludes, XLinks, application-specific markup like the `img` element in XHTML, or anything else. It is strictly about the DTD.

Whatever values you pick for the `version`, `encoding`, and `standalone` attributes, and whether you include `encoding` and `standalone` attributes at all, you should provide an XML declaration. It only takes a few bytes and makes it much easier for both people and parsers to process your document.

Item 2   Mark Up with ASCII if Possible

Despite the rapid growth of Unicode in the last few years, the sad fact is that many text editors and other tools are still tied to platform- and nationality-dependent character sets such as Windows-1252, Mac-Roman, and SJIS. The only characters all these sets have in common are the 128 ASCII letters, digits, punctuation marks, and control characters. These characters are the only ones that can be reliably displayed and edited across the wide range of computers and software in use today. Thus, if it's not too big a problem, try to limit your markup to the ASCII character set. If you're writing in English, this is normally not a problem.

On the other hand, this principle is not written in stone, especially if you're not working in English. If you're writing a simple vocabulary for a local French bank without any international ambitions, you will probably want to include all the accents commonly used in French for words like *relevé* (statement) and *numéro* (number). For instance, a bank statement might look like this:

```
<?xml version="1.0" encoding="ISO-8859-1"?>
<Relevé xmlns="http://namespaces.petitebanque.com/">
```

```
<Banque>PetiteBanque</Banque>
<Compte>
   <Numéro>00003145298</Numéro>
   <Type>épargne</Type>
   <Propriétaire>Jean Deaux</Propriétaire>
</Compte>
<Date>2003-30-02</Date>
<SoldeDOuverture>5266.34</SoldeDOuverture>
<Transaction type="dépôt">
   <Date>2003-02-07</Date>
   <Somme>300.00</Somme>
</Transaction>
<Transaction type="transfert">
   <Compte>
      <Numéro>0000271828</Numéro>
      <Type>courant</Type>
      <Propriétaire>Jean Deaux</Propriétaire>
   </Compte>
   <Date>2003-02-07</Date>
   <Somme>200.00</Somme>
</Transaction>
<Transaction type="dépôt">
   <Date>2003-02-15</Date>
   <Somme>512.32</Somme>
</Transaction>
<Transaction type="retrait">
   <Date>2003-02-15</Date>
   <Somme>200.00</Somme>
</Transaction>
<Transaction type="retrait">
   <Date>2003-02-25</Date>
   <Somme>200.00</Somme>
</Transaction>
<SoldeDeFermeture>5478.64</SoldeDeFermeture>
</Relevé>
```

However, this code is likely to cause trouble if the document ever crosses national or linguistic boundaries. For instance, if programmers at the bank's Athens branch open the same document in a text editor, they're likely to see something like this:

```
<?xml version="1.0" encoding="ISO-8859-1"?>
<Relevɩ xmlns="http://namespaces.petitebanque.com/">
  <Banque>PetiteBanque</Banque>
  <Compte>
    <Numɩro>00003145298</Numɩro>
    <Type>ɩpargne</Type>
    <Propriɩtaire>Jean Deaux</Propriɩtaire>
  </Compte>
  <Date>2003-30-02</Date>
  <SoldeDOuverture>5266.34</SoldeDOuverture>
  <Transaction type="dɩpτt">
    <Date>2003-02-07</Date>
    <Somme>300.00</Somme>
  </Transaction>
  <Transaction type="transfert">
    <Compte>
      <Numɩro>0000271828</Numɩro>
      <Type>courant</Type>
      <Propriɩtaire>Jean Deaux</Propriɩtaire>
    </Compte>
    <Date>2003-02-07</Date>
    <Somme>200.00</Somme>
  </Transaction>
  <Transaction type="dɩpτt">
    <Date>2003-02-15</Date>
    <Somme>512.32</Somme>
  </Transaction>
  <Transaction type="retrait">
    <Date>2003-02-15</Date>
    <Somme>200.00</Somme>
  </Transaction>
  <Transaction type="retrait">
    <Date>2003-02-25</Date>
    <Somme>200.00</Somme>
  </Transaction>
  <SoldeDeFermeture>5478.64</SoldeDeFermeture>
</Relevɩ>
```

The e's with accents acute have morphed into iotas, and the o's with carets have turned into lowercase taus.

Indeed, even crossing platform boundaries within the same country may cause problems. Were the same document opened on a Mac, the developers would likely see something like this:

```
<?xml version="1.0" encoding="ISO-8859-1"?>
<RelevÈ xmlns="http://namespaces.petitebanque.com/">
  <Banque>PetiteBanque</Banque>
  <Compte>
    <NumÈro>00003145298</NumÈro>
    <Type>Èpargne</Type>
    <PropriÈtaire>Jean Deaux</PropriÈtaire>
  </Compte>
  <Date>2003-30-02</Date>
  <SoldeDOuverture>5266.34</SoldeDOuverture>
  <Transaction type="dÈpÙt">
    <Date>2003-02-07</Date>
    <Somme>300.00</Somme>
  </Transaction>
  <Transaction type="transfert">
    <Compte>
      <NumÈro>0000271828</NumÈro>
      <Type>courant</Type>
      <PropriÈtaire>Jean Deaux</PropriÈtaire>
    </Compte>
    <Date>2003-02-07</Date>
    <Somme>200.00</Somme>
  </Transaction>
  <Transaction type="dÈpÙt">
    <Date>2003-02-15</Date>
    <Somme>512.32</Somme>
  </Transaction>
  <Transaction type="retrait">
    <Date>2003-02-15</Date>
    <Somme>200.00</Somme>
  </Transaction>
  <Transaction type="retrait">
    <Date>2003-02-25</Date>
    <Somme>200.00</Somme>
  </Transaction>
```

```
<SoldeDeFermeture>5478.64</SoldeDeFermeture>
</RelevÈ>
```

In this case, the lowercase e's with accents acute have changed to upper-case E's with accents grave, and the accented o's have also changed. This isn't quite as bad, but it's more than enough to confuse most software applications and not a few people.

The encoding declaration fixes these issues for XML-aware tools such as parsers and XML editors. However, it doesn't help non-XML-aware systems like plain text editors and regular expressions. (See Item 29.) There's a lot of flaky code out there in the world in less than perfect systems.

Using Unicode instead of ISO-8859-1 for the character set goes a long way toward fixing this particular problem. (See Item 38.) However, this opens up several lesser but still significant problems.

1. Many text editors can't handle Unicode. Even editors that can often have trouble recognizing Unicode documents.
2. The only glyphs (graphical representations of characters from a particular font) you can rely on being available across a variety of systems cover the ASCII range. Even a system that can process all Unicode characters may not be able to display them.
3. Keyboards don't have the right keys for more than a few languages. The basic ASCII characters are the only characters likely to be available anywhere in the world. Indeed, even a few ASCII characters are problematic. I once purchased a French keyboard in Montreal that did not have a single quote key.
4. The string facilities of many languages and operating systems implicitly assume single-byte characters. This includes the char data type in C. Java is slightly better but still can't handle all Unicode characters.

None of these problems are insurmountable. Programmers' editors that properly handle Unicode are available for almost all systems of interest. You can purchase or download fonts that cover most Unicode blocks, though you may have to mix and match several fonts to get full coverage. Input methods, multi-key combinations, and graphical keymaps allow authors to type accented characters and ideographic characters even on U.S. keyboards. It is possible to write Unicode-savvy Java, C, and Perl code provided you have a solid understanding of Unicode and know exactly where those languages' usual string and character types are inadequate. Just be aware that if you do use non-ASCII characters for your markup, these issues will arise.

One final caveat: I am primarily concerned with *markup* here, that is, element and attribute names. I am not talking about element content and attribute values. To the extent that such content is written in a natural human language, that content really needs to be written in that language with all its native characters intact. For instance, if a customer's name is Thérèse Barrière, it should be written as Thérèse Barrière, not Therese Barriere. (In some jurisdictions there are even laws requiring this.) Non-ASCII content raises many of the same issues as non-ASCII markup. However, the need for non-ASCII characters is greater here, and the problems aren't quite as debilitating.

While the situation is improving slowly, for the time being, documents will be more easily processed in an international, heterogeneous environment if they contain only ASCII characters. ASCII is a lowest common denominator and a very imperfect one at that. However, it is the lowest common denominator. In the spirit of being liberal in what you accept but conservative in what you generate, you should use ASCII when possible. If the text you're marking up is written in any language other than English, you'll almost certainly have to use other character sets. Just don't choose to do so gratuitously. For example, don't pick ISO-8859-1 (Latin-1) just so you can tag a curriculum vitae with `<resumé>` instead of `<resume>`.

Item 3   Stay with XML 1.0

Everything you need to know about XML 1.1 can be summed up in two rules.

1. Don't use it.
2. (For experts only) If you speak Mongolian, Yi, Cambodian, Amharic, Dhivehi, Burmese, or a very few other languages and you want to write your markup (not your text but your markup) in these languages, you can set the `version` attribute of the XML declaration to 1.1. Otherwise, refer to rule 1.

XML 1.1 does several things, one of them marginally useful to a few developers, the rest actively harmful.

- It expands the set of characters allowed as name characters.
- The C0 control characters (except for NUL) such as form feed, vertical tab, BEL, and DC1 through DC4 are now allowed in XML text provided they are escaped as character references.
- The C1 control characters (except for NEL) must now be escaped as character references.
- NEL can be used in XML documents but is resolved to a line feed on parsing.
- Parsers may (but do not have to) tell client applications that Unicode data was not normalized.
- Namespace prefixes can be undeclared.

Let's look at these changes in more detail.

New Characters in XML Names

XML 1.1 expands the set of characters allowed in XML names (that is, element names, attribute names, entity names, ID-type attribute values, and so forth) to allow characters that were not defined in Unicode 2.0, the version that was extant when XML 1.0 was first defined. Unicode 2.0 is fully adequate to cover the needs of markup in English, French, German, Russian, Chinese, Japanese, Spanish, Danish, Dutch, Arabic, Turkish, Hebrew, Farsi, Thai, Hindi, and most other languages you're likely to be familiar with as well as several thousand you aren't. However, Unicode 2.0 did miss a few important living languages including Mongolian, Yi, Cambodian, Amharic, Dhivehi, and Burmese, so if you want to write your markup in these languages, XML 1.1 is worthwhile.

However, note that this is relevant only if we're talking about *markup,* particularly element and attribute names. It is not necessary to use XML 1.1 to write XML data, particularly element content and attribute values, in these languages. For example, here's the beginning of an Amharic translation of the Book of Matthew written in XML 1.0.

```
<?xml version="1.0" encoding="UTF-8">
<book>
<title>የማቴዎስ  ወንጌል</title>
<chapter number="፩">
<title>የኢየሱስ የትውልድ ሐረግ</title>
<verse number="፩">
    የዳዊት ልጅ፡ የአብርሃም ልጅ የሁ ነው የኢየሱስ ክርስቶስ የትውልድ ሐረግ የሚከተለው ነው፤
```

```
</verse>
<verse number="፪">
  ከከርሃም ይስሐቅነ ወለደ፤
  ይስሐቅ ያዕቆብነ  ወለደ፤
  ያዕቆብ ይሁዳነና ወነድሞቹነ ወለደ፤
</verse>
</chapter>
</book>
```

Here the element and attribute names are in English although the content
and attribute values are in Amharic. On the other hand, if we were to
write the element and attribute names in Amharic, we would need to use
XML 1.1.

```
<?xml version="1.1" encoding="UTF-8">
```

⟨መጽሐፋ⟩

⟨ክርስት⟩የማቴዎስ ወንጌል⟨/ክርስት⟩

⟨ምዕራፋ ዌጥር="፩"⟩

⟨ክርስት⟩የኢየሱስ የትውʹ ልድ ሐረግ⟨/ክርስት⟩

⟨ቤት ዌጥር="፩"⟩

የዳዊት ልጅ፤ የከከርሃም ልጅ የሁ ነው የኢየሱስ ክርስቶስ የትውʹ ልድ ሐረግ የሚከተለውʹ ነው

⟨/ቤት⟩

⟨ቤት ዌጥር="፪"⟩

  ከከርሃም ይስሐቅነ ወለደ፤

  ይስሐቅ ያዕቆብነ ወለደ፤

  ያዕቆብ ይሁዳነና ወነድሞቹነ ወለደ፤

⟨/ቤት⟩

⟨/ምዕራፋ⟩

⟨/መጽሐፋ⟩

This is plausible. A native Amharic speaker might well want to write
markup like this. However, the loosening of XML's name character rules
have effects far beyond the few extra languages they're intended to enable.
Whereas XML 1.0 is conservative (everything not permitted is forbidden),

XML 1.1 is liberal (everything not forbidden is permitted). XML 1.0 lists the characters you can use in names. XML 1.1 lists the characters you can't use in names. Characters XML 1.1 allows in names include:

- Symbols like the copyright sign (©)
- Mathematical operators such as ±
- Superscript 7 (^{7})
- The musical symbol for a six-string fretboard
- The zero-width space
- Private-use characters
- Several hundred thousand characters that aren't even defined in Unicode and probably never will be

XML 1.1's lax name character rules have the potential to make documents much more opaque and obfuscated.

C0 Control Characters

The first 32 Unicode characters with code points from 0 to 31 are known as the C0 controls. They were originally defined in ASCII to control teletypes and other monospace dumb terminals. Aside from the tab, carriage return, and line feed they have no obvious meaning in text. Since XML is text, it does not include binary characters such as NULL (#x00), BEL (#x07), DC1 (#x11) through DC4 (#x14), and so forth. These noncharacters are historical relics. XML 1.0 does not allow them. This is a good thing. Although dumb terminals and binary-hostile gateways are far less common today than they were twenty years ago, they are still used, and passing these characters through equipment that expects to see plain text can have nasty consequences, including disabling the screen. (One common problem that still occurs is accidentally paging a binary file on a console. This is generally quite ugly and often disables the console.)

A few of these characters occasionally do appear in non-XML text data. For example, the form feed (#x0C) is sometimes used to indicate a page break. Thus moving data from a non-XML system such as a BLOB or CLOB field in a database into an XML document can unexpectedly cause malformedness errors. Text may need to be cleaned before it can be added to an XML document. However, the far more common problem is that a document's encoding is misidentified, for example, defaulted as UTF-8 when it's really UTF-16 or ISO-8859-1. In this case, the parser will notice unexpected nulls and throw a well-formedness error.

XML 1.1 fortunately still does not allow raw binary data in an XML document. However, it does allow you to use character references to escape the C0 controls such as form feed and BEL. The parser will resolve them into the actual characters before reporting the data to the client application. You simply can't include them directly. For example, the following document uses form feeds to separate pages.

```
<?xml version="1.1">
<book>
  <title>Nursery Rhymes</title>
  <rhyme>
    <verse>Mary, Mary quite contrary</verse>
    <verse>How does your garden grow?</verse>
  </rhyme>
  &#x0C;
  <rhyme>
    <verse>Little Miss Muffet sat on a tuffet</verse>
    <verse>Eating her curds and whey</verse>
  </rhyme>
  &#x0C;
  <rhyme>
    <verse>Old King Cole was a merry old soul</verse>
    <verse>And a merry old soul was he</verse>
  </rhyme>
</book>
```

However, this style of page break died out with the line printer. Modern systems use stylesheets or explicit markup to indicate page boundaries. For example, you might place each separate page inside a `page` element or add a `pagebreak` element where you wanted the break to occur, as shown below.

```
<?xml version="1.1">
<book>
  <title>Nursery Rhymes</title>
  <rhyme>
    <verse>Mary, Mary quite contrary</verse>
    <verse>How does your garden grow?</verse>
  </rhyme>
  <pagebreak/>
  <rhyme>
```

```
    <verse>Little Miss Muffet sat on a tuffet</verse>
    <verse>Eating her curds and whey</verse>
  </rhyme>
  <pagebreak/>
  <rhyme>
    <verse>Old King Cole was a merry old soul</verse>
    <verse>And a merry old soul was he</verse>
  </rhyme>
</book>
```

Better yet, you might not change the markup at all, just write a stylesheet that assigns each rhyme to a separate page. Any of these options would be superior to using form feeds. Most uses of the other C0 controls are equally obsolete.

There is one exception. You still cannot embed a null in an XML document, not even with a character reference. Allowing this would have caused massive problems for C, C++, and other languages that use null-terminated strings. The null is still forbidden, even with character escaping, which means it's still not possible to directly embed binary data in XML. You have to encode it using Base64 or some similar format first. (See Item 19.)

C1 Control Characters

There is a less common block of C1 control characters between 128 (#x80) and 159 (#x9F). These include start of string, end of string, cancel character, privacy message, and a few other equally obscure characters. For the most part these are even less useful and less appropriate for XML documents than the C0 control characters. However, they were allowed in XML 1.0 mostly by mistake. XML 1.1 rectifies this error (with one notable exception, which I'll address shortly) by requiring that these control characters be escaped with character references as well. For example, you can no longer include a "break permitted here" character in element content or attribute values. You have to write it as ‚ instead.

This actually does have one salutary effect. There are a lot of documents in the world that are labeled as ISO-8859-1 but actually use the nonstandard Microsoft Cp1252 character set instead. Cp1252 does not include the C1 controls. Instead it uses this space for extra graphic characters such as €, Œ, and ™. This causes significant interoperability problems when moving documents between Windows and non-Windows systems, and these problems are not always easy to detect.

By making escaping of the C1 controls mandatory, such mislabeled documents will now be obvious to parsers. Any document that contains an unescaped C1 character labeled as ISO-8859-1 is malformed. Documents that correctly identify themselves as Cp1252 are still allowed.

The downside to this improvement is that there is now a class of XML documents that is well-formed XML 1.0 but not well-formed XML 1.1. XML 1.1 is not a superset of XML 1.0. It is neither forward nor backward compatible.

NEL Used as a Line Break

The fourth change XML 1.1 makes is of no use to anyone and should never have been adopted. XML 1.1 allows the Unicode next line character (#x85, NEL) to be used anywhere a carriage return, line feed, or carriage return–line feed pair is used in XML 1.0 documents. Note that a NEL doesn't mean anything different than a carriage return or line feed. It's just one more way of adding extra white space. However, it is incompatible not only with the installed base of XML software but also with all the various text editors on UNIX, Windows, Mac, OS/2, and almost every other non-IBM platform on Earth. For instance, you can't open an XML 1.1 document that uses NELs in emacs, vi, BBEdit, UltraEdit, jEdit, or most other text editors and expect it to put the line breaks in the right places. Figure 3–1 shows what happens when you load a NEL-delimited file into emacs. Most other editors have equal or bigger problems, especially on large documents.

If so many people and platforms have such problems with NEL, why has it been added to XML 1.1? The problem is that there's a certain huge monopolist of a computer company that doesn't want to use the same standard everyone else in the industry uses. And—surprise, surprise—its name isn't Microsoft. No, this time the villain is IBM. Certain IBM mainframe software, particularly console-based text editors like XEdit and OS/390 C compilers, do not use the same two line-ending characters (carriage return and line feed) that everybody else on the planet has been using for at least the last twenty years. Instead those text editors use character #x85, NEL.

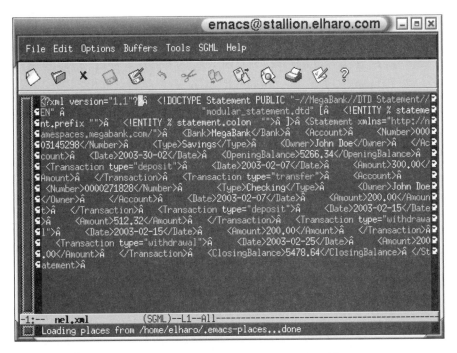

Figure 3–1 Loading a NEL-Delimited File into a Non-IBM Text Editor

If you're one of those few developers writing XML by hand with a plain console editor on an IBM mainframe, you should upgrade your editor to support the line-ending conventions the rest of the world has standardized on. If you're writing C code to generate XML documents on a mainframe, you just need to use \x0A instead of \n to represent the line end. (Java does not have this problem.) If you're reading XML documents, the parser should convert the line endings for you. There's no need to use XML 1.1.

Unicode Normalization

For reasons of compatibility with legacy character sets such as ISO-8859-1 (as well as occasional mistakes) Unicode sometimes provides multiple representations of the same character. For example, the e with accent acute (é) can be represented as either the single character #xE9 or with the two characters #x65 (e) followed by #x301 (combining accent acute). XML 1.1 suggests that all generators of XML text should normalize such alternatives into a canonical form. In this case, you should use the single character rather than the double character.

However, both forms are still accepted. Neither is malformed. Furthermore, parsers are explicitly prohibited from doing the normalization for the client program. They may merely report a nonfatal error if the XML is found to be unnormalized. In fact, this is nothing that parsers couldn't have done with XML 1.0, except that it didn't occur to anyone to do it. Normalization is more of a strongly recommended best practice than an actual change in the language.

Undeclaring Namespace Prefixes

There's one other new feature that's effectively part of XML 1.1: namespaces 1.1, which adds the ability to undeclare namespace prefix mappings. For example, consider the following API element.

```
<?xml version="1.0" encoding="UTF-8">
<API xmlns:public="http://www.example.com"
     xmlns:private="http://www.example.org" >
  <title>Geometry</title>
  <cpp xmlns:public="" xmlns:private="">
    class CRectangle {
      int x, y;
      public:void set_values (int,int);
      private:int area (void); }
  </cpp>
</API>
```

A system that was looking for qualified names in element content might accidentally confuse the `public:void` and `private:int` in the `cpp` element with qualified names instead of just part of C++ syntax (albeit ugly C++ syntax that no good programmer would write). Undeclaring the public and private prefixes allows them to stand out for what they actually are, just plain unadorned text.

In practice, however, very little code looks for qualified names in element content. Some code does look for these things in attribute values, but in those cases it's normally clear whether or not a given attribute can contain qualified names. Indeed this example is so forced precisely because prefix undeclaration is very rarely needed in practice and never needed if you're only using prefixes on element and attribute names.

That's it. There is nothing else new in XML 1.1. It doesn't move namespaces or schemas into the core. It doesn't correct admitted mistakes in the design of XML such as attribute value normalization. It doesn't simplify XML by removing rarely used features like unparsed entities and notations. It doesn't even clear up the confusion about what parsers should and should not report. All it does is change the list of name and white space characters. This very limited benefit comes at an extremely high cost. There is a huge installed base of XML 1.0–aware parsers, browsers, databases, viewers, editors, and other tools that don't work with XML 1.1. They will report well-formedness errors when presented with an XML 1.1 document.

The disadvantages of XML 1.1 (including the cost in both time and money of upgrading all your software to support it) are just too great for the extremely limited benefits it provides most developers. If you're more comfortable working in Mongolian, Yi, Cambodian, Amharic, Dhivehi, or Burmese and you only need to exchange data with other speakers of one of these languages (for instance, you're developing a system exclusively for a local Amharic-language newspaper in Addis Ababa where everybody speaks Amharic), you can set the `version` attribute of the XML declaration to 1.1. Everyone else should stick to XML 1.0.

Item 4   Use Standard Entity References

No reasonably sized keyboard could possibly include all the characters in Unicode. U.S. keyboards are especially weak when it comes to typing in foreign languages with unusual accents and non-Latin scripts. XML allows you to use either character references or entity references to address this problem. In general, named entity references like `&Ecaron;` should be preferred to character references like `&#x011B;` because they're easier on the human beings who have to read the source code.

While there are no standards for how to name these entity references, there are some useful entity sets bundled with XHTML, DocBook, and MathML. Since these are all modular specifications, you can even use the DTDs that define their entity sets without pulling in the rest of the application. For example, if you just want to use the standard HTML entity references many designers have already memorized like `&copy;` and ` `, you could add the following lines to your DTD.

```
<!ENTITY nbsp   " ">
<!ENTITY iexcl  "&#161;">
<!ENTITY cent   "&#162;">
<!ENTITY pound  "&#163;">
<!ENTITY curren "&#164;">
<!ENTITY yen    "&#165;">
<!ENTITY brvbar "&#166;">
<!ENTITY sect   "&#167;">
<!ENTITY uml    "&#168;">
<!ENTITY copy   "&#169;">
...
```

Better yet, you could store local copies of the relevant DTDs in the same directory as your own DTD and just point to them.

```
<!ENTITY % HTMLlat1 PUBLIC
    "-//W3C//ENTITIES Latin 1 for XHTML//EN"
    "xhtml-lat1.ent">
%HTMLlat1;

<!ENTITY % HTMLsymbol PUBLIC
    "-//W3C//ENTITIES Symbols for XHTML//EN"
    "xhtml-symbol.ent">
%HTMLsymbol;

<!ENTITY % HTMLspecial PUBLIC
    "-//W3C//ENTITIES Special for XHTML//EN"
    "xhtml-special.ent">
%HTMLspecial;
```

If you're using catalogs (Item 47), you can use the public IDs to locate the local caches of these entity sets.

Even if you're defining your own entity references for a particular subset of Unicode, I still suggest using the standard names. The HTML names are far and away the most popular, so if there's an HTML name for a certain character, by all means use it. For example, I would never call Unicode character 0xA0, the nonbreaking space, anything other than .

If HTML does not have a standard name for a character, I normally turn to DocBook next. Its entity names are based on the standard SGML entity names. (These are among the SGML features that got dropped out of

XML in the process of making it simple enough for mere mortals to use.) They aren't as well known as the HTML entity names, but they are much more comprehensive and are an international standard. The SGML entity names include those listed below.

ISO 8879:1986//ENTITIES Added Math Symbols: Arrow Relations//EN// XML

ISO 8879:1986//ENTITIES Added Math Symbols: Binary Operators// EN//XML

ISO 8879:1986//ENTITIES Added Math Symbols: Delimiters//EN//XML

ISO 8879:1986//ENTITIES Added Math Symbols: Negated Relations// EN//XML

ISO 8879:1986//ENTITIES Added Math Symbols: Ordinary//EN//XML

ISO 8879:1986//ENTITIES Added Math Symbols: Relations//EN//XML

ISO 8879:1986//ENTITIES Box and Line Drawing//EN//XML

ISO 8879:1986//ENTITIES Russian Cyrillic//EN//XML

ISO 8879:1986//ENTITIES Non-Russian Cyrillic//EN//XML

ISO 8879:1986//ENTITIES Diacritical Marks//EN//XML

ISO 8879:1986//ENTITIES Greek Letters//EN//XML

ISO 8879:1986//ENTITIES Monotoniko Greek//EN//XML

ISO 8879:1986//ENTITIES Greek Symbols//EN//XML

ISO 8879:1986//ENTITIES Alternative Greek Symbols//EN//XML

ISO 8879:1986//ENTITIES Added Latin 1//EN//XML

ISO 8879:1986//ENTITIES Added Latin 2//EN//XML

ISO 8879:1986//ENTITIES Numeric and Special Graphic//EN//XML

ISO 8879:1986//ENTITIES Publishing//EN//XML

ISO 8879:1986//ENTITIES General Technical//EN//XML

Finally, for mathematically oriented characters like $\oint$ and $\oplus$, I turn to MathML 2.0. Its entity sets, found at http://www.w3.org/TR/MathML2/ chapter6.html, cover more of the special characters that Unicode 3.0 and later define for mathematics than the pure SGML mathematical entity sets.

Item 5   Comment DTDs Liberally

DTDs can be as obfuscated as C++ code written by a first-year undergrad. You should use lots of comments to explain exactly what's going on. Well-written DTDs such as the modular XHTML DTD often contain more than twice as many lines of comments as actual code. The list that follows shows some of the information you should include in a DTD.

- Who wrote it and how to contact them
- The copyright and use conditions that apply to the DTD
- The version of the DTD
- The namespace URI
- The PUBLIC and SYSTEM identifiers for the DTD
- The root elements
- A brief description of the application the DTD models
- The purpose and content of each parameter entity defined
- The purpose and content of each general entity defined
- The meaning of each element declared by an ELEMENT declaration
- The meaning of each attribute declared in an ATTLIST declaration
- The meaning of each notation declared in a NOTATION declaration
- Additional constraints on elements and attributes that cannot be specified in a DTD, for example, that a length attribute must contain a positive integer

For example, let's consider a DTD designed for bank statements like the ones your bank sends you at the end of every month. If the account isn't very active a typical document might look like this:

```
<?xml version="1.0"?>
<!DOCTYPE Statement PUBLIC "-//MegaBank//DTD Statement//EN"
                           "statement.dtd">
<Statement xmlns="http://namespaces.megabank.com/">
  <Bank>MegaBank</Bank>
  <Account>
    <Number>00003145298</Number>
    <Type>Savings</Type>
    <Owner>John Doe</Owner>
  </Account>
  <Date>2003-30-02</Date>
  <OpeningBalance>5266.34</OpeningBalance>
  <Transaction type="deposit">
    <Date>2003-02-07</Date>
    <Amount>300.00</Amount>
  </Transaction>
  <Transaction type="transfer">
    <Account>
      <Number>0000271828</Number>
      <Type>Checking</Type>
      <Owner>John Doe</Owner>
```

```
    </Account>
    <Date>2003-02-07</Date>
    <Amount>200.00</Amount>
  </Transaction>
  <Transaction type="deposit">
    <Date>2003-02-15</Date>
    <Amount>512.32</Amount>
  </Transaction>
  <Transaction type="withdrawal">
    <Date>2003-02-15</Date>
    <Amount>200.00</Amount>
  </Transaction>
  <Transaction type="withdrawal">
    <Date>2003-02-25</Date>
    <Amount>200.00</Amount>
  </Transaction>
  <ClosingBalance>5478.64</ClosingBalance>
</Statement>
```

You already saw this example in French in Item 2. We'll be looking at different aspects of it in several later items too, but for now let's think about what's appropriate for the DTD.

The Header Comment

The DTD should start with one long comment that lists lots of metadata about the DTD. Generally, this would start with a title specifying the XML application the DTD describes. For example:

```
MegaBank Account Statement DTD, Version 1.1.2
```

This would normally be followed with some copyright notice. For example:

```
Copyright 2003 MegaBank
```

Alternately, you could use the copyright symbol:

```
© 2003 MegaBank
```

Do **not** use a *c* inside parentheses:

```
(c) 2003 MegaBank
```

This is not recognized by the international treaty that establishes copyright law in most countries. For similar reasons do not use both the word *Copyright* and the symbol like this:

```
Copyright © 2003 MegaBank
```

Neither of these forms is legally binding. I wouldn't want to rely on the difference between © and (c) in a defense against a claim of copyright infringement, but as a copyright owner I wouldn't want to count on them being considered the same either. If the genuine symbol is too hard to type because you're restricted to ASCII, just use the word *Copyright* with a capital *C* instead.

Now that the DTD has been copyrighted, the next question is, who do you want to allow to use the DTD and under what conditions? If the DTD is purely for internal use and you don't want to allow anyone else to use it, a simple © 2003 `MegaBank` statement may be all you need. However, by default such a statement makes the DTD at least technically illegal for anyone else to use, copy, or distribute without explicit permission from the copyright owner. If it is your intention that this DTD be used by multiple parties, you should include language explicitly stating that. For example, this statement would allow third parties to reuse the DTD but not to modify it:

```
This DTD may be freely copied and redistributed.
```

If you want to go a little further, you can allow other parties to modify the DTD. For example, one of the most liberal licenses common among DTDs is the W3C's, which states:

```
Permission to use, copy, modify and distribute the XHTML
Basic DTD and its accompanying documentation for any purpose
and without fee is hereby granted in perpetuity, provided
that the above copyright notice and this paragraph appear in
all copies. The copyright holders make no representation
about the suitability of the DTD for any purpose.
```

Often some authorship information is also included. As well as giving credit where credit is due (or assigning blame), this is important so that users know who they can ask questions of or report bugs to. Depending on circumstances the contact information may take different forms. For instance, a private DTD inside a small company might use a personal name and a phone extension while a large public DTD might provide the name and URL of a committee. Whichever form it takes, there should be some means of contacting a party responsible for the DTD. For example:

```
Prepared by the MegaBank Interdepartment XML Committee
Joseph Quackenbush, editor <jquackenbush@megabank.com>
http://xml.megabank.com/
```

If you modify the DTD, you should add your name and contact information and indicate how the DTD has been modified. However, you should also retain the name of the original author. For example:

```
International Statement DTD prepared for MegaBank France to
satisfy EEC banking regulations by Stefan Hilly
<shilly@megabank.fr>

Original prepared by the MegaBank Interdepartment XML Committee
Joseph Quackenbush, editor <jquackenbush@megabank.com>
http://xml.megabank.com/
```

Following the copyright and authorship information, the next thing is normally a brief description of the XML application the DTD describes. For example, the bank statement application might include something like this:

```
This is the DTD for MBSML, the MegaBank Statement Markup
Language. It is used for account statements sent to both
business and consumer customers at the end of each month.
Each document represents a complete statement for a single
account. It handles savings, checking, CD, and money market
accounts. However, it is not used for credit cards or loans.
```

This is often followed by useful information about the DTD that is not part of the DTD grammar itself. For example, the following comment describes the namespace URI, the root element, the public ID, and the customary system ID for this DTD.

```
All elements declared by this DTD are in the
http://namespaces.megabank.com/statement namespace.

Documents adhering to this DTD should have the root element
Statement.

This DTD is identified by these PUBLIC and SYSTEM identifiers:

    PUBLIC "-//MegaBank//DTD Statement//EN"
    SYSTEM "http://dtds.megabank.com/statement.dtd"
```

```
The system ID may be pointed at a local copy of the DTD
instead. For example,
```

```
<!DOCTYPE Statement PUBLIC "-//MegaBank//DTD Statement//EN"
                          "statement.dtd">
```

```
The internal DTD subset should *not* be used to customize
the DTD.
```

Some DTDs also include usage instructions or detailed lists of changes in the current version. There's certainly nothing wrong with this, but I normally prefer to point to some canonical source of documentation for the application. For example:

```
For more information see http://xml.megabank.com/statement/
```

This pretty much exhausts the information that's customarily stored in the header.

Declarations

Next come the individual declarations, and in well-commented DTDs each such declaration should also have a comment expanding on it in more detail. Let's begin with a simple element declaration, such as this one for an amount:

```
<!ELEMENT Amount (#PCDATA)>
```

All the declaration tells us is that the amount contains text and no child elements. It does not say whether this is an amount of money, an amount of time, an amount of oranges, or anything else. According to this declaration all of the following are valid:

```
<Amount>$3.45</Amount>
<Amount>3.45</Amount>
<Amount>-3.45</Amount>
<Amount>(3.45)</Amount>
<Amount>3.45 EUR</Amount>
<Amount>+3.45 EUR</Amount>
<Amount>23</Amount>
<Amount />
<Amount>Oh Susanna, won't you sing a song for me?</Amount>
```

Naturally, the application likely has somewhat more rigid requirements than this. Although you can't enforce these requirements with a DTD, it is a very good idea to list them in a comment like this:

```
<!-- An amount element contains an amount of money, using two
     decimal places of precision for decimalized currencies;
     e.g.,

       <Amount>3.45</Amount>

     Nondecimalized currencies such as yen are given as
     an integer; e.g.

       <Amount>3450</Amount>

     A leading minus sign is used to indicate a negative
     number.
     White space is not allowed. -->
<!ELEMENT Amount (#PCDATA)>
```

The same is true for attribute values. For example, consider this ATTLIST declaration that declares a currency attribute. The type is NMTOKEN, but what else can be said about it?

```
<!ATTLIST Amount currency NMTOKEN "USD">
```

The following comment makes it clear that the value of the currency attribute is a three-letter ASCII currency code as defined by ISO 4217:2001 *Codes for the Representation of Currencies and Funds*. The default value can be read from the ATTLIST declaration, but it doesn't hurt to be more explicit.

```
<!-- Currencies are given as one of the three-letter codes
     defined by ISO 4217. Codes for countries where we have
     branches are:

     AUD  Australian Dollar
     BRL  Brazilian Real
     BSD  Bahaman Dollar
     CAD  Canadian Dollar
     CHF  Swiss Franc
     DKK  Danish Krone
     EUR  European Currency Unit (Euro, formerly known as ECU)
     GBP  British Pound
     JPY  Japanese Yen
```

```
KYD  Cayman Dollar
MXN  Mexican Peso (new)
MXP  Mexican Peso (old)
USD  American Dollar

 The complete list can be found at
 http://www.gnucash.org/docs/C/xacc-isocurr.html.

 The default currency is U.S. dollars.
-->
```

Sometimes when one type of value, such as money or currency, is going to be used for multiple elements in the DTD, it's useful to define it as a named parameter entity that can be referenced from different locations in the DTD. In this case, the comment moves on to discuss the parameter entity.

```
<!-- A money element uses two decimal places of precision for
     decimalized currencies and an integer for nondecimalized
     currencies. Noninteger, nondecimal currencies are not
     supported. A leading minus sign is used to indicate a
     negative number. White space is not allowed. -->
<!ENTITY % money "(#PCDATA)">

<!ELEMENT Amount %money;>
```

General entities should also be commented. Sometimes if there are a lot of them, they're all related, and the names are descriptive enough, you can settle for a single comment for a group of entities. For example, this batch declares several currency symbols.

```
<!-- Currency symbols used in statements -->
<!ENTITY YenSign   "&#0xA5;">
<!ENTITY PoundSign "&#0xA3;">
<!ENTITY EuroSign  "&#0x20AC;">
```

On the other hand, sometimes an entity is unique and needs its own comment. For example, this external general entity loads the bank's current privacy policy from a remote URL.

```
<!-- The privacy policy printed on each statement is prepared
     by the legal department and updated from time to time.
     The following URL has the most recent version at any
     given time. -->
```

```
<!ENTITY privacy SYSTEM
        "http://legal.megabank.com/privacy.xml">
```

Comments can also be used and generally should be used for declarations of elements with complex types. For example, consider the following declaration of a `transaction` element.

```
<!-- A transaction element represents any action that moves
     money into or out of an account, including, but not
     limited to:

     * A withdrawal
     * A deposit
     * A transfer
     * A loan payment
     * A fee
     * Interest credit

-->
<!ELEMENT Transaction (Account?, Date, Amount)>
```

The comment gives a much clearer picture of just what a `transaction` element is for than the mere fact that each transaction has an optional account, followed by one date and one amount.

DTDs can be quite opaque and obscure, perhaps not as obfuscated as poorly written C++ but certainly worse than clean Python code. Even when the element and attribute names are properly verbose and semantic, it's always helpful to include comments clarifying the many things the declarations themselves can't say. Remember, in some cases the DTD isn't even used for direct validation. Its primary purpose is documentation. But even when a DTD is used for validation, its use as documentation is still very important. Proper commenting makes DTDs much more effective documentation for an application.

Item 6   Name Elements with Camel Case

There are no standard naming conventions for XML. I've seen XML applications that use all capitals, all small letters, separate words with hyphens, separate words with underscores, and more. Without being too fanatical about it, I recommend camel case, usingInternalCapitalization

InLieuOfWhiteSpaceLikeThis, simply because our eyes are better trained to follow it.

In the programming sections of Usenet, case conventions are second only to indentation as a source of pointless erudition and time-wasting flameage. There are many good naming and case conventions, most of which have nothing to strongly recommend them over any other. Most modern languages like Java, Delphi, and C# have tended to adopt one convention, even if they don't enforce it in the compiler, in order to facilitate the legibility of code between different people and groups. It doesn't matter which convention is picked as long as a single convention is chosen.

XML, unfortunately, does not have any recommended naming or case conventions for element and attribute names. Multiple conventions such as those listed below are used in practice.

- XSLT uses all lower case with hyphens separating words, as in `xsl:value-of`, `xsl:apply-templates`, `xsl:for-each`, and `xsl:attribute-set`.
- The W3C XML Schema Language uses camel case with an initial lowercase letter, as in `xsd:complexType`, `xsd:simpleType`, `xsd:gMonthDay`, and `xsi:schemaLocation`.
- DocBook uses lower case exclusively and never separates the words, as in `para`, `firstname`, `biblioentry`, `chapterinfo`, `methodsynopsis`, and `listitem`.
- MathML uses lower case exclusively, does not separate the words, and furthermore often abbreviates the words, as in `mi` (math italic), `mn` (math number), `mfrac` (math fraction), `msqrt` (math square root), and `reln` (relation).
- SOAP 1.2 uses camel case with initial capitals for element names (`env:Body`, `env:Envelope`, `env:Header`, and so on) and camel case with an initial lowercase letter for attributes (`encodingStyle`, `env:role`, `env:mustUnderstand`, and so on).
- XHTML uses lower case exclusively with fairly short, abbreviated names, as in `p`, `div`, `head`, `h1`, `tr`, `td`, `img`, and so on.

The one style you tend not to see is exclusively upper case like this:

```
<STATEMENT xmlns="http://namespaces.megabank.com/">
  <BANK>MegaBank</BANK>
  <ACCOUNT>
```

```
    <NUMBER>00003145298</NUMBER>
    <TYPE>Savings</TYPE>
    <OWNER>John Doe</OWNER>
  </ACCOUNT >
  <DATE>2003-30-02</DATE>
  <OPENINGBALANCE>5266.34</OPENINGBALANCE>
  <CLOSINGBALANCE>5266.34</CLOSINGBALANCE>
</STATEMENT>
```

The reason is simple: In English and other case-aware languages (not, for example, Chinese and Hebrew) human eyes are trained to recognize words by their shape. After the first or second grade, readers do not sound out each letter when trying to identify a word. At least with common words like *first, case,* and *language,* we recognize the entire word as a unit. The ascenders and descenders of letters like *d, g, l, k,* and *j* are major contributors to the overall shape of a word. HOWEVER, IN UPPER CASE ALL LETTERS HAVE EXACTLY THE SAME HEIGHT, SO A SENTENCE WRITTEN IN PURE UPPER CASE IS MUCH HARDER TO READ. See what I mean? Consequently, a document will be much easier to read if you stick to lower case or a mix of upper and lower case.

XML vocabularies do tend to be verbose. Most vocabularies prefer to spell out the complete names of things rather than abbreviating. A few applications, such as DocBook and XHTML (in which a significant fraction of the user base authors by hand), use at least some abbreviations, but in general it's considered good form to spell out all words completely. This naturally raises the question of how to break the words. Spaces aren't legal in XML, but the next best thing is an underscore, as shown below.

```
<Opening_Balance>5266.34</Opening_Balance>
<Closing_Balance>5266.34</Closing_Balance>
```

Surprisingly, this tends not to be very common. The hyphen is a little more common but is eschewed because many data binding APIs can't easily map names containing hyphens to class names. The two most common conventions are camel case and pure lower case. However, pure lower case creates excessively long new words that are not easily recognized by their shape since they're unfamiliar. Camel case is much closer to what readers subconsciously expect. It is cleaner, easier to follow, and easier to debug. Thus I recommend using camel case.

Naturally, this recommendation does vary a little by language. If you're writing your markup in a language like Hebrew or Chinese that does not distinguish upper and lower case, you can pretty much ignore this entire item. If you're marking up in a language like German where the nouns are distinguished by capitalization, you might choose to capitalize only the nouns. However, in English and many other languages, camel case is the most appropriate choice.

I do not have a strong opinion about whether the first letter of a camel-cased element or attribute name should be lower or upper case. As a Java programmer, I'm accustomed to seeing class names begin with uppercase letters and field names begin with lowercase letters. Probably because of that, an initial uppercase letter for elements and an initial lowercase letter for attributes seems more correct to me, but I freely admit that I can't rationalize that feeling. C# and Delphi programmers often have the opposite preference. All I can really recommend is that you pick one convention and stick with it.

Item 7   Parameterize DTDs

No one XML application can serve all uses. No one DTD can describe every necessary document. As obvious as this statement seems, there have been a number of failed efforts to develop DTDs that describe all possible documents in a given field, even fields as large as all business documents. A much more sensible approach is to design DTDs so they can be customized for different local environments. Elements and attributes can be added to or removed from particular systems. Names can be translated into the local language. Even content models can be adjusted to suit the local needs.

You cannot override attribute lists or element declarations in a DTD. However, you can override entity definitions, and this is the key to making DTDs extensible. If the attribute lists and element declarations are defined by reference to parameter entities, redefining the parameter entity effectively changes all the element declarations and attribute lists based on that parameter entity. When writing a parameterized DTD, almost everything of interest is defined as a parameter entity reference, including:

- Element names
- Attribute names
- Element content models

- Attribute types
- Attribute lists
- Namespace URIs
- Namespace prefixes

The extra level of indirection allows almost any aspect of the DTD to be changed. For example, consider a simple XML application that describes bank statements. A traditional monolithic DTD for this application might look like the listing below.

```
<!ELEMENT Statement (Bank, Account, Date, OpeningBalance,
                     Transaction*, ClosingBalance)>
<!ATTLIST Statement
    xmlns CDATA #FIXED "http://namespaces.megabank.com/">

<!ELEMENT Account (Number, Type, Owner)>
<!ELEMENT Number         (#PCDATA)>
<!ELEMENT Type           (#PCDATA)>
<!ELEMENT Owner          (#PCDATA)>
<!ELEMENT OpeningBalance (#PCDATA)>
<!ELEMENT ClosingBalance (#PCDATA)>
<!ELEMENT Bank           (#PCDATA)>
<!ELEMENT Date           (#PCDATA)>
<!ELEMENT Amount         (#PCDATA)>
<!ELEMENT Transaction (Account?, Date, Amount)>
<!ATTLIST Transaction
    type (withdrawal | deposit | transfer) #REQUIRED>
```

(I've stripped out most of the comments to save space. You can see them in Item 5 though. Of course, this example is a lot simpler than any real bank statement application would be.)

We can parameterize the DTD by defining each of the element and attribute names, content models, and types as parameter entity references. For example, the Number element could be defined like this:

```
<!ENTITY % Number "Number">
<!ELEMENT %Number; (#PCDATA)>
```

However, you normally shouldn't parameterize just the name. You should also parameterize the content model.

```
<!ENTITY % Number.content " #PCDATA ">
<!ELEMENT %Number; (%Number.content;)>
```

This is longer and less clear, but it is much more extensible. For example, suppose that in a particular special document you want to change the content model from simple PCDATA to a branch code followed by a customer code like this:

```
<Number>
  <BranchCode>00003</BranchCode>
  <CustomerCode>145298</CustomerCode>
</Number>
```

You can do this in the internal DTD subset by overriding the `Number.content` parameter entity reference.

```
<!DOCTYPE Statement PUBLIC "-//MegaBank//DTD Statement//EN"
                            "modular_statement.dtd" [
  <!ENTITY % Number.content " BranchCode, CustomerCode ">
  <!ELEMENT BranchCode    (#PCDATA)>
  <!ELEMENT CustomerCode  (#PCDATA)>
]>
```

Of course you can also do this in other DTDs that import the original DTD as well as in the internal DTD subset. You just need to be careful that the new entity definitions appear before the original entity definitions. (Declarations in the internal DTD subset are considered to come before everything in the external DTD subset.)

The same principles apply for elements such as `Transaction` with more complicated content models. Every element name is replaced by a parameter entity reference that points to the name. Every content model is replaced by a parameter entity reference that points to the content model. For example, the complete parameterized declaration of `Transaction` might look like this:

```
<!ENTITY % AccountElement      "Account">
<!ENTITY % DateElement         "Date">
<!ENTITY % AmountElement       "Amount">
<!ENTITY % TransactionElement "Transaction">
<!ENTITY % TransactionContent
          "%AccountElement;?, %DateElement;,
%AmountElement;">
<!ELEMENT %TransactionElement; ( %TransactionContent; )>
```

One of the most common adjustments to content models is adding an extra child element. While this can be done by redefining the complete content entity, it's even better to prepare for this in advance by defining an empty extra entity, as shown below.

```
<!ENTITY % Transaction.extra "">
<!ENTITY % TransactionContent
  "%AccountElement;?, %DateElement;, %AmountElement;
  %Transaction.extra;">
```

By default this adds nothing to the content model. However, redefining `Transaction.extra` allows new elements to be added.

```
<!ELEMENT ApprovedBy (#PCDATA)>
<!ENTITY % Transaction.extra ", ApprovedBy">
```

This works even better with choices than with sequences thanks to the insignificance of order. With a sequence we can add the new elements only at the end. With a choice, the new elements can appear anywhere.

Parameterizing Attributes

Attribute declarations also benefit from parameterization. For example, the `type` attribute of the `Transaction` element can be declared as follows.

```
<!ENTITY % TypeAtt "type">
<!ENTITY % type.extra "">
<!ATTLIST %TransactionElement; %TypeAtt;
  (withdrawal | deposit | transfer %type.extra;)
  #REQUIRED>
```

Now you can change the name of the attribute by redefining the `TypeAtt` entity or add an additional value by redefining the `type.extra` entity. For example, the redefinition below adds a `balanceInquiry` type.

```
<!ENTITY % type.extra " |  balanceInquiry ">
```

Parameterizing Namespaces

One of the biggest benefits of parameterization is that it lets you vary the namespace prefix. The fundamental principle of namespaces is that the prefix doesn't matter, only the URI matters. For instance, `Statement`, `mb:Statement`, and `bank:Statement` are all the same just as long as `Statement` is in the default namespace http://namespaces.megabank.com/ and `mb:Statement` and `bank:Statement` are in contexts where the `mb` and `bank` prefixes are mapped to the http://namespaces.megabank.com/ URI. Only the local name and URI matter. The prefix (or lack thereof) doesn't.

However, DTDs violate this principle. In a DTD only the qualified name matters. The parser validates against the prefix and local name. It ignores the namespace URI. You cannot change the prefix without changing the DTD to match. However, parameterization provides a way out of this trap. First, define the prefix and the colon as separate parameter entity references.

```
<!ENTITY % statement.prefix "stmt">
<!ENTITY % statement.colon  ":">
```

Next, define the names using these parameter entities.

```
<!ENTITY % Date.qname "%statement.prefix;%statement.colon;Date">
<!ENTITY % Transaction.qname
          "%statement.prefix;%statement.colon;Transaction">
<!ENTITY % Amount.qname
          "%statement.prefix;%statement.colon;Amount">
<!ENTITY % Account.qname
          "%statement.prefix;%statement.colon;Account">

<!ENTITY % TransactionContent
          "%Account.qname;?, %Date.qname;, %Amount.qname;">
```

You'll normally also want to parameterize the namespace declaration using either an `xmlns` or `xmlns:prefix` attribute, typically on the root element. For example:

```
<!ENTITY % NamespaceDeclaration
          "xmlns%statement.colon;%statement.prefix;">
<!ATTLIST %statement.prefix;%statement.colon;%Statement.name;
  %NamespaceDeclaration; CDATA
  #FIXED "http://namespaces.megabank.com/">
```

To adjust the prefix used in a particular instance document just override `statement.prefix` and `statement.colon` in the internal DTD subset to match what appears in the instance document. For example, the following code sets the prefix to bank.

```
<!DOCTYPE Statement PUBLIC "-//MegaBank//DTD Statement//EN"
                           "modular_statement.dtd" [
  <!ENTITY % statement.prefix "bank">
  <!ENTITY % statement.colon  ":">
]>
```

To use the default namespace set both `statement.prefix` and `statement.colon` to the empty string.

```
<!DOCTYPE Statement PUBLIC "-//MegaBank//DTD Statement//EN"
                           "modular_statement.dtd" [
  <!ENTITY % statement.prefix "">
  <!ENTITY % statement.colon  "">

]>
```

Warning *When parameterizing namespace prefixes like this, it is essential that you do not skip any steps. In particular, you must use the double indirection of defining entity references for both the element's qualified name and for its local name and prefix. Do not try something like this:*

```
<!ELEMENT %statement.prefix;%statement.colon;Number
                                        (%Number.content;)>
```

For various technical reasons, this will fail. In brief, without the double indirection the parser adds extra space around the resolved entities so that the resolved declaration is malformed.

Full Parameterization

After full parameterization, the entire DTD resembles the listing below.

```
<!ENTITY % statement.prefix "stmt">
<!ENTITY % statement.colon  ":">

<!ENTITY % NamespaceDeclaration
            "xmlns%statement.colon;%statement.prefix;">
```

```
<!ENTITY % Statement.qname
             "%statement.prefix;%statement.colon;Statement">
<!ENTITY % Bank.qname
             "%statement.prefix;%statement.colon;Bank">
<!ENTITY % Date.qname
             "%statement.prefix;%statement.colon;Date">
<!ENTITY % Transaction.qname
             "%statement.prefix;%statement.colon;Transaction">
<!ENTITY % Amount.qname
             "%statement.prefix;%statement.colon;Amount">
<!ENTITY % Account.qname
             "%statement.prefix;%statement.colon;Account">
<!ENTITY % Number.qname
             "%statement.prefix;%statement.colon;Number">
<!ENTITY % Owner.qname
             "%statement.prefix;%statement.colon;Owner">
<!ENTITY % Type.qname
             "%statement.prefix;%statement.colon;Type">
<!ENTITY % OpeningBalance.qname
             "%statement.prefix;%statement.colon;OpeningBalance">
<!ENTITY % ClosingBalance.qname
             "%statement.prefix;%statement.colon;ClosingBalance">

<!ATTLIST %Statement.qname; %NamespaceDeclaration;
    CDATA #FIXED "http://namespaces.megabank.com/">

<!ELEMENT %Statement.qname; (
  %Bank.qname;,
  %Account.qname;,
  %Date.qname;,
  %OpeningBalance.qname;,
  (%Transaction.qname;)*,
  %ClosingBalance.qname;)
>

<!ELEMENT Account (%Number.qname;, %Type.qname;, %Owner.qname;)>

<!ELEMENT %Number.qname; (#PCDATA)>
<!ELEMENT %Type.qname; (#PCDATA)>
<!ELEMENT %Owner.qname; (#PCDATA)>
```

```
<!ELEMENT %OpeningBalance.qname; (#PCDATA)>
<!ELEMENT %ClosingBalance.qname; (#PCDATA)>
<!ELEMENT %Bank.qname; (#PCDATA)>
<!ELEMENT %Date.qname; (#PCDATA)>
<!ELEMENT %Amount.qname; (#PCDATA)>

<!ENTITY % TransactionContent
     "%Account.qname;?, %Date.qname;, %Amount.qname;">
<!ELEMENT %Transaction.qname; ( %TransactionContent; )>

<!ENTITY % TypeAtt    "type">
<!ENTITY % type.extra "">
<!ATTLIST %Transaction.qname; %TypeAtt;
  (withdrawal | deposit | transfer %type.extra; )
  #REQUIRED
```

The downside is that this DTD is a lot less legible than the unparameterized DTD. However, the fully parameterized DTD is also much more extensible.

There are limits to all this. Sometimes you don't want to allow a DTD to be easily customized, or you want to allow it to be customized in some ways but not in others—for example, allowing elements to be added but not removed or reordered but not renamed. Generally, this is possible using the right combination of parameter entity references. I've perhaps overparameterized here to make a point, but you're free to pick and choose only those pieces that are helpful in your systems.

Conditional Sections

As the next step, we can allow particular documents to enable or disable particular parts of the DTD. This is accomplished with INCLUDE and IGNORE sections. The basic syntax for these directives appears below.

```
<![INCLUDE[
  <!-- Declarations the parser reads -->
]]>
<![IGNORE[
  <!-- Declarations the parser ignores -->
]]>
```

Note that the syntax is the same except for the keyword. By defining the keyword as a parameter entity reference, you can provide a switch customizers can use to turn sections of the DTD on or off. These can be individual declarations or groups of related declarations.

For example, some bank subsidiaries with different systems might wish to leave out an explicit closing balance since it can be calculated from the opening balance and the individual transactions. To enable this, you'd first define a parameter entity such as this one:

```
<!ENTITY % IncludeClosingBalance "INCLUDE">
```

Next, you'd place the declaration of the ClosingBalance element inside a conditional section that can be either included or ignored depending on the value of the IncludeClosingBalance entity.

```
<![%IncludeClosingBalance;[
  <!ELEMENT %ClosingBalance.qname; (#PCDATA)>
]]>
```

What about the content models that use ClosingBalance? How can they be parameterized? This is quite tricky, but it can be done. You'll need two declarations, one for the case that includes the closing balance and one for the case that doesn't. You'll need to define two parameter entities that identify the two cases. Do this both inside and after the conditional block that decides whether or not to use closing balances.

```
<![%IncludeClosingBalance;[
  <!ELEMENT %ClosingBalance.qname; (#PCDATA)>
  <!ENTITY  AddClosingBalance     "INCLUDE">
  <!ENTITY  DontAddClosingBalance "IGNORE">
]]>
<!ENTITY  AddClosingBalance     "IGNORE">
<!ENTITY  DontAddClosingBalance "INCLUDE">
```

Inside the conditional block the entities have the value to be used if the closing balance is included. After the conditional block the entities have the value to be used if the closing balance is not included. Order matters here. We're relying on the fact that the first declaration the parser encounters takes precedence when picking between the two possibilities.

Next, wrap the two different declarations of the Statement element in their own conditional sections based on the AddClosingBalance and DontAddClosingBalance entities.

```
<![%AddClosingBalance;[
  <!ELEMENT %Statement.qname; (
  %Bank.qname;,
  %Account.qname;,
  %Date.qname;,
  %OpeningBalance.qname;,
  (%Transaction.qname;)*,
  %ClosingBalance.qname;)
>
]]>
<![%DontAddClosingBalance;[
<!ELEMENT %Statement.qname; (
  %Bank.qname;,
  %Account.qname;,
  %Date.qname;,
  %OpeningBalance.qname;,
  (%Transaction.qname;)*)
>
]]>
```

I don't recommend going this far for all declarations in all DTDs, but when you need this much flexibility, this approach is very convenient.

Parameterization recognizes the reality that one size does not fit all. Different systems need to supply and support different information. Making DTDs parameterizable enables them to be customized and reused in ways never envisioned by the original developers. At a minimum you should allow for parameterization that does not remove information from the document: changing namespace prefixes and adding attributes and content to elements. Allowing the complete redefinition of element content models is perhaps a little more dangerous. It has the potential to break processes that depend on the information guaranteed to be provided by a document valid against the unparameterized DTD. However, even this can be useful as long as application software takes proper care not to assume too much and the customized DTD uses a different public ID so it's easily distinguished from the uncustomized variant. Parameterization is not always necessary for tightly coupled systems inside one organization, but its enhanced flexibility is very important for the loosely coupled systems of the Internet, where widely dispersed organizations routinely use applications for tasks the original developers never imagined.

Item 8   Modularize DTDs

Large, monolithic DTDs are as hard to read and understand as large, monolithic programs. While DTDs are rarely as large as even medium-sized programs, they can nonetheless benefit from being divided into separate modules, one to a file. Furthermore, this allows you to combine different DTDs in a single application. For example, modularization allows you to include your own custom vocabularies in XHTML documents.

Modularization divides a DTD into multiple, somewhat independent units of functionality that can be mixed and matched to suit. A master DTD integrates all the parts into a single driver application. Parameterization is based on internal parameter entities. Modularization is based on external parameter entities. However, the techniques are much the same. By redefining various entities, you choose which modules to include where.

I'll demonstrate with another variation of the hypothetical MegaBank statement application used in earlier items. This time we'll look at a statement that's composed of several more or less independent parts. It begins with a batch of information about the bank branch where the account is held, then the list of transactions, and finally a series of legal fine print covering things like the bank's privacy policy and where to write if there's a problem with the statement. This latter part is written in XHTML. Example 8–1 is a complete bank statement that demonstrates all the relevant parts.

Example 8–1 | A Full Bank Statement

```
<?xml version="1.0"?>
<!DOCTYPE Statement PUBLIC "-//MegaBank//DTD Statement//EN"
                          "statement.dtd">
<Statement xmlns="http://namespaces.megabank.com/">
  <Bank>
    <Logo href="logo.jpg" height="125" width="125"/>
    <Name>MegaBank</Name>
    <Motto>We Really Pretend to Care</Motto>
    <Branch>
      <Address>
        <Street>666 Fifth Ave.</Street>
```

```
        <City>New York</City>
        <State>NY</State>
        <PostalCode>10010</PostalCode>
        <Country>USA</Country>
    </Address>
  </Branch>
</Bank>
<Account>
  <Number>00003145298</Number>
  <Type>Savings</Type>
  <Owner>John Doe</Owner>
  <Address>
      <Street>123 Peon Way</Street>
      <Apt>28Z</Apt>
      <City>Brooklyn</City>
      <State>NY</State>
      <PostalCode>11239</PostalCode>
      <Country>USA</Country>
  </Address>
</Account>
<Date>2003-30-02</Date>
<AccountActivity>
    <OpeningBalance>5266.34</OpeningBalance>
    <Transaction type="deposit">
      <Date>2003-02-07</Date>
      <Amount>300.00</Amount>
    </Transaction>
    <Transaction type="transfer">
      <Account>
        <Number>0000271828</Number>
        <Type>Checking</Type>
        <Owner>John Doe</Owner>
      </Account>
      <Date>2003-02-07</Date>
      <Amount>200.00</Amount>
    </Transaction>
    <Transaction type="deposit">
      <Date>2003-02-15</Date>
      <Amount>512.32</Amount>
    </Transaction>
```

```
      <Transaction type="withdrawal">
        <Date>2003-02-15</Date>
        <Amount>200.00</Amount>
      </Transaction>
      <Transaction type="withdrawal">
        <Date>2003-02-25</Date>
        <Amount>200.00</Amount>
      </Transaction>
      <ClosingBalance>5488.66</ClosingBalance>
  </AccountActivity>
  <Legal>
    <html xmlns="http://www.w3.org/1999/xhtml">
      <body style="font-size: xx-small">
        <h1>Important Information About This Statement</h1>
        <p>
          In the event of an error in this statement,
          please submit complete details in triplicate to:
        </p>

        <p>
          MegaBank Claims Department
          3 Friday's Road
          Adamstown
          Pitcairn Island
        </p>

        <p>
          We'll get back to you in four to six weeks.
          (We're not sure which four to six weeks, but we do
          know it's bound to be some period of four to six
          weeks, sometime.)
        </p>

        <h2>Privacy Notice</h2>
        <p>
          You have none. Get used to it. We will sell your
          information to the highest bidder, the lowest
          bidder, and everyone in between. We'll give it
          away to anybody who can afford a self-addressed
          stamped envelope. We'll even trade it for a
          lifetime supply of Skinny Dip Thigh Cream &trade;.
```

```
        It's not like it costs us anything.
      </p>
    </body>
    </html>
  </Legal>
</Statement>
```

As usual, a real-world document would be considerably more complex and contain a lot more data, but this is enough to present the basic ideas.

Leaving aside comments, a modular DTD normally starts in a driver module. This is a DTD fragment that declares a couple of crucial entity references, such as those defining the namespace URI and prefix, then loads the other modules. For example, in the bank statement application, a driver DTD might look something like Example 8–2.

Example 8–2 | The Statement DTD Driver Module

```
<!ENTITY % NS.prefixed "IGNORE" >
<!ENTITY % stmt.prefix "" >

<!ENTITY % stmnt-qnames.mod SYSTEM "stmnt-qnames.mod" >

<!ENTITY % stmnt-framework.mod SYSTEM "stmnt-framework.mod" >
%stmnt-framework.mod;

<!ENTITY % stmnt-structure.mod SYSTEM "stmnt-structure.mod" >
%stmnt-structure.mod;

<!ENTITY % stmnt-address.mod SYSTEM "stmnt-address.mod" >
%stmnt-address.mod;

<!ENTITY % stmnt-branch.mod SYSTEM "stmnt-branch.mod" >
%stmnt-branch.mod;

<!ENTITY % stmnt-transaction.mod SYSTEM "stmnt-transaction.mod" >
%stmnt-transaction.mod;

<!ENTITY % stmnt-legal.mod SYSTEM "stmnt-legal.mod" >
%stmnt-legal.mod;
```

Since all the modules are loaded via entity references, this allows local bank branches and subsidiaries to substitute their own modules by redefining those entities or by writing a different driver.

In this case, the various parts have been loaded in the following order.

1. Specify whether namespace prefixes are used. (Here they aren't, by default.)
2. Define the location of the qualified names module. This will be loaded by the framework.
3. Define and load the framework, which is responsible for loading common DTD parts that cross module boundaries, such as the qualified names module, the entities module, and any common content models or attribute definitions shared by multiple elements.
4. Define and load the structure module, which is responsible for merging the different modules into a single DTD for a complete document.
5. Define the separate modules that comprise different, somewhat independent parts of the application. Here there are four:
   a. The address module
   b. The branch module
   c. The transaction module
   d. The legal module

Conditional sections can control which modules are or are not included. This makes the DTD a little harder to read, which is why I didn't show it this way in the first place; but they're essential for customizability. Example 8–3 demonstrates.

Example 8–3 | The Conditionalized Statement DTD Driver Module

```
<!ENTITY % NS.prefixed "IGNORE" >
<!ENTITY % stmt.prefix "" >

<!-- Address Module   -->
<!ENTITY % stmnt-address.module "INCLUDE" >
<![%stmnt-address.module;[
<!ENTITY % stmnt-address.mod
    SYSTEM "stmnt-address.mod" >
%stmnt-address.mod;]]>

<!ENTITY % stmnt-branch.module "INCLUDE" >
<![%stmnt-branch.module;[
<!ENTITY % stmnt-branch.mod
    SYSTEM "stmnt-branch.mod" >
%stmnt-branch.mod;]]>
```

```
<!ENTITY % stmnt-qnames.mod
    SYSTEM "stmnt-qnames.mod" >

<!ENTITY % stmnt-framework.mod SYSTEM "stmnt-framework.mod" >
%stmnt-framework.mod;

<!ENTITY % stmnt-transaction.module "INCLUDE" >
<![%stmnt-transaction.module;[
<!ENTITY % stmnt-transaction.mod
    SYSTEM "stmnt-transaction.mod" >
%stmnt-transaction.mod;]]>

<!ENTITY % stmnt-legal.module "INCLUDE" >
<![%stmnt-legal.module;[
<!ENTITY % stmnt-legal.mod SYSTEM "stmnt-legal.mod" >
%stmnt-legal.mod;]]>
```

Not all pieces can be turned on or off. Generally, the framework and the qualified names modules are required and thus are not wrapped in conditional sections.

Now let's take a look at what you might find inside the individual modules. The qualified names module (Example 8–4), which has not yet been loaded, only referenced, defines the names of elements that will be used in different content models using the parameterization techniques shown in Item 7.

Example 8–4 | The Qualified Names Module

```
<!ENTITY % Statement.qname
    "%statement.prefix;%statement.colon;Statement">
<!ENTITY % Bank.qname
    "%statement.prefix;%statement.colon;Bank">
<!ENTITY % Date.qname
    "%statement.prefix;%statement.colon;Date">
<!ENTITY % Transaction.qname
    "%statement.prefix;%statement.colon;Transaction">
<!ENTITY % Amount.qname
    "%statement.prefix;%statement.colon;Amount">
<!ENTITY % Account.qname
    "%statement.prefix;%statement.colon;Account">
<!ENTITY % Number.qname
```

```
        "%statement.prefix;%statement.colon;Number">
<!ENTITY % Owner.qname
        "%statement.prefix;%statement.colon;Owner">
<!ENTITY % Type.qname
        "%statement.prefix;%statement.colon;Type">
<!ENTITY % OpeningBalance.qname
        "%statement.prefix;%statement.colon;OpeningBalance">
<!ENTITY % ClosingBalance.qname
        "%statement.prefix;%statement.colon;ClosingBalance">

<!ENTITY % Logo.qname "%statement.prefix;%statement.colon;Logo">
<!ENTITY % Name.qname "%statement.prefix;%statement.colon;Name">
<!ENTITY % Motto.qname
        "%statement.prefix;%statement.colon;Motto">
<!ENTITY % Branch.qname
        "%statement.prefix;%statement.colon;Branch">
<!ENTITY % Address.qname
        "%statement.prefix;%statement.colon;Address">
<!ENTITY % Street.qname
        "%statement.prefix;%statement.colon;Street">
<!ENTITY % Apt.qname "%statement.prefix;%statement.colon;Apt">
<!ENTITY % City.qname "%statement.prefix;%statement.colon;City">
<!ENTITY % State.qname
        "%statement.prefix;%statement.colon;State">
<!ENTITY % PostalCode.qname
        "%statement.prefix;%statement.colon;PostalCode">
<!ENTITY % Country.qname
        "%statement.prefix;%statement.colon;Country">
<!ENTITY % AccountActivity.qname
        "%statement.prefix;%statement.colon;AccountActivity">
<!ENTITY % Legal.qname
        "%statement.prefix;%statement.colon;Legal">
```

The framework module shown in Example 8–5 actually loads the qualified names module. In addition, it loads any general modules used across the DTD, such as those for defining common attributes or character entities. In other words, the framework module defines those modules that cross other module boundaries.

Example 8–5 | The Framework Module

```
<!ENTITY % stmnt-qname.mod SYSTEM "stmnt-qnames.mod" >
%stmnt-qname.mod;

<!ENTITY % stmnt-attribs.module "INCLUDE" >
<![%stmnt-attribs.module;[
<!ENTITY % stmnt-attribs.mod SYSTEM "stmnt-attribs.mod" >
%stmnt-attribs.mod;
]]>

<!ENTITY % stmnt-model.module "INCLUDE" >
<![%stmnt-model.module;[%stmnt-model.mod;
]]>

<!ENTITY % stmnt-charent.module "INCLUDE" >
<![%stmnt-charent.module;[
<!ENTITY % stmnt-charent.mod SYSTEM "stmnt-charent.mod" >
%stmnt-charent.mod;
]]>
```

The structure module (Example 8–6) defines the root element. It provides the overall architecture of a statement document, that is, a `Statement` element that contains a variety of child elements mostly drawn from other modules.

Example 8–6 | The Structure Module

```
<!ELEMENT %Statement.qname; (
  %Bank.qname;,
  %Account.qname;,
  %Date.qname;,
  %AccountActivity.qname;,
  %Legal.qname;
)>

<!ENTITY % NamespaceDeclaration
    "xmlns%statement.colon;%statement.prefix;">

<!ATTLIST %Statement.qname; %NamespaceDeclaration;
            CDATA #FIXED "http://namespaces.megabank.com/">
```

The final step is to define the individual modules for the different classes of content. Example 8–7 demonstrates the transaction module. It's very similar to the parameterized version of the DTD shown in Item 7.

Example 8–7 | The Transaction Module

```
<!ELEMENT %AccountActivity.qname; (
    %OpeningBalance.qname;,
    (%Transaction.qname;)*,
    %ClosingBalance.qname;
)>

<!ENTITY  % OpeningBalance.content " #PCDATA ">
<!ELEMENT %OpeningBalance.qname; (%OpeningBalance.content;)>
<!ENTITY  % ClosingBalance.content " #PCDATA ">
<!ELEMENT %ClosingBalance.qname; (%ClosingBalance.content;)>
<!ENTITY  % Amount.content " #PCDATA ">
<!ELEMENT %Amount.qname; (%Amount.content;)>
<!ENTITY  % Date.content " #PCDATA ">
<!ELEMENT %Date.qname; (%Date.content;)>

<!ENTITY  % TransactionContent
    "%Account.qname;?, %Date.qname;, %Amount.qname;">
<!ELEMENT %Transaction.qname; ( %TransactionContent; )>

<!ENTITY % TypeAtt     "type">
<!ENTITY % type.extra "">
<!ATTLIST %Transaction.qname; %TypeAtt;
  (withdrawal | deposit | transfer %type.extra; )
  #REQUIRED
>
```

Notice how almost everything has been parameterized with entity references so that almost any piece can be changed independent of the other pieces. The other modules are similar. In general, the dependencies are limited and unidirectional. The modules depend on the framework and the document model, but not vice versa. This allows you to add and remove modules by adjusting the document model and the framework alone. You can change the individual parts of the module by redefining the various entities. Together with parameterization this makes the DTD extremely flexible. Not all DTDs require this level of customizability, but for those that do, modularization is extremely powerful.

Item 9   Distinguish Text from Markup

All legal text characters that can appear anywhere in an XML document can appear in #PCDATA. This includes characters like < and & that may have to be escaped with character or entity references. When an API presents the content of a node containing such a character to your code, it will give you the actual character, not the escaping text. Similarly, when you create such a node, the string you use should contain the actual character, not the entity or character reference.

Consider the following DocBook `programlisting` element. A CDATA section is used to embed a literal sequence of XML text.

```
<programlisting><![CDATA[<value>
  <double>28657</double>
 </value>]]></programlisting>
```

Everything inside the CDATA section is content, not markup. The content of this `programlisting` element is the text shown below.

```
<value>
  <double>28657</double>
</value>
```

A CDATA section is not required for this trick to work. For instance, consider the following variation of the above element.

```
<programlisting>&lt;value&gt;
  &lt;double&gt;28657&lt;/double&gt;
 &lt;/value&gt;</programlisting>
```

The content of this element is exactly the same.

```
<value>
  <double>28657</double>
</value>
```

In this case the markup of the entity references `&lt;` and `&gt;` is resolved to produce the text < and >. However, that's just syntax sugar. It does not affect the content in any way.

Now consider the reverse problem. Suppose you're creating an XML document in something at least a little more XML-aware than a text editor. Possibilities include:

- A tree-based editor like <Oxygen/> or XMLSPY
- A WYSIWYG application like OpenOffice Writer or Apple's Keynote that saves its data into XML
- A programming API such as DOM, JDOM, or XOM

In all cases, the creating tool will provide separate means to insert markup and text. The tool is responsible for escaping any reserved characters like <, >, or & when it saves the document. You do not need to do this. Indeed, if you try to pass something like `&lt;double&gt;28657 &lt;/double&gt;` into a method that expects to get plain text, it will actually save something like `&amp;lt;double&amp;gt;28657 &amp;lt;/double&amp;gt;`.

Similarly, you cannot type `<double>28657</double>` into a user interface widget that creates text and expect it to create an element. If you try it, in the serialized document you will get something like `&lt;double& gt;28657&lt;/double&gt;`. Instead, you should use the user interface widget or method call designed for creating a new element.

The key thing to remember is this: Just because something looks like an XML tag does not always mean it *is* an XML tag. Context matters. XML documents are made of markup that sometimes surrounds PCDATA, but that's the limit of the nesting. You can put PCDATA inside markup, and you can put markup inside markup, but you can't put markup inside PCDATA. CDATA sections are just an alternative means of escaping text. They are not a way to embed markup inside PCDATA.

Item 10   White Space Matters

XML defines white space as the Unicode characters space (0x20), carriage return (0x0D), line feed (0x0A), and tab (0x09), as well as any combination of them. Other invisible characters, such as the byte order mark and the nonbreaking space (0xA0), are treated the same as visible characters, such as A and $.

White space is significant in XML character data. This can be a little surprising to programmers who are used to languages like Java where white space mostly isn't significant. However, remember that XML is a markup language, not a programming language. An XML document contains data, not code. The data parts of a program (that is, the string literals) are precisely where white space does matter in traditional code. Thus it really shouldn't be a huge surprise that white space is significant in XML.

For example, the following two shape elements are not the same.

```
<shape>star</shape>
```

```
<shape>
     star
</shape>
```

Depending on the context, a particular XML application may choose to treat these two elements the same. However, an XML parser will faithfully report all the data in both shape elements to the client application. If the client application chooses to trim the extra white space from the content of the second element, that's the client application's business. XML has nothing to do with it.

The xml:space Attribute

The xml:space attribute can indicate the significance (or lack thereof) of white space within a particular element. It has two legal values, default and preserve. The value default means that the application may treat white space in the element in whatever fashion is customary for that application. For instance, it might trim off or compress excess white space. The value preserve means that white space is significant, even if it normally isn't, and the application should not adjust the white space in any way.

For example, the xml:space attribute of the text element below indicates that white space is significant and should be preserved.

```
<text xml:space="preserve">
   I try to make XML lean
   Without extra white space between
   But when I forgo
   All the spaces I know
   My markup is not at all clean.
</text>
```

However, even without this attribute, the parser would *still* report all white space in the element content to the client application. It is the responsibility of the client application to inspect the value of the `xml:space` attribute and normalize the white space accordingly (or not).

Ignorable White Space

Another special case that really isn't all that special is white space in element content, sometimes misleadingly called *ignorable white space*. This is white space in an element whose element declaration specifies that it can contain only child elements and not PCDATA. For example, suppose the PhoneNumber element has the following declaration.

```
<!ELEMENT PhoneNumber (CountryCode, AreaCode, Number)>
```

Now consider the valid PhoneNumber element below.

```
<PhoneNumber>
  <CountryCode>01</CountryCode>
  <AreaCode>212</ AreaCode >
  <Number>555-1234</ Number >
</PhoneNumber>
```

Because the DTD says this element can only contain these three child elements, the white space is ignorable. It is assumed to exist only for formatting and not to have any real purpose. Nonetheless, the parser will *still* report all of it to the client application. In most APIs, there will be no distinction between this white space and any other nonignorable white space. The notable exception here is SAX. SAX will pass this white space to the `ignorableWhiteSpace()` method rather than to the `characters()` method, so the client application can distinguish ignorable from nonignorable white space.

Tags and White Space

Inside tags the white space story is quite different. These three shape elements are the same for all intents and purposes.

```
<shape>star</shape>

<shape
            >star</shape>

<shape     >star</shape>
```

Parsers will not distinguish one from the other, and your code should not depend on the difference.

Similarly, white space in a document's prolog, epilog, and DTD is not considered. For example, these three documents are essentially the same.

```
<?xml version="1.0"?>
<?xml-stylesheet type="text/css" href="root.css"?>
<!DOCTYPE root SYSTEM "data.dtd">
<root>
  contents
</root>
```

```
<?xml version="1.0"?>

<?xml-stylesheet type="text/css" href="root.css"?>

<!DOCTYPE root SYSTEM "data.dtd">

<root>
  contents
</root>
```

```
<?xml version="1.0"?><?xml-stylesheet type="text/css"
                               href="root.css"?><!DOCTYPE
 root SYSTEM "data.dtd">
<root>
  contents
</root>
```

White Space in Attributes

The final and trickiest case are attribute values. Depending on attribute type, the parser *normalizes* attribute values before reporting them to the client application. First it converts all tabs, carriage returns, and line feeds to one space each. This is done for all attributes. Next, if the attribute has a declared type and that type is anything other than CDATA, the parser also condenses all runs of space to a single space and finally trims all leading and trailing white space from the value. However, the parser does not perform this second step for attributes that have type CDATA or are undeclared.

For example, consider the following document. The parser will trim the leading and trailing white space from the `year` attribute because it has type NMTOKEN, but it will not trim the white space from the `source` attribute that has type CDATA or the `group` attribute that is undeclared.

```
<?xml version="1.0"?>
<!DOCTYPE motto [
  <!ATTLIST motto year    NMTOKEN #IMPLIED
                  source CDATA   #IMPLIED
]>
<motto year=" 1908 " source=" Scouting  for  Boys " group="
BSA ">
  Be prepared
</motto>
```

It is not necessary for the document to be valid in order for normalization to apply—indeed, the document above is not valid—only that the attribute be declared on the element where it appears and that the parser read that declaration. All conforming XML parsers are required to read the internal DTD subset (up to the first external parameter entity reference they don't read) and use ATTLIST declarations in the internal DTD subset to decide whether to normalize or not. However, if an attribute is declared in the external DTD subset, then nonvalidating parsers may or may not read the declaration. This means validating and nonvalidating parsers can report different values for the same attribute, as can two nonvalidating parsers. The values will differ only in white space, but this can still be important. If this is a concern, make sure you use either a fully validating parser or a nonvalidating parser that is known to read the external DTD subset.

Note *Tim Bray, one of the primary authors of XML 1.0, has admitted that normalization of attribute values was a mistake. In his words, "Why the $#%%!@! should attribute values be 'normalized' anyhow? This was a pure process failure: at no point during the 18-month development cycle of XML 1.0 did anyone stand up and say 'why are you doing this?' I'd bet big bucks that if someone had, the silly thing would have died a well-deserved death."[1]*

---

1. "Re: Attribute normalisation and character entities," posted on the xml-dev mailing list, January 27, 2000. Accessed in June 2003 at http://www.lists.ic.ac.uk/hypermail/xml-dev/xml-dev-Jan-2000/1085.html.

Schemas

The W3C XML Schema Language uses the `whiteSpace` facet to specify whether white space in an attribute or element with a simple type should be preserved, replaced, or collapsed.

- *Preserved white space* is like `xml:space="preserve"`; that is, all white space is considered to be significant.
- *Replaced white space* replaces all tabs, carriage returns, and line feeds with a single space each. Thus the number of white space characters is preserved but their type may be changed.
- *Collapsed white space* first replaces all carriage returns and line feeds with a single space each, then replaces each run of consecutive spaces with a single space, and finally trims all leading and trailing white space.

However, once again this only offers a hint to the client application. The parser will *still* report all white space to the client application in the same way it would without the schema. Indeed, the `whiteSpace` facet doesn't even change the set of valid content for an element. For example, suppose the `shape` element is declared in a schema like the one below.

```
<xsd:element name="shape">
  <xsd:simpleType>
    <xsd:restriction base="xsd:string">
      <xsd:whiteSpace value="collapse"/>
    </xsd:restriction>
</xsd:element>
```

The following three elements are all still valid.

```
<shape> triangle    rectangle   square  </shape>

<shape>triangle rectangle square</shape>

<shape>
      triangle
      rectangle
      square
</shape>
```

Bottom line: White space is significant in XML documents except in the prolog, epilog, and tags. Parsers report all white space in element content and attribute values to the client application. Depending on the DTD, the `xml:space` attribute, and the value of the `whiteSpace` facet in the schema, parsers may indicate that white space is or is not significant. However, it will all be reported. It is up to each individual application to determine the rules by which white space is treated.

2 Structure

Designing an XML application is an exercise in modeling a problem domain, similar in many respects to designing a class hierarchy in an object-oriented programming language or defining the tables that make up a database schema. It involves mapping a real-world system into the constructs the language makes available. In the case of XML, you map real-world information into trees, elements, and attributes. The mapping may be implicit or it may be described in a schema written in some language such as RELAX NG, DTDs, Schematron, or the W3C XML Schema Language.

Part 2 discusses the issues that arise when performing such mappings. It shows you which XML structures are appropriate for which kinds of data and which ones aren't appropriate at all as a repository for significant data. (XML has a lot of syntax sugar that, while useful for authoring, doesn't offer a lot of additional expressiveness.) This section covers tools and techniques for designing and documenting such mappings as namespaces and schemas. It also provides a few hints for ensuring that your models are both representative now and extensible in the future.

Item 11   Make Structure Explicit through Markup

All structure in an XML document should be indicated through XML tags, not through other means. XML parsers are designed to process tags. They do not see any other form of structure in the data, explicit or implicit. Using anything except tags and their attributes to delineate structure makes the data much harder to read. In essence, programmers who write software to process such documents must invent mini-parsers for the non-XML structures in the data.

For example, in the bank statement XML application we examined in Part 1, a transaction could theoretically be represented like this:

```
<Transaction>Withdrawal 2003 12 15 200.00</Transaction>
```

This would require applications reading the data to know that the first field is the kind of transaction, the second field is the year, the third is the month, the fourth is the day, and the last is the amount. In most cases a client application would have to split this data along the white space to further process it. On the other hand, the client application has less work to do and can operate more smoothly if it's presented with data marked up like this:

```
<Transaction type="withdrawal">
  <Date>2003-12-15</Date>
  <Amount>200.00</Amount>
</Transaction>
```

Here each useful unit of information can be seen as the complete content of an element or an attribute.

Tag Each Unit of Information

The key idea is that what's between two tags should be the minimum unit of text that can usefully be processed as a whole. It should not need to be further subdivided for the common use cases. An Amount element contains a complete amount and nothing else. The amount is a single thing, a whole unit of information, in this case a number. It does not have internal structure that any application is likely to care about.

Occasionally the question of what constitutes a unit may depend on where and how the data is used. For example, consider the Date element in the above Transaction element. It contains implicit markup based on the hyphen. It could instead be written like this:

```
<Date>
  <Year>2003<Year>
  <Month>12</Month>
  <Day>15</Day>
</Date>
```

Whether this is useful or not depends on how the dates will be used. If they're merely formatted on a page as is or passed to an API that knows how to create Date objects from strings like 2003-12-15, you may not need to separate out the month, day, and year as separate elements. Generally, whether to further subdivide data depends on the use to which the information will be put and the operations that will be performed on it. If dates are intended purely to notate a particular moment in history, then a format like `<Date>2003-12-15</Date>` is appropriate. This would be useful for figuring out whether it's time to drink a bottle of wine, determining whether a worker is eligible for retirement benefits, or calculating how much time remains on a car's warranty, for example. In none of these cases is the individual day, month, or even year very significant. Only the combination of these quantities matters. That dates are even divided into these quantities in the first place is mostly a fluke of astronomy and the planet we live on, not something intrinsic to the nature of time.

On the other hand, consider weather data. Since weather varies with the seasons and has a roughly periodic structure tied to the years and the months, it does make sense to compare weather from one February to the next, without necessarily considering the year. Other real-world data tied to annual and monthly cycles includes birthdays, pay periods, and financial results. If you're modeling this sort of data, you will want to be able to separate months, days, and years from each other. In this case, more structured markup such as `<date><year>2003</year><month>12</month><day>15</day></date>` is appropriate. The question is really whether processes manipulating this data are likely to want to treat the text as a single unit of information or as a composite of more fundamental data.

However, just because you don't need to extract the individual components of a date does not mean that no one who works with the data will need to do that. Generally, I prefer to err on the side of too much markup rather than too little. Larger chunks of data can normally be formed by manipulating the parent or ancestor elements when necessary. It is easier to remove structure when processing than to add it.

The classic example of what *not* to do is Scalable Vector Graphics (SVG). SVG uses huge amounts of non-XML-based markup. For example, consider the following `polygon` element.

```
<polygon points="350,75 379,161 469,161 397,215 423,301
                 350,250 277,301 303,215 231,161 321,161" />
```

In particular, look at the value of the `points` attribute. That's not just a string of characters—it's a sequence of x, y coordinates. An SVG processor cannot simply work with the attribute value. Instead, it first has to divide the attribute value into matching pairs and decide which are x's and which are y's. The proper approach would have been to define the coordinates as child elements.

```
<polygon>
  <point x="350" y="75"/>
  <point x="379" y="161"/>
  <point x="469" y="161"/>
  <point x="397" y="215"/>
  <point x="423" y="301"/>
  <point x="350" y="250"/>
  <point x="277" y="301"/>
  <point x="303" y="215"/>
  <point x="231" y="161"/>
  <point x="321" y="161"/>
</polygon>
```

This way the XML processor would present the coordinates to the application already nicely parsed. This also demonstrates the important point that attributes don't support structure very well. (See Item 12.) Structured data normally needs to be stored in element hierarchies. Only the lowest, most unstructured pieces should be put in attributes.

The reason for this bad design was to avoid excessive file size and verbosity. However, terseness of markup is an explicit nongoal of XML. If you really care that much about how many characters a user must type, you shouldn't be using XML in the first place. In this case, however, terseness truly has no benefits. Almost all practical SVG is either generated by a computer program or drawn in a WYSIWYG application such as Adobe Illustrator. Software can easily handle a more verbose, pure XML format. Indeed, it would be considerably easier to write such SVG processing and generating software if all the structures were based on XML. File size is even less important. SVG documents are routinely gzipped in practice anyway, which rapidly eliminates any significant differences between the less and more verbose formats. (See Item 50.)

SVG goes even further in the wrong direction by incorporating the non-XML Cascading Style Sheets (CSS) format. For example, a polygon can be filled, stroked, and colored like this:

```
<polygon style="fill: red; stroke: blue; stroke-width: 10"
         points="350,75 379,161 469,161 397,215 423,301
                 350,250 277,301 303,215 231,161 321,161" />
```

Fortunately for the most important and common styles, SVG also allows an attribute-based alternative. For example, this is an equivalent polygon:

```
<polygon fill="red" stroke="blue" stroke-width="10"
        points="350,75 379,161 469,161 397,215 423,301
                350,250 277,301 303,215 231,161 321,161" />
```

Nonetheless, because the CSS `style` attribute is allowed, an SVG renderer needs both an XML parser and a CSS parser. It's easier to write a CSS parser than an XML parser, but it's still a nontrivial amount of work. Furthermore, it's much harder to detect violations of CSS. Its less draconian error handling makes it easier to produce incorrect SVG documents that may not be noticed by authors. SVG is less interoperable and reliable than it would be if it were pure XML.

XSL Formatting Objects (XSL-FO), by contrast, is an example of how to properly integrate XML formats with legacy formats such as CSS. It maintains the CSS property names, values, and meanings. However, it replaces CSS's native structure with an XML equivalent. XSL-FO doesn't have polygons, but here's a paragraph whose color is blue, whose background color is red, and whose border is ten pixels wide:

```
<fo:block color="blue" background-color="red" border="10px">
  The text of the paragraph goes here.
</fo:block>
```

This has all the advantages of familiarity with CSS but none of the disadvantages of non-XML structure. The semantics of CSS are retained while the syntax is changed to more convenient XML.

Avoid Implicit Structure

You need to be especially wary of implicit markup, often indicated by white space. For example, consider the simple case of a name:

```
<Name>Lenny Bruce</Name>
```

The name is sometimes treated as a single thing, but quite often you need to extract the first name and last name separately, most commonly to sort by last name. This seems easy enough to do: just split the string on the white space. The first name is everything before the space. The last name is everything after the space. Of course, this algorithm falls apart as soon as you add middle names:

```
<Name>Lenny Alfred Bruce</Name>
```

You may decide that you don't really care about middle names, that they can just be appended to the first name. You're just going to sort by last name anyway. However, now consider what happens when the last name contains white space:

```
<Name>Stefania de Kennessey</Name>
```

The obvious algorithm assigns people the wrong last name. This can be quite offensive to the person whose name you've butchered, not that I haven't seen a lot of naïve software that does exactly this.

What about titles? For example, consider these names:

```
<Name>Mr. Lenny Bruce</Name>
<Name>Dr. Benjamin Spock</Name>
<Name>Timothy Leary, Ph.D.</Name>
<Name>William Kunstler, Esq.</Name>
<Name>Ms. Anita Hoffman</Name>
<Name>Prof. John H. Exton, M.D., Ph.D.</Name>
```

Given a large list of likely titles you can probably design an algorithm that accounts for these, but what seemed like a simple operation is rapidly complexifying in the face of real-world data.

Finally, let's recall that not all cultures put the family name last. For example, in Japan the family name normally comes first:

```
<Name>Kawabata Yasunari</Name>
```

Thus when sorting Japanese names you sort by first name rather than last name. Do you really want to try to design a system that can guess whether a string is a Japanese name or an English one? To make matters worse, often, but not always, when Japanese names are translated into English the order of the names is reversed:

```
<Name>Yasunari Kawabata</Name>
```

In fact, Japanese written in Kanji normally doesn't even use white space between the family and given name:

```
<Name> 川端康成 </Name>
```

The problem is a lot messier than it looks at first glance.

All of this goes away as soon as you use explicit markup to identify the different components of a name, instead of relying on software to sort it out.

```
<Name><Given>Lenny</Given> <Family>Bruce</Family></Name>
<Name><Given>Lenny <Middle>Alfred</Middle> Bruce</Family></Name>
<Name>
  <Given>Stefania</Given> <Family>de Kennessey</Family>
</Name>
<Name>
  <Title>Mr.</Title> <Given>Lenny</Given> <Family>Bruce</Family>
</Name>
<Name>
  <Title>Dr.</Title>
  <Given>Benjamin</Given> <Family>Spock</Family>
</Name>
<Name>
  <Given>Timothy</Given>
  <Family>Leary</Family>, <Title>Ph.D.</Title>
</Name>
<Name>
  <Given>William</Given>
  <Family>Kunstler</Family>, <Title>Esq.</Title>
</Name>
<Name>
  <Title>Ms.</Title> <Given>Anita</Given>
  <Family>Hoffman</Family>
<Name>
  <Title>Prof.</Title>
  <Given>John</Given> <MiddleInitial>H.</MiddleInitial>
  <Family>Exton</Family>,
  <Title>M.D.</Title>, <Title>Ph.D.</Title>
</Name>
<Name><Family>川端 </Family><Given>康成 </Given></Name>
<Name><Family>Kawabata</Family> <Given>Yasunari</Given></Name>
<Name><Given>Yasunari</Given> <Family>Kawabata</Family></Name>
```

Another example of abuse of white space occurs in narrative documents that attempt to treat white space as significant, as in the following poem.[1]

---

1. "Now" by Eleanor Alexander, republished in *The County Series of Contemporary Poetry No. IX, Middlesex Poetry* (High Holborn, U.K.: Fowler Wright Ltd., 1928).

```
<poem type="sonnet" poet="Eleanor Alexander">
  For me, my friend, no grave-side vigil keep
  With tears that memory and remorse might fill;
  Give me your tenderest laughter earth-bound still,
  And when I die you shall not want to weep.
  No epitaph for me with virtues deep
  Punctured in marble pitiless and chill:
  But when play time is over, if you will,
  The songs that soothe beloved babes to sleep.

  No lenten lilies on my breast and brow
  Be laid when I am silent; roses red,
  And golden roses bring me here instead,
  That if you love or bear me I may know;
  I may not know, nor care, when I am dead:
  Give me your songs, and flowers, and laughter now.
</poem>
```

Here the line breaks indicate the end of a verse, and the blank lines indicate the end of a stanza. However, this can be problematic when the content is displayed in an environment where the lines are wrapped or the white space is otherwise adjusted for typographical reasons. Furthermore, these white-space-based constraints can't be validated with respect to either XML (every stanza contains one or more lines) or poetry (the first stanza of a sonnet has eight lines; the second has six). Authors are likely to make mistakes when the white space is too significant. It's much better to make the stanza and line division explicit, as shown below.

```
<poem type="sonnet" poet="Eleanor Alexander">
  <stanza>
    <line>For me, my friend, no grave-side vigil keep</line>
    <line>With tears that memory and remorse might fill;</line>
    <line>
      Give me your tenderest laughter earth-bound still,</line>
    <line>And when I die you shall not want to weep.</line>
    <line>No epitaph for me with virtues deep</line>
    <line>Punctured in marble pitiless and chill:</line>
    <line>But when play time is over, if you will,</line>
    <line>The songs that soothe beloved babes to sleep.</line>
  </stanza>
```

```
<stanza>
  <line>No lenten lilies on my breast and brow</line>
  <line>Be laid when I am silent; roses red,</line>
  <line>And golden roses bring me here instead,</line>
  <line>That if you love or bear me I may know;</line>
  <line>I may not know, nor care, when I am dead:</line>
  <line>
    Give me your songs, and flowers, and laughter now.</line>
  </stanza>
</poem>
```

I think the only time you should insist on exact white space preservation is when the white space is actually a significant component of the content, as in the poetry of e.e. cummings or Python source code.

Computer source code, whether in Python or in other languages, is a special case. It has a huge amount of structure that just does not lend itself to expression in XML. Furthermore, parsers for this structure exist and are as common and useful as parsers for XML. (They're generally bundled as parts of compilers.) Most importantly, there are only two normal uses for source code embedded in XML documents:

1. Passing the code to a compiler
2. Displaying the complete, unformatted code to an end user, as in a programming tutorial

In neither of these cases is the process reading the XML likely to want to subdivide the data into smaller parts and treat them individually, even though these parts demonstrably exist. Thus it makes sense to leave the structure in source code implicit.

Where to Stop?

At the absolute extreme I've seen it suggested (facetiously) that an integer such as 6587 should be written like this:

```
<integer>
  <thousands>6</thousands>
  <hundreds>5</hundreds>
  <tens>8</tens>
  <ones>7</ones>
</integer>
```

Obviously, this is going too far. It would be far more troublesome to process than a simple, unmarked-up number. After all, almost everyone who wants to use a number treats it as an atomic quantity rather than a composition of single digits. However, this does suggest a good rule of thumb for where to stop inserting tags. Anything that will normally be treated as a single atomic value should not be further divided by markup. However, if a value is composed of smaller parts that will need to be addressed individually, they should be marked up.

Here are a few other common edge cases and my thoughts on why I would or wouldn't further divide them.

- *Numbers with units such as 7px, 8.5kg, or 108db:* Neither the unit nor the number means anything in isolation. It doesn't help much to know that a mass is denoted in kilograms without knowing how many kilograms. Similarly, there's not much point to knowing that the mass is 3.2 if you don't know whether that's 3.2 grams, 3.2 kilograms, or 3.2 metric tons. Thus I prefer to write such quantities as `<mass>7.5kg</mass>` and `<speed>32mph</speed>`.

- *Time:* The division of time into hours, minutes, and seconds is very similar to the date case. Indeed, a date is just a somewhat more coarsely grained measure of time, and times can be appended to dates to more precisely identify a moment. However, *durations* of time are a different story. These include quantities such as the flight time from San Jose to New York or the number of minutes that can be recorded on a video tape in SP mode. Here it is the total time that matters, not the beginning point and end point. The division of time into 24 hours per day, 60 minutes per hour, and 60 seconds per minute is a historical relic of Babylonian astronomy and their base-60 number system, not anything fundamentally related to natural quantities (a point proved by the fact that durations can be flattened to a total number of minutes or seconds rather than using three different units). Thus I tend to treat a duration as a single quantity and write it using a form like `<FlightTime>6h32m</FlightTime>` instead of a more structured form such as `<FlightTime><hours>6</hours><minutes>32</minutes></FlightTime>`.

- *Lists:* Both DTDs and schemas define list data types that can describe content separated by white space. In DTDs, these include attributes declared to have type IDREFS or ENTITIES. In schemas this includes any element or attribute declared with a list type. I really don't like this. This may be the only way to store plural quantities such as a list of entities or numbers in attributes. However, when faced with potentially plural things I prefer to use child elements. Overuse of attributes leads to markup that's hard to manage.

- *URLs:* A URL (or URI) has a lot of internal structure. For instance, the URL http://www.cafeconleche.org:80/books/xmljava/chapters/ ch09s07.html#d0e15480 has a protocol, a host (which itself has a host name, a domain name, and a top-level domain), a port, a file path, and a fragment identifier. Theoretically, you could mark this up like so:

```
<url>
   <protocol>http</protocol>
   <host>www.cafeconleche.org</host>
   <port>80</port>
   <file>/books/xmljava/chapters/ch09s07.html</file>
   <fragment>d0e15480</fragment>
</url>
```

However, in practice this is almost never done, and with good reason. Almost every use of a URL, from passing it to a method in a programming API to copying it and pasting into the browser location bar to painting it on the side of a building, expects to receive an entire URL, not a piece of one. In those rare cases where you need to divide a URL into its component parts, most APIs provide adequate support. Thus it's best not to subdivide the URL beyond what everyone expects.

In general, if I suspect that an element might usefully be further divided, I will divide it. XML has the opposite of the Humpty-Dumpty problem: It's much easier to put the pieces back together again when content is split by tags than it is to break it apart when there aren't enough tags. Having too much markup in your data is rarely a practical problem. Having too little markup is much more cumbersome.

Item 12   Store Metadata in Attributes

There's a recurring mild flame war on the xml-dev mailing list about when one should use attributes and when one should use elements. There's a slightly hotter one about whether one should ever use attributes at all. The bottom line is that it's really up to you. Do what feels right for your application. Most developers prefer to use attributes for metadata as opposed to the data itself, but this is a very rough rule of thumb at best. Of course, what's data and what's metadata depends heavily on who is reading your documents for what purpose.

One way to determine whether information is metadata or not is to ask yourself whether a person reading the text would want to see it. For example, consider the following paragraph from the XML Base specification:

> The set of characters allowed in xml:base attributes is the same as for XML, namely [Unicode]. However, some Unicode characters are disallowed from URI references, and thus processors must encode and escape these characters to obtain a valid URI reference from the attribute value.[1]

If I were to mark this up in DocBook, every word above would be part of the element content.

```
<para id="p32">
  The set of characters allowed in <markup>xml:base</markup>
  attributes is the same as for XML, namely
  <ulink url="http://www.w3.org/TR/xmlbase/#Unicode"
  >[Unicode]</ulink>. However, some Unicode characters
  are disallowed from URI references, and thus processors
  <ulink type="Must, May, etc." url=
  "http://www.w3.org/TR/xmlbase/#dt-must">must</ulink> encode
  and escape these characters to obtain a valid URI reference
  from the attribute value.
</para>
```

However, the following parts would be stored in attribute values.

- IDs
- Styles
- URLs of the remote links
- Titles of the remote links
- Revision dates
- Author's name

---

1. XML Base W3C Recommendation, June 27, 2001. Accessed online in June 2003 at http://www.w3.org/TR/xmlbase/#escaping.

What unifies all these pieces of data is that the reader doesn't want to see any of them as part of the normal flow of text. They're useful, and they have a purpose. For instance, without the URL in the `url` attribute, the browser doesn't know where a link goes to. Without the `id` attribute, other pages can't link to this paragraph. Without revision tracking information, the author can't review and accept or reject changes. However, none of these things matter to the end reader, who just wants to read words in a row. Some of the attribute values may affect how the text is presented to the reader, for example, whether a word is italicized or whether a link is underlined. But in no case does the reader actually want to see the text that makes up the attribute value. After all, this would be much more confusing.

> p32 The set of characters allowed in xml:base attributes is the same as for XML, namely [Unicode http://www.w3.org/TR/xmlbase/ #Unicode]. However, some Unicode characters are disallowed from URI references, and thus processors must Must, May, etc. http://www. w3.org/TR/xmlbase/#dt-must encode and escape these characters to obtain a valid URI reference from the attribute value.

In a few special circumstances, the reader may want to see the content of the attribute value. For instance, when the user moves the mouse over a link, the browser may show the link title or URL in a tooltip or the browser status bar. However, this is extra information that still isn't provided as part of the normal flow of text.

The dividing line between data and metadata isn't nearly as clear in record-like documents as it is in narrative documents. Different users may be interested in different aspects of the content. What is irrelevant data for one user may well be the whole point for another reader. There are often several reasonable ways to divide the data between element content and attribute values. Nonetheless, the same basic principle applies: If the information is core, place it in element content. Reserve attributes for housekeeping information such as arbitrary ID numbers.

Although the rough distinction between data and metadata is a useful way to decide whether or not to place some simple text in an attribute, there is one rule that trumps this: Structured data should be part of element content. Attribute values contain undifferentiated text. They have no substructure, at least none that's accessible to the XML parser. An attribute value can contain a number, a URL, a date, a time, or some other atomic value. However, more complicated structures often require division into component parts, and you can only reasonably do this with elements. For example, consider this `blockquote` element where the `src` attribute is used to identify the source of the quote.

```
<blockquote src="Christopher Locke, "Post-Apocalypso," in
   The Cluetrain Manifesto
   (Cambridge, MA: Perseus Books, 1999), p. 175">
   <p>
     There never was any grand plan on the Internet, and there
     isn't one today. The Net is just the Net. But it
     <em>has</em> provided an  extraordinarily efficient means
     of communication to people so long ignored, so long
     invisible, that they're only now figuring out what to do
     with it. Funny thing: lawless, planless, management-free,
     they're figuring out what to do with the Internet much
     faster than government agencies, academic institutions,
     media conglomerates, and Fortune-class corporations.
   </p>
</blockquote>
```

There are many different units of information in the `src` attribute: the author, the title of the chapter, the title of the book, the publisher, the page number, and so on. Perhaps these could be divided into separate attributes as shown below.

```
<blockquote author_name="Christopher Locke"
            chapter_title="Post-Apocalypso"
            book_title="The Cluetrain Manifesto"
            page_number="175"
            publisher_name="Perseus Books"
            publisher_city="Cambridge"
            year="1999">
...
```

However, this loses track of the substructure, such as the difference between first and last name or the order. For instance, I carefully wrote the original citation so that it adheres to the rules of the *Chicago Manual of Style*. Once the citation has been split into separate attributes, that's no longer true.

Even worse, what if the chapter has more than one author? There can be only one attribute with the name `author` on any given element, but there's no limit to the number of child elements it can have. No, what's really called for here is a child `source` element, even though the source is obviously metadata about the quotation rather than core information.

```
<blockquote>
  <p>
    There never was any grand plan on the Internet, and there
    isn't one today. The Net is just the Net. But it
    <em>has</em> provided an  extraordinarily efficient means
    of communication to people so long ignored, so long
    invisible, that they're only now figuring out what to do
    with it. Funny thing: lawless, planless, management-free,
    they're figuring out what to do with the Internet much
    faster than government agencies, academic institutions,
    media conglomerates, and Fortune-class corporations.
  </p>

  <source>
    <author>
      <name><given>Christopher<given> <family>Locke</family>
      </name>
    </author>
    <chapter>
      <title>Post-Apocalypso</title>
    </chapter>
    <book>The Cluetrain Manifesto</book>
    <page>175</page>
    <publisher>Perseus Books</publisher>
    <publisher_city>Cambridge, MA</publisher_city>
    <year>1999</year>
  </source>
</blockquote>
```

Once the substructure is expressed with elements, it's straightforward for a stylesheet to show or hide any parts of the content you do or do not want shown. For example, you might want to include the name of the author, the title of the book, the year, and the page number but leave out the publisher and chapter title. The following CSS rules accomplish that.

```
source, author, book, year, page { display: inline }
publisher, publisher_city, chapter { display: none }
```

You really couldn't do that if you had just one big attribute to work with.

Elements have one final advantage over attributes: They are much more extensible in the face of future changes. For example, many libraries like to give the author's birth year in their card catalogs. With elements this is easy to add.

```
<author>
  <name><given>Christopher<given> <family>Locke</family></name>
  <born>1950</born>
</author>
```

With attributes, adding additional content is much more cumbersome.

One common use of attributes that I think does clearly meet the characteristic of being metadata that belongs in an attribute rather than data for a child element is the need to identify the subtype of a particular element. For instance, in HTML and XHTML you often see elements annotated with a `class` attribute, most commonly `div` and `span`.

```
<div class="sect2">...</<div>
<div class="titlepage">...</div>
<div class="informalexample">...</div>
<div class="summary">...</div>
<span class="person">...</span>
<span class="book">...</span>
<img class="equation" src="maxwell.gif" width="120"
height="30"/>
```

Here, the `class` attribute is extending the normally fairly fixed HTML vocabulary. Identifying elements by class enables the author to apply different styles or processing rules to elements of different classes, even though they have the same name. This, I think, is clearly metadata. It is metadata in the same way that an element name is metadata. In effect these attributes are substituting for invalid element names. Thus they belong in the start-tag, just like an element name. If you find you're using such attributes frequently, it indicates that your markup vocabulary is not a good fit to your data.

DocBook uses the `role` attribute in a similar way to allow authors to attach arbitrary roles to elements that the designers of DocBook did not anticipate. A little more formally, the DocBook `systemitem` element has a `class` attribute whose value is given as an enumerated list of specific types of `systemitem` such as `domainname`, `ipaddress`, `newsgroup`, and `username`.

```
<phrase role="formula">H2O</phrase>
<phrase role="prescription">Paxil, 20 mg</phrase>
<personname role="plumber">
  <firstname>Laurence</firstname>
  <lastname>Bienvenue</lastname>
</personname>
<systemitem class="domainname">www.cluetrain.com</systemitem>
<systemitem class="username">eharold</systemitem>
```

DocBook treats this very sensibly. If a particular role or class is found to be used frequently in practice, it's a strong candidate for addition to the next version of DocBook as an element. Indeed several current DocBook elements such as `environvar` and `prompt` started life as `systemitem` classes or mere roles.

In the end, if you have any doubt about whether information is metadata or data, I suggest that you place it in element content. There's little an attribute can do that an element can't, but much that an element can do that an attribute can't. The costs of mismarking data that should be elements as attributes are much higher than the costs of mismarking data that should be attributes as elements.

Item 13 Remember Mixed Content

XML was designed for narrative documents meant to be read by humans: books, novels, plays, poems, technical manuals, and most especially web pages. Its use for record-oriented data was a happy accident. Narrative documents have a number of characteristics that are not often true of more record-like data. The most significant is mixed content. For example, consider this simple paragraph taken from the second edition of the XML specification.

```
<p diff="add">This second edition is <emph>not</emph> a new
version of XML (first published 10 February 1998); it merely
incorporates the changes dictated by the first-edition errata
(available at <loc
href="http://www.w3.org/XML/xml-19980210-errata">
http://www.w3.org/XML/xml-19980210-errata</loc>) as a
convenience to readers. The errata list for this second
edition
```

```
is available at <loc href=
"http://www.w3.org/XML/xml-V10-2e-errata">
http://www.w3.org/XML/xml-V10-2e-errata</loc>.</p>
```

It has seven children in the following order:

1. A text node starting "This second edition is"
2. The `emph` element
3. A text node starting " a new version of XML"
4. A `loc` element
5. A text node starting ") as a convenience"
6. A `loc` element
7. A text node containing a single period

The text is on the same level of the tree as the child elements. It is a crucial part of the meaning of the paragraph. It cannot be ignored.

Nonetheless, numerous tools and APIs blithely assume mixed content simply doesn't exist. They also often assume that order doesn't matter and that documents are not recursive. These assumptions are true of relational tables. While these assumptions may also be accurate about XML formats that are little more than database dumps (for instance, RSS 0.9.x), they are definitely not true of most real-world XML. They aren't even true of as many specific applications as their inventors often think. For example, RSS was originally designed to provide simple record-like news items like the following one.

```
<item>
  <title>Xerlin 1.3 released</title>
  <description>
    Xerlin 1.3, an open source XML Editor written in Java,
    has been released. Users can extend the application via
    custom editor interfaces for specific DTDs. New features
    in version 1.3 include XML Schema support, WebDAV
    capabilities, and various user interface enhancements.
    Java 1.2 or later is required.
  </description>
  <link>http://www.cafeconleche.org/#news2003April7</link>
</item>
```

However, it rapidly became apparent that this wasn't enough to meet the needs of most web sites. In particular, site authors often wanted to put mixed content in the description as shown next.

```
<description>
  <a href="http://www.xerlin.org"><strong>Xerlin
  1.3</strong></a>,an open source XML Editor written in
  <a href="http://java.sun.com/">Java</a>, has been
  released. Users can extend the application via custom
  editor interfaces for specific DTDs. New features in
  version 1.3 include:
  <ul>
     <li>XML Schema support</li>
     <li>WebDAV capabilities</li>
     <li>Various user interface enhancements</li>
  </ul>
  Java 1.2 or later is required.
</description>
```

However, since RSS doesn't allow this, authors and vendors instead converged on the truly awful solution of escaping the markup for eventual display as HTML.

```
<description>
    &lt;a href="http://www.xerlin.org">&lt;strong>Xerlin
    1.3&lt;/strong>&lt;/a>, an open source XML Editor written
    in &lt;a href="http://java.sun.com/">Java&lt;/a>, has
    been released. Users can extend the application via
    custom editor interfaces for specific DTDs. New features
    in version 1.3 include:
     &lt;ul>
       &lt;li>XML Schema support&lt;/li>
       &lt;li>WebDAV capabilities&lt;/li>
       &lt;li>Various user interface enhancements&lt;/li>
     &lt;/ul>
    Java 1.2 or later is required.
  </description>
```

This ugliness wasn't created just so mixed content can be avoided. It also avoids the use of namespaces (Item 20) and modularization (Item 8). But fear of mixed content is certainly a major contributing factor. What's really telling in this example is that the community promptly hacked their own uglier version of mixed content back into RSS, even though the original developers had tried to avoid it. Mixed content is not a mistake. It is not something to be feared. It is at the core of much of the information XML is designed to mark up.

Tools that fail to handle mixed content properly range from simple programs such as XML pretty printers to complete data binding APIs. One particularly perverse API I encountered read mixed content but reordered it so all the plain text nodes came after all the child elements. Many other tools came into existence without support for mixed content and had to undergo complicated and expensive retrofitting when the need to support it became obvious.

Another common problem is software that claims to be able to handle mixed content but was never extensively tested with narrative documents. I've brought more than one XML editor to its knees by loading in a book written in DocBook. Too often programmers introduce bugs into their code based on mistaken notions of what XML documents can look like. For example, a programmer who forgets about mixed content may try to store the children of an element as a list of `Element` objects, rather than a more generic list of `Object` or `Node` objects. True XML software needs to be prepared to handle all the many forms XML can take, including both narrative and record-like documents.

The underlying cause of these problems is that the designers started with the question "How do I convert an object into an XML document?" rather than the much tougher question "How do I convert an XML document into an object?" A variant starts with the question "How do I convert a relational table to an XML document?" but the underlying problem is the same. This is a toothpaste problem: It's a lot easier to squirt XML out of an object than to push it back in. Most of these tools claim to be able to read XML documents into Java or C++, but they fail very quickly as soon as you start throwing real-world documents at them. Generally speaking, the developers designing these tools are laboring under numerous faulty assumptions, including the following.

- Documents have W3C XML Schema Language schemas. (The vast majority don't.)
- Documents have some kind of schema. (Many, perhaps most, don't.)
- Documents that actually have schemas of some kind do in fact adhere to those schemas. (Often untrue.)
- You know the sorts of structures you're going to encounter before you see the documents. In other words, the documents are predictable.

(Not an unreasonable assumption, but nonetheless it is often untrue in practice.)

- Mixed content doesn't exist. (Patently false.)
- XML documents are fairly flat. In particular they have nearly tabular structures. (The database mapping folks tend to make this assumption. The object folks are a little less likely to fall into this particular trap.)

The same issues arise when developers try to store XML data in relational tables. XML documents are not tables. You can force them in, in a variety of very ugly ways, but this is simply not the task a relational database is designed for. You'll be happier with a database and API designed for XML from the start that doesn't try to pretend XML is simpler than it really is.

The fact is, XML documents considered in their full generality are extremely complicated. They are not tables. They are not objects. Any reasonable model for them has to take this complexity into account. Their structures very rarely match the much more restrictive domains of tables and objects. You can certainly design mappings from XML to classes, but unless you're working in a very limited domain, it's questionable whether you can invent anything much simpler than JDOM. And if you are working in a restricted domain, all you really need is a standard way of serializing and deserializing instances of particular classes to and from a particular XML format. This can be almost hidden from the client programmer. Be wary of tools that implicitly subset XML and handle only some kinds of XML documents. Robust, reliable XML processing needs to use tools that are ready to handle all of XML, including mixed content.

Item 14   Allow All XML Syntax

XML applications should be designed around elements and attributes. You can use a schema or a DTD to constrain which elements and attributes are allowed where and what their legal content is. You may also impose additional constraints that affect the content of the document but cannot be expressed in a schema. For example, you might require that the ID attribute of an Employee element must be the actual ID of a current or past employee. All of these are constraints on the content and structure of the document. They generally reflect the *semantics* of a particular application domain.

Despite some early hype about search engines that understood web pages because you used a Shoe tag instead of an LI tag (some of which I was guilty of myself, I freely admit), XML is not a semantic language. It is a *syntactic* language. Semantics are properly defined by the individual applications built out of XML rather than by XML itself. With the almost negligible exception of xml:lang, there is nothing semantic in XML. XML is only syntax.

It is your role as a developer to define the semantics that are appropriate for your application using the underlying XML syntax. However, it is not your role as a developer to change, add to, or restrict XML's underlying syntax. Doing so destroys XML's value proposition of a compatible interoperable data format. Once you have decided to use XML, you have committed to supporting all of XML: tags, PCDATA, attributes, CDATA sections, document type declarations, comments, processing instructions, entity references, character references, and so on. You do not have the right to throw away any of this. Your application must handle all of it. Fortunately, this is not hard to do because the XML parser handles all this for you. Changing the definition of XML actually requires a lot more work because you can't rely on standard parsers. You have to write your own.

It takes no more effort on your part to allow CDATA sections, comments, processing instructions, and so on in your documents than it does to forbid them. If you don't care about these, you can freely ignore them when processing a document that contains them. You just shouldn't say that they are disallowed.

The classic example of what not to do is SOAP. SOAP explicitly requires that documents contain neither a document type declaration nor any processing instructions. There are a number of problems with these requirements, most notably:

- Most schema languages cannot verify these constraints. Checking that no processing instructions are present actually requires walking the entire tree of a SOAP document. For this reason SOAP doesn't actually require processors to verify the constraints. A constraint that isn't verified is no constraint at all.
- SOAP requests and responses cannot be validated against a DTD, even if the receiver wishes to do so. This removes a powerful tool from the developer's toolbox.

- Both SOAP requests and responses are envelopes intended to wrap other elements from different namespaces and vocabularies. However, when these content elements are copied from existing XML documents and systems, they must first be carefully inspected for any processing instructions. They cannot be sent as is. This imposes a significant burden on a SOAP server or client.
- SOAP requests and responses can't be easily passed through processing chains that use processing instructions for their intended purposes of defining processing in a particular environment.
- Developers who have a real need to use processing instructions or a document type declaration will probably invent hacks that shoehorn the results into comments or empty elements instead, thus reintroducing all the problems the original constructs cause for SOAP while creating additional problems for generic XML systems that don't recognize the special comments and elements.

Perhaps worst of all is the pollution of the XML environment such subsetting engenders. Because SOAP is so completely broken with respect to normal XML processing, vendors are pushing special purpose parsers that process SOAP documents but not all well-formed XML 1.0 documents. Furthermore, as I write this, some members of the SOAP community are lobbying the W3C to bless their subset and not require XML parsers to support the pieces of XML syntax they disapprove of. This is an interoperability disaster.

There are reasons the SOAP specification chose to forbid processing instructions and document type declarations. Forbidding document type declarations means that all content is present in a single document. This eliminates the possibility of external entities that launch multiple connections to remote servers or even enable a denial-of-service attack. Forbidding processing instructions helps eliminate covert channels. It means that all information must be passed through the SOAP vocabulary all processors should understand. However, forbidding these constructs also eliminates many important uses. There are other ways to mitigate these problems that don't require limiting the syntax of XML.

A better approach, in my opinion, is taken by XML-RPC, which neither requires nor forbids document type declarations and processing instructions. It is (perhaps unintentionally) agnostic about these constructs. You can use them if you wish, but generic XML-RPC servers and clients will mostly ignore them. The parser may read the document type declaration and use it to resolve external entity references and supply default attribute values, but this is completely transparent to the program receiving data from the parser, as it should be.

Restricting the syntax an application is willing to parse confuses the role of parser and client application. The parser is responsible for working with tags, entity references, CDATA sections, document type declarations, and so forth and translating all of this into labeled structures for the client program. The client program should only operate on the output of the parser. It should not require the parser to do other than it would normally do. Restricting the syntax an application is willing to accept (as opposed to the structure it will accept) prevents it from using general purpose tools and makes your job as a developer much harder for no good reason. Properly designed XML applications neither notice nor care how the information is syntactically encoded because the parser handles all that work for them. Why make your job harder? Allow all legal XML syntax in your XML applications.

Item 15   Build on Top of Structures, Not Syntax

Entity references, CDATA sections, character references, empty-element tags, and the like are just syntax sugar. They make it a little easier to include certain hard-to-type constructs in XML documents. They do not in any way change a document's information content. Many parsers will not even tell you whether such syntax sugar was used or not. Your documents should convey the same meaning if each of these is replaced with an equivalent representation of the same content.

XML processing can be thought of as a five-layer stack as shown in Figure 15–1. Each layer of data is processed to generate the successively more abstract, more useful layer that follows it. Binary data is converted into characters. Characters are converted into syntax. Syntax is processed to form structures. Finally structures are interpreted to form semantics. Each layer has its place and each layer is necessary. However, it's important not to mix them. A program processing XML can safely operate on only a single layer. Programs that attempt to operate on multiple layers simultaneously risk corrupting the clean, well-formed nature of XML.

Normally processing begins with binary data that is translated into Unicode text according to a particular encoding. It may be necessary to first

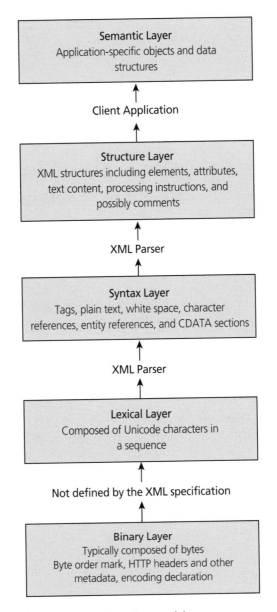

Figure 15–1 The Five-Layer XML Processing Model

strip off and interpret metadata from the binary stream to locate the XML document. For example, when reading an XML document from a web server over a socket, you would have to read and remove the HTTP header while storing the information the header contained about the document's content type and encoding. (See Item 45.) Once the beginning of the document has been located, the parser will read ahead far enough to detect the encoding. Once the parser is confident it knows the encoding, it backs up to the beginning of the document and begins converting bytes into Unicode characters. This may happen before the XML parser begins its work and is technically not a part of XML, although for convenience most XML parsers at least have options to perform some of this work, especially encoding detection. In Java the APIs for the binary layer are `java.io.InputStream` and `java.io.OutputStream`.

The Unicode characters form the lexical layer. In Java the APIs for this layer are `java.io.Reader` and `java.io.Writer`. These are not specifically XML APIs because this data is not necessarily XML until well-formedness has been verified. The only well-formedness check that can be performed at this level is verifying that the characters are all legal in an XML document; for example, that there are no vertical tabs or unmatched halves of surrogate pairs in the data stream.

The parser then reads the raw Unicode characters to recognize the low-level syntax of an XML document: tags, characters, entity references, CDATA section delimiters, and so forth.[1] This is the layer where most of the well-formedness rules defined by XML's BNF grammar are checked. There are very few existing APIs that truly expose the constructs in this layer, partially because it's not always recognized as a separate layer and partially because few programs really need to operate at this level, mostly just source-code-level XML editors. However, a number of APIs have dug holes for themselves by mixing a few pieces of this layer in with the next higher structure layer.

The parser combines these low-level syntax items into higher-level information structures: elements, attributes, text nodes, processing instructions, and so forth. During this process, the parser checks the XML well-formedness constraints that the XML specification calls out separately because they cannot be encoded in the BNF grammar. The most important of these is that each start-tag has a matching end-tag. At this point many of the details about exactly how the information was encoded are deliberately lost. For instance, the parser will merge the text inside a

---

1. In a traditional compiler we'd say this step is performed by the lexer rather than the parser. However, in XML the distinction between lexers and parsers is rarely made, and lexers are not normally available separate from parsers.

CDATA section with the text outside the CDATA section without in any way noting which characters came from inside and which from outside. Most common XML APIs operate primarily at the structure layer. These include SAX, DOM, JDOM, and XOM. Both DOM and SAX parsers can optionally mix in a lot of syntax layer information, but neither is required to support this.

Finally, the parser passes the information about these high-level structures to the client program that invoked the parser. This client program then acts on these structures to produce semantic objects and data structures that are appropriate for its local process. This is the domain of data binding APIs such as JAXB, Castor, and Zeus. These attempt to completely hide the fact that the data came from XML and treat it as some kind of programming object.

A clean program that processes XML works exclusively with a single layer. Almost always, the appropriate layer to work with is the structure layer. In this layer, a well-designed program processes the elements, attributes, text, and other post-parse content. It is responsible for transforming from the structure layer to the semantic layer. It does not involve itself with syntactic issues such as whether a dollar sign was typed as $, $, $, $, or even <![CDATA[$]]>. It has even less interest in lexical and binary layer issues such as which character encoding the document uses. The parser handles all of this before the program ever sees the document.

Note *There is perhaps one exception to this rule. Source-code-level, generic XML editors such as XMLSPY, XED, and jEdit do need access to the syntax layer in order to preserve the appearance of the document. For instance, they do not want to change a named entity reference to a numeric character reference or vice versa. They may even allow for partially malformed documents because users may want to type content after start-tags before they type the end-tags. Thus these tools tend to operate on the syntax layer rather than the structure layer. However, XML editors are a very special case in the realm of XML software. The very unusual needs of these tools should not influence the design of other, more conventional applications.*

Particularly common confusions about layers include the following:

- Treating empty-element tags different from the equivalent start-tag and end-tag pairs

- Using CDATA sections as pseudo-elements that contain malformed markup
- Considering character and entity references as somehow different from their replacement text
- Skipping or forbidding the document type declaration

Let's explore some of the problems that commonly arise as a result of these layer confusions.

Empty-Element Tags

Developers trained in database theory often latch onto the empty-element tag (e.g., `<para/>`) as a way to indicate a null value, which they rightly consider to be distinct from 0 or the empty string. From their perspective this makes sense. `<para>AA</para>` is a `para` element whose value is the string "AA". `<para>A</para>` is a `para` element whose value is the string "A". `<para></para>` is a `para` element whose value is the empty string. Finally, `<para/>` is a `para` element whose value is null.

This is all perfectly sensible, but it does not reflect the way XML parsers actually behave. An XML parser will produce exactly the same data from `<para></para>` as from `<para/>`. There is no detectable difference between the two. They both have the same value, and that value is the empty string, not null.

The right way to indicate a null element is to attach an extra attribute to the element. In particular, the W3C XML Schema Language defines an attribute for exactly this purpose, `xsi:nil`. The customary `xsi` prefix is mapped to the namespace URL http://www.w3.org/2001/XMLSchema-instance, and as always the prefix can change as long as the URL stays the same. For example, the following `para` element genuinely has a null value.

```
<para xmlns:xsi="http://www.w3.org/2001/XMLSchema-instance"
      xsi:nil="true"/>
```

A schema-aware parser may actually report the value of this element as being null. However, it's more likely you'll have to explicitly test each empty element for the presence of an `xsi:nil` attribute. For example, in DOM to convert an `Element` object known to be empty to a string, you might write code something like this:

```
String elementText;
String isNil = element.getAttributeNS(
 "http://www.w3.org/2001/XMLSchema-instance", nil);
if ("true".equals(isNil)) {
 elementText == null;
}
else { // there is no xsi:nil attribute or its value is false
   elementText = "";
}
```

It is an error to set xsi:nil="true" on a nonempty element. However, the difference between two tags and one is not important. The para element below is also nil.

```
<para xmlns:xsi="http://www.w3.org/2001/XMLSchema-instance"
      xsi:nil="true"></para>
```

CDATA Sections

CDATA sections are probably the most frequently abused drugs in the XML pharmacy. The normal reason for this abuse is to embed non-well-formed HTML inside an XML document. For example, the description element in a catalog entry might contain an entire web page for a product.

```
<Vehicle>
  <price>30000</price>
  <inStock>4</inStock>
  <color>black</color>
  <description><![CDATA[
    <html>
      <title>The G2 SUV</title>
      <body>
        <img src=g2suv.jpg height=100 width=100>
        The G2 SUV is one of our best-selling models.
        <p>

        It's built on a truck base for all the stability of a
        pickup driving down a bumpy country road.
        <p>

        It gets an astonishing eight miles to the liter.
        <p>
```

```
        <hr>
        <a href=G3SUV.html>Next Car</a>
      </body>
    </HTML>
  ]]></description>
</Vehicle>
```

Given this structure, it's temptingly easy to write code that extracts the contents of the `description` element and writes the raw text into a file or onto a network socket that expects to receive HTML.

Even worse is the case where the CDATA section is not the exclusive contents of an element but is instead one of several children, so that it becomes almost a pseudo-element. For example, imagine that the above catalog entry did not contain a separate `description` element child, just a CDATA section holding HTML.

```
<Vehicle>
  <price>30000</price>
  <inStock>4</inStock>
  <color>black</color>
  <![CDATA[
    <html>
      <title>The G2 SUV</title>
      <body>
        <img src=g2suv.jpg height=100 width=100>
        The G2 SUV is one of our best-selling models.
        <p>

        It's built on a truck base for all the stability of a
        pickup driving down a bumpy country road.
        <p>

        It gets an astonishing eight miles to the liter.
        <p>
        <hr>
        <a href=G3SUV.html>Next Car</a>
      </body>
    </HTML>
  ]]>
</Vehicle>
```

This kind of structure causes major problems for all sorts of XML tools. It severely limits the validation that can be performed with a DTD or a schema. It is extremely difficult to transform properly with XSLT. DOM parsers may or may not separate out the CDATA sections from the surrounding text, and SAX parsers might not even notice the CDATA sections.

The solution in both cases is simple: Make the HTML well-formed and treat it as an `html` element rather than raw text:

```
<Vehicle>
  <price>30000</price>
  <inStock>4</inStock>
  <color>black</color>
  <html>
    <title>The G2 SUV</title>
    <body>
      <img src="g2suv.jpg" height="100" width="100" />
      <p>
        The G2 SUV is one of our best-selling models.
      </p>
      <p>
        It's built on a truck base for all the stability of a
        pickup driving down a bumpy country road.
      </p>

      <p>
        It gets an astonishing eight miles to the liter.
      </p>
      <hr />
      <a href="G3SUV.html">Next Car</a>
    </body>
  </html>
</Vehicle>
```

If you want to get the text from the HTML, you'll have to serialize the root `html` element, just like you'd serialize any other XML element. In DOM3 you can use the `DOMWriter` class.

The general rule for CDATA sections is that nothing should change if the CDATA section is replaced by its content text with all < and & characters suitably escaped. CDATA sections are meant as a convenience for human authors, especially those writing books about markup like the one you're reading right now. They are not meant to replace elements for indicating the structure and semantics of content to hide malformed markup inside an XML document.

Character and Entity References

Entity and character references are also often abused. Many XML parser APIs sometimes let you see which entity any given character came from (though not all do, and in SAX and DOM this ability is not implemented by all parsers). However, you shouldn't rely on this, and no parsers will tell you whether each character came from raw text or a character reference.

The classic example of what not to do here is to mix XML's escaping mechanisms with your application's escaping mechanism. For instance, an application could specify that a string of text beginning with a literal dollar sign (\$, Unicode character 36) is a variable reference. For example, the following `Para` element includes a variable reference.

```
<Para>Hello $name</Para>
```

This is fine. However, it does require some way to escape the dollar sign when it's used as just a dollar sign. I've occasionally seen applications that attempt to use XML character references for such escaping. For example, this would not be a variable reference.

```
<Para>Hello &#36;name</Para>
```

This is a bad design that makes it impossible to parse these documents correctly with standard APIs like SAX and DOM or standard parsers like Crimson and Ælfred because they won't distinguish between a literal \$ and `&#36;`. Instead a custom parser is required. This makes development much harder than it needs to be.

The mistake is tying application-level semantics (how to tell what's a variable and what isn't) to syntactic aspects of the document that the parser hides. The correct approach is to define a new escaping mechanism that's visible above the XML parser layer instead of below it. For example, you could declare that all variables begin with a `$`, whichever way that character was typed. However, a double dollar sign would be converted to a single plain text dollar sign. For example, these `Para` elements would each contain a variable reference.

```
<Para>Hello $name</Para>
<Para>Hello &#36;name</Para>
```

However, these two would not.

```
<Para>Hello $$name</Para>
<Para>Hello &#36;&#36;name</Para>
```

Design your processing software and XML applications so that they depend only on those aspects of XML that parsers reliably report: element boundaries, text content, attribute values, and processing instructions. Do not write markup that depends on syntax that the parser may resolve before reporting to the client application: CDATA sections, entity references, attribute order, character references, comments, whether attributes are defaulted from the DTD or included in the instance document, and so on. You may indeed be able to write software that supports such lower-level syntax using one particular parser or API. However, you won't be able to validate it with standard schema languages, and I guarantee that you'll confuse document authors who won't always follow your rules. Worst of all, many and perhaps most XML parsers and APIs won't be able to fully process your documents, even if you can. Build applications on top of the structure layer, and let the parser do the hard work of sorting out the syntax.

Item 16   Prefer URLs to Unparsed Entities and Notations

Unparsed entities and notations are one of the weirder parts of the XML specification. They're not well understood in the community and are not properly implemented in all APIs. There's little you can do with an unparsed entity you can't do with a URL in an attribute value anyway, so there's not a lot of need for them. They're mostly a holdover from SGML and the pre-Web world.

For example, suppose you want to embed images in a variety of formats in your documents. This is a completely reasonable thing to do. The unparsed entity approach is to first define notations for all the different image formats in the DTD.

```
<!NOTATION GIF  SYSTEM "image/gif">
<!NOTATION JPEG SYSTEM "image/jpeg">
```

```
<!NOTATION PNG  SYSTEM "image/png">
<!NOTATION SVG  SYSTEM "image/svg+xml">
```

Unfortunately, there's no standard format for notation values. I've used MIME types here because that seems reasonable. However, there's no guarantee that any particular program will recognize these types. The parser will simply tell the client application what the notation is. It will not tell the client application how to interpret data with this notation. (Some parsers and APIs won't even do that much.)

Having defined the notations, the next step is to define the unparsed entities. This is normally done in the internal DTD subset so that different documents can load different entities. For example, the following document type declaration defines two unparsed entities, one named PUPPY for a JPEG image at the relative URL images/fido.jpg and the other named LOGO for an SVG image at the absolute URL http://www.example.com/images/cup.svg:

```
<!ENTITY PUPPY SYSTEM "images/fido.jpg" NDATA JPEG>
<!ENTITY LOGO  SYSTEM
    "http://www.example.com/images/cup.svg" NDATA SVG>
```

Unparsed entities like these cannot be referenced with a simple entity reference as parsed entities can be. Instead, you have to declare an attribute with type ENTITY and place the name of the unparsed entity in that attribute value. For example, the following line declares that the source attribute of the Image element has type ENTITY.

```
<!ATTLIST Image source ENTITY>
```

Finally, in the instance document you would add an Image element with a source attribute.

```
<Image source="PUPPY"/>
```

That's a huge amount of work, especially for what little it buys you. There is a much simpler alternative: Put the URL for the image in the source attribute directly.

```
<Image source="images/fido.jpg"/>
```

In every API I've seen it is much easier to read the URL directly out of the attribute than to load it from the entities declared in the DTD. For example, in SAX loading an unparsed entity from an attribute requires first storing all the entities declared in the DTD using an implementation of the DTDHandler interface such as the one below.

```
import org.xml.sax.*;
import java.util.Hashtable;

public class UnparsedEntityCache implements DTDHandler {

  private Hashtable entities = new Hashtable();

  public void unparsedEntityDecl(String name, String publicID,
   String systemID, String notationName) {
    entities.put(name, systemID);
  }

  public String getUnparsedEntity(String name) {
    return (String) entities.get(name);
  }

}
```

Then you need to reference this data structure from inside the startElement method.

```
public void startElement(String namespaceURI, String
localName,
 String qualifiedName, Attributes attributes) {

  Attribute source = attributes.getValue("source");
  String url = cache.getUnparsedEntity(source);
  // Download the image from the URL...

}
```

Here's the equivalent code that loads the same URL directly from an attribute. No separate cache is required.

```
public void startElement(String namespaceURI, String
localName,
 String qualifiedName, Attributes attributes) {

  String url = attributes.getValue("source");
  // Download the image from the URL...

}
```

I think you'll agree this is much simpler (and reading unparsed entities is actually much easier in SAX than in every other common API).

If you want something marginally more standard, you can always use XLinks instead. For example:

```
<Image xmlns:xlink="http://www.w3.org/1999/xlink"
       xlink:type="simple" xlink:actuate="onLoad"
       xlink:show="embed" xlink:href="images/fido.jpg"/>
```

The one thing the unparsed entity offers that a direct URL in an attribute value doesn't is the notation. However, in practice, the data type can often be determined from the file name or the metadata associated with the URL stream. For example, HTTP includes a `Content-Type` header that specifies the MIME type for all images it transmits.

```
HTTP/1.1 200 OK
Date: Thu, 30 Jan 2003 15:55:18 GMT
Server: Apache/1.3.27 (Unix) DAV/1.0.3 mod_fastcgi/2.2.12
Last-Modified: Tue, 28 Apr 1998 13:31:47 GMT
Content-Length: 900
Connection: close
Content-Type: image/gif
```

Notations can also be used to identify the type of an element rather than an unparsed entity. The only XML application I've ever seen that actually uses this approach is DocBook, which uses the `linespecific` notation to identify elements in which white space should be preserved. For example:

```
<!NOTATION linespecific SYSTEM "linespecific">
<!ATTLIST programlisting format NOTATION (linespecific) >
```

However, this is mostly a holdover from DocBook's SGML legacy. In XML, the preferred way to do this is with an `xml:space` attribute.

```
<!ATTLIST programlisting xml:space #FIXED "preserve">
```

You can imagine other uses for notation type attributes. For example, you could use them to assign data types to elements.

```
<!NOTATION decimal SYSTEM
   "http://www.w3.org/TR/xmlschema-2/#decimal">
<!ATTLIST  weight type NOTATION (decimal) >
```

However, the W3C Schema Working Group chose to go with a global `xsi:type` attribute instead.

```
<!ATTLIST weight xsi:type NMTOKEN (decimal) >
```

In effect, the Working Group chose to use namespaces and a predefined attribute rather than notations. In general, this seems to be the way the wind is blowing. Most parsers and APIs have some support for notations, but if you actually rely on them in your applications, you're just going to confuse most users. This is a case where the simpler, more direct solution is much preferred.

Item 17 Use Processing Instructions for Process-Specific Content

Processing instructions are certainly useful, but they can be a source of interoperability problems. They are not normally validated, and many processes ignore them by default. SOAP, the Extensible Messaging and Presence Protocol (XMPP), and a few other applications have even chosen to forbid them (in violation of Item 14, I'll note). Be careful not to use processing instructions for information that really deserves to be part of the markup instead. The correct purpose of processing instructions is, naturally enough, to give instructions to particular processes that read the XML document. The following characteristics normally indicate that a processing instruction is warranted.

- The information is intended only for a very particular process, often a purely local one, not for a large portion of the programs that will read a document.
- The instruction describes how a particular process acts on the data in the document. It does not describe or add to the data itself.
- The processing instruction is a unit that can be treated in isolation. It does not extend across a range of the XML document.
- The content of the processing instruction does not need to be validated.
- The content of the processing instruction is simple and not very XML-like.
- The processing instruction logically applies to the entire document, not to a specific element, even the root element.
- The processing instruction applies to multiple document types.

When are processing instructions not appropriate? I can think of two main criteria:

- When their content is closely related to the content of the document itself
- When they have structure that extends beyond a single processing instruction

In both cases, processing instructions are being used as a sort of pseudo-tag. This sidesteps the normal XML parsing and validation process and eliminates some of the customary benefits of XML. Let's explore these criteria by investigating common usages of processing instructions, both good and bad.

Style Location

The classic example of a processing instruction, far and away the most familiar one used in practice, is the `xml-stylesheet` processing instruction that tells web browsers where to find the stylesheet for a particular instance document. For example, consider the following document, which describes a chess game.

```
<?xml version="1.0"?>
<?xml-stylesheet type="text/css" href="chess.css"?>
<game>
  <move>f3</move>
  <move>e5</move>
  <move>g4</move>
  <move>Qh4++</move>
</game>
```

The content of the document is completely related to chess. It can be used for many purposes, not just for display to people but also as input to chess-playing programs like Deep Junior. The styles used to format this content for a person are not a fundamental part of the data. They are extra meta-information intended only for one class of process: browser display. There's no way for any one XML application to anticipate the needs of all the different processes that will operate on its documents. Thus it's completely reasonable to include process-specific information in processing instructions when that information extends beyond the bounds of the application itself.

In general, the `xml-stylesheet` processing instruction satisfies almost all the rules for when to use a processing instruction.

- It provides extra information for processes such as web browsers that format a document for display to people. Other kinds of applications are uninterested in its content.
- It locates the stylesheet to be applied to the document. It does not say anything about what is in the document.
- It can be treated as a unit. The processing instruction contains all the information needed to process it. It is not context dependent. It does not have any structure beyond the processing instruction itself.
- If the processing instruction format is wrong, nothing too terrible will happen. At worst a default stylesheet will be applied instead.
- A stylesheet applies to the entire document, not just to one element in the document.
- The `xml-stylesheet` processing instruction can be and is used in many different XML applications including DocBook, SVG, MathML, XHTML, and informally defined custom applications that authors invent on the fly.

The one criterion that's a little iffy is the complexity of the processing instruction. The `xml-stylesheet` processing instruction uses a pseudo-attribute format that makes it look a lot like an XML empty-element tag. However, of the major APIs only JDOM provides support for parsing these pseudo-attributes (and it's a little buggy here). If a real empty-element tag with real attributes were used instead, all XML parsers would be able to read the real attributes. You can imagine something like this:

```
<?xml version="1.0"?>
<game>
  <stylesheet type="text/css" href="chess.css" />
  <move>f3</move>
  <move>e5</move>
  <move>g4</move>
  <move>Qh4++</move>
</game>
```

However, the positioning raises a lot of questions about what exactly the `stylesheet` element applies to. For instance, does it apply to the entire game element or just the move elements within it? Could each move element possess its own `stylesheet` element that overrides the parent element's?

Worse yet, this interferes with validation of the game element, which must now declare that it can contain a stylesheet element.

Perhaps attributes in some other namespace could be used instead, as shown below.

```
<?xml version="1.0"?>
<game xmlns:ss="http://www.example.com/stylesheet"
      ss:type="text/css" ss:href="chess.css">
  <move>f3</move>
  <move>e5</move>
  <move>g4</move>
  <move>Qh4++</move>
</game>
```

This solves the problem of scope. Clearly each style attribute has scope within the element where it appears. However, this approach is still bulky, and it still interferes with validation. On the other hand, this makes it much easier to mix different stylesheets into different parts of the document.

Still, I think a processing instruction in the document prolog is the right solution here. It neatly hits the 80/20 point. The few applications with more complex needs can define a more complex solution such as the namespaced attributes. Most applications don't need anything that complex.

Overlapping Markup

Not all markup fits neatly into tree structures. The classic case of overlapping markup is tracking the structure of a text such as *The Aeneid* along with the identity of the scribe (usually a medieval monk) who copied it. This can be important for recognizing likely transcription errors, determining which sources multiple monasteries in different areas shared, whether different versions of a text were extant in the ancient world, and more. It's not uncommon for one scribe to pick up in the middle of a paragraph where another monk left off, as shown below.

```
<Scribe name="Marcus">
<Stanza>
  <Verse>ARMA virumque cano, Troiae qui primus ab oris</Verse>
  <Verse>Italiam, fato profugus, Laviniaque venit</Verse>
```

```
  <Verse>litora, multum </Scribe>
  <Scribe name="Josephus">ille et terris iactatus et alto</Verse>
  <Verse>vi superum saevae memorem Iunonis ob iram;</Verse>
  <Verse>multa quoque et bello passus,
          dum conderet urbem,</Verse>
  <Verse>inferretque deos Latio, genus unde Latinum,</Verse>
  <Verse>Albanique patres, atque altae moenia Romae.</Verse>
</Stanza>

<Stanza>
  <Verse>Musa, mihi causas memora, quo numine laeso,</Verse>
  <Verse>quidve dolens,</Scribe>
  <Scribe name="Marcus"> regina deum tot volvere casus</Verse>
  <Verse>insignem pietate virum, tot adire labores</Verse>
  <Verse>impulerit.   Tantaene animis caelestibus irae?</Verse>
</Stanza>
</Scribe>
```

This is completely malformed XML. One occasional solution is to use processing instructions to mark the beginning and end of the authorship.

```
<?beginscribe name="Marcus"?>
<Stanza>
  <Verse>ARMA virumque cano, Troiae qui primus ab oris</Verse>
  <Verse>Italiam, fato profugus, Laviniaque venit</Verse>
  <Verse>litora, multum <?beginscribe name="Josephus"?>
          ille et terris iactatus et alto</Verse>
  <Verse>vi superum saevae memorem Iunonis ob iram;</Verse>
  <Verse>multa quoque et bello passus,
          dum conderet urbem,</Verse>
  <Verse>inferretque deos Latio, genus unde Latinum,</Verse>
  <Verse>Albanique patres, atque altae moenia Romae.</Verse>
</Stanza>

<Stanza>
  <Verse>Musa, mihi causas memora, quo numine laeso,</Verse>
  <Verse>quidve dolens,
  <?beginscribe name="Marcus"?>
          regina deum tot volvere casus</Verse>
  <Verse>insignem pietate virum, tot adire labores</Verse>
```

```
<Verse>impulerit.  Tantaene animis caelestibus
irae?</Verse>
</Stanza>
```

On the one hand, this is well-formed XML. On the other hand, this doesn't really do anything you couldn't do with empty elements. Revision tracking presents similar issues because users may revise and delete ranges of text that do not necessarily coincide neatly with element boundaries. In both cases, the source of the difficulty is the same. The lexical issues of characters in a row don't always match up with the tree structure of well-formed XML. You can't always fit all useful information into a single tree.

I think empty elements are a much better fit here than processing instructions. The content of the instructions in examples like this is really a key part of the markup. It's not just supplementary information for one particular process. It reflects real information about the content. Thus it properly belongs in tags, not processing instructions. If the tag structure is too limiting, it's time to consider whether XML really fits the data in the first place. XML is a round hole that works very well with round pegs. Square pegs might better be pounded into different holes.

One somewhat more plausible use of begin and end processing instructions occurred in a spell checking program that recognized `<?begin-nospell?>` and `<?end-nospell?>` instructions to identify words that should not be checked, such as foreign words, proper names, and technical terms. For example:

```
<para>
  Francine read <title>Processing
  <?begin-nospell?>XML<?end-nospell?> with Java</title> in
  its French translation, <?begin-nospell?><title>Traitement
  de XML avec Java</title>.
</para>
```

In this case, overlapping markup is not a fundamental issue, as it is in the classic text example. However, such processing instructions can still fail to nest properly within elements. Worse, unlike overlapping elements caused by misplaced start- and end-tags, the parser will not detect this as an error. And people will and do make such errors. Did you notice that I left off the last `<?end-nospell?>` instruction in the above example?

Page Formatting

Another common use of processing instructions is in page formatting. Figuring out exactly where to break words, columns, pages, and so forth is a very difficult problem for a machine. TeX probably does a better job of this than anything else, and it still doesn't always get it right. Human intervention is normally necessary for high-quality typesetting. Processing instructions like those shown below are often used for this purpose.

```
<?xml version="1.0"?>
<game>
  <?begin-keep-together?>
  <date>2003-10-24</date>
  <white>Jane Smith</white>
  <black>Alice Jones</black>
  <?end-keep-together?>
  <?page-break?>
  <move>f3</move>
  <move>e5</move>
  <move>g4</move>
  <move>Qh4++</move>
</game>
```

I think this is reasonable in applications not related to publishing, such as this simple chess vocabulary, in which a stylesheet will be used to produce pages. While ideally the stylesheet and formatting engine would be smart enough to figure out where to put everything, the reality is that these tools just aren't good enough to handle real-world documents. Indeed, it may not even be theoretically possible to do so. If you're using the common chain of XML→XSLT→XSL-FO→PDF, it may not be possible to determine where objects are placed until the final layout step that chooses sizes for everything. However, without the sizes, you can't calculate whether or not a break is needed from within the XSLT stylesheet. Processing instructions are a necessary escape.

On the other hand, I do not think this is appropriate for publishing-related vocabularies such as DocBook, XSL-FO, and OpenOffice. Keeps and breaks should be elements in these vocabularies, just like paragraphs, lists, tables, and other aspects of layout. XHTML would accomplish this by using CSS keeps and breaks properties attached to elements with particular IDs. This works, but it does require at least one custom stylesheet for each document. It's sometimes (though not always) more convenient to keep all of a document's unique markup in one place.

Out-of-Line Markup

Books like this one sometimes include complete XML documents as examples, sometimes just fragments thereof. To keep the examples correct, it's very useful if the fragments are automatically extracted from complete documents that can be validated, checked for well-formedness, and verified to be correct. This requires some way to mark off the portions of the document that will be extracted and included. Since processing instructions are ignored by validators and most other processes that don't expect to see them, they make an excellent tool for this purpose. For example, the following document uses `<?begin-extract?>` and `<?end-extract?>` processing instructions to select the checkmating move.

```
<?xml version="1.0"?>
<game>
   <move>f3</move>
   <move>e5</move>
   <move>g4</move>
   <?begin-extract?><move>Qh4++</move><?end-extract?>
</game>
```

Here an empty element would not work as well because it might interfere with validation. Furthermore, a processing instruction only describes how this document will be used by one very particular process (the auto-assembly of a different document). It is not in any way a key part of the document's own information.

An alternative approach would be to use XPointers to extract the relevant subtrees or ranges. Then the document need not carry additional markup at all. The problem with this (besides the lack of effective tool support for XPointer) is that XPointer operates on a processed form of the document created by the XPath data model. In this case, we really do want to operate on the lexical layer and extract particular characters, not particular nodes. We might even use a non-XML-aware tool like a regular expression to do this. (Just look for the text between `<?begin-extract?>` and `<?end-extract?>`). Thus, unlike most other cases involving overlapping markup, it may well be acceptable if a pair of extract instructions begins in the middle of one element and finishes somewhere outside that element.

Misuse of Processing Instructions

Clearly, processing instructions should not be used for information that is properly part of the domain of the XML application. For example, it would be inappropriate to use processing instructions to specify when and where a particular chess game was played. Markup like the following is to be eschewed.

```
<?xml version="1.0"?>
<?game-info date="2003-10-24" white="Jane Smith"
                           black="Alice Jones"?>
<game>
  <move>f3</move>
  <move>e5</move>
  <move>g4</move>
  <move>Qh4++</move>
</game>
```

Instead, additional elements and attributes should be added to the vocabulary to encode the additional information.

```
<?xml version="1.0"?>
<game>
  <date>2003-10-24</date>
  <white>Jane Smith</white>
  <black>Alice Jones</black>
  <move>f3</move>
  <move>e5</move>
  <move>g4</move>
  <move>Qh4++</move>
</game>
```

For the same reason, when the whole purpose of an XML application is to display content to end users, presentation style information should be encoded in the markup. It would be inappropriate, for example, to add an `xml-stylesheet` processing instruction to an XHTML document. Instead, you should use the elements and attributes XHTML provides for this purpose: `link`, `style`, and so forth.

One reason developers sometimes use processing instructions where they shouldn't is to include necessary information the DTD or schema doesn't provide a place for. However, this means you can't use the basic XML tools to extract the structure from these instructions, as you can from elements. You also run the risk that other processes will, intentionally or not, strip out the processing instructions from the document. For instance, by default an XSLT transformation throws away all processing instructions that are not targeted by the stylesheet.

Ideally, what needs to be done in this case is to update the DTD or schema. However, even if that isn't possible, this shouldn't stop you from adding the extra elements you need. XML is the *Extensible* Markup Language. You can add pieces to it that aren't expected. Invalid documents can still be usefully processed.

Processing instructions should be used to provide clues to specific processes that operate on the document. They should be used for information that is orthogonal to the document's own content. And they should be used with great caution. Processing instructions should not be your first resort. Always try to fit the data into the element markup and content if it's at all reasonably possible. However, sometimes it isn't, and processing instructions become a useful escape hatch from the usual strictures of XML.

Item 18   Include All Information in the Instance Document

An XML document is not the same thing as an XML file. XML provides a bewildering array of options for building documents and infosets out of multiple pieces. Among them are the following:

- External parsed entity references
- Internal parsed entity references
- XInclude
- Default attribute values from the DTD
- Default attribute values from the schema

These can be useful shortcuts for authoring, but they are death traps for interoperable documents. Many XML processors do not read the external DTD subset and cannot resolve any entity references defined therein. They also cannot apply default attribute values. Few current XML parsers can read a schema and apply default attribute values found there. Almost no XML parsers perform XInclusion by default. And even though it doesn't conform to the XML specification, there are even a few processors that don't read the internal DTD subset, so attribute values defined there may not be accessible in all environments.

For maximum portability and robustness, include all necessary information in the instance document itself. Do not rely on default attribute values, notations, types, entity references, or anything else that can be discovered only by processing the schema or DTD. Make the instance document self-contained. You may choose to use schema defaults while authoring, but before publishing your documents to the world, be sure to resolve all of them so that a processor without access to anything other than the document itself can still correctly process the document.

For example, consider the following XHTML+SVG+MathML document.

```
<!DOCTYPE html PUBLIC
    "-//W3C//DTD XHTML 1.1 plus MathML 2.0 plus SVG 1.1//EN"
    "xhtml-math-svg/xhtml-math-svg-flat.dtd">
<html>
<head>
  <title>Equation of the Unit Circle</title>
</head>
<body>

<h1>Equation of the Unit Circle</h1>

<div>
  <math>
    <mrow>
      <mrow>
        <msup><mi>x</mi><mn>2</mn></msup>
        <mo>+</mo>
        <msup><mi>y</mi><mn>2</mn></msup>
      </mrow>
      <mo>=</mo>
      <mn>1</mn>
    </mrow>
  </math>
</div>

<div>
  <svg:svg width="5cm" height="5cm"
           viewBox="0 0 500 500" version="1.1">
```

```
            <svg:circle cx="250" cy="250" r="100"
                        stroke="black" stroke-width="10" />
    </svg:svg>
</div>

</body>
</html>
```

It relies on namespace declaration attributes that are not present in the instance document. Instead they are defaulted in from the DTD. A browser that does not read the DTD will not know about them, will not recognize the MathML or SVG elements, may not recognize the XHTML elements, will erroneously conclude that this document is namespace malformed, and may reject the document.

Instead, the document should be written like this, with all namespace declarations spelled out explicitly.

```
<!DOCTYPE html PUBLIC
    "-//W3C//DTD XHTML 1.1 plus MathML 2.0 plus SVG 1.1//EN"
    "xhtml-math-svg/xhtml-math-svg-flat.dtd">
<html xmlns="http://www.w3.org/1999/xhtml">
<head>
  <title>Equation of the Unit Circle</title>
</head>
<body>
<h1>Equation of the Unit Circle</h1>

<div>
  <math xmlns="http://www.w3.org/1998/Math/MathML">
    <mrow>
      <mrow>
        <msup><mi>x</mi><mn>2</mn></msup>
        <mo>+</mo>
        <msup><mi>y</mi><mn>2</mn></msup>
      </mrow>
      <mo>=</mo>
      <mn>1</mn>
    </mrow>
  </math>
</div>
```

```
<div>
  <svg:svg xmlns:svg="http://www.w3.org/2000/svg"
    width="5cm" height="5cm" viewBox="0 0 500 500" version="1.1">
      <svg:circle cx="250" cy="250" r="100"
                  stroke="black" stroke-width="10" />
  </svg:svg>
</div>
</body>
</html>
```

The extra declarations are redundant with the information in the DTD, but they make the whole document more reliable. All processors will be able to handle this document, even if they don't read the DTD.

For another example, consider entity references, as in this fragment of XHTML.

```
<p>
  The Greek word for father is
  &pi;&alpha;&tau;&rho;&omicron;&sigmaf;.
</p>
```

In order to understand the content of this fragment, a processor must read the DTD. If it has failed to do so, it will not be able to correctly report the text. It would be much better to use the actual characters in the body of the document.

```
<p>The Greek word for father is πατροσ.</p>
```

If this is simply not feasible given the limits of the local software and fonts, you should use character references instead.

```
<p>
  The Greek word for father is
  &#x3C0;&#x3B1;&#x3C4x;&#x3C1x;&#x3BF;&#x3C2;.
</p>
```

This is more opaque in source form but much more easily interpreted by a generic XML parser.

None of this is to say that you should not use DTDs or schemas for valida-tion. A document can stand completely on its own and still have a DTD or a schema or both. However, those features of DTDs and schemas that augment the infoset, as opposed to merely defining validation rules, have proven to be problematic. When publishing a document, strive to make it completely self-contained. Think of entities, default attribute values, and the like as authoring tools, not publishing tools. One easy way to merge these pieces together is by using an XSLT stylesheet that performs the identity transformation.

```
<xsl:template match="@*|node()">
  <xsl:copy>
    <xsl:apply-templates select="@*|node()"/>
  </xsl:copy>
</xsl:template>
```

The resulting output will have added in all default attribute values and resolved all entities. A couple of XSLT engines can even be configured to resolve XIncludes as well.

Reversing the perspective, consider not the producers of documents but the consumers. Consumers cannot assume that documents are self-contained. In the spirit of being liberal in what you accept but conservative in what you produce, when receiving a document from a third party you should do your utmost to read the external DTD subset, resolve all external entity references, and apply all default attribute values. You should only use parsers that can do this, especially for DTDs. While most APIs allow you to turn off resolution of external entity references and ignore the external DTD subset, you should almost never do so. Reading the external DTD subset will cost you little in the case where it isn't necessary and may save your bacon in the case where it is. Programs that repeatedly read the same external DTD subsets can use the public identifiers, catalogs, and various caching strategies to cache the DTDs so repeated trips back to a server are not necessary. (See Item 47.)

This is especially useful with web browsers and XHTML, and indeed it's sanctioned by the XHTML specification. Web browsers that support XHTML have, for practical intents and purposes, internally cached the XHTML DTD. Thus when they encounter a document whose public ID labels it as XHTML, they do not need to read the DTD. They already know how to resolve entity references like `&Theta;` and `&alpha;`. However, this option is not available to a general purpose XML parser that does not know which specific XML applications it will encounter. Such a processor must read the external DTD subset before it can confidently replace all entities.

In brief, be liberal in what you read and conservative in what you write. Always include all necessary information in the document itself, but be prepared to handle the case where other document producers have not been so wise.

Item 19   Encode Binary Data Using Quoted Printable and/or Base64

It's questionable whether including binary data in XML documents is a good idea at all. You're often better off just pointing to it with a URL. However, if you do have a genuine need to keep binary information together with text in one document, there are a number of straightforward algorithms for encoding arbitrary byte sequences as text. These include the following:

- UUEncode
- hexBinary
- Quoted printable
- Base64

Only the last two are worth considering. UUEncode is not precisely defined and varies significantly in practice between different implementations. hexBinary is simple to implement, but it at least doubles the size of every file. Quoted printable and Base64 are much more efficient. Quoted printable is suitable for text data that is not well-formed XML. Base64 is suited for truly nontext data like JPEG images or QuickTime movies.

Quoted Printable

The quoted printable encoding was designed for e-mail, but it works surprisingly well in XML. It can encode any ASCII or UTF-8 text including characters that are not normally allowed in XML documents, such as form feed, vertical tab, null, and the reserved XML characters less than sign (<), greater than sign (>), and ampersand (&). Most importantly, most of the ASCII text is intact and can be read by a normal browser. Only the problematic characters need to be escaped.

The basic algorithm uses just five rules.

1. Each byte can be encoded as an equals sign (=) followed by two hexadecimal digits; for example, a less than sign can be represented as =3C. Only capital letters are used for the hexadecimal digits A–F.

2. The bytes with values between 33 and 60, inclusive, and 62 through 126, inclusive, may be represented as the ASCII characters. However, for use with XML we need to modify that a bit and always encode 60 (the less than sign) and 62 (the greater than sign) as =3C and =3E, respectively. The ampersand must be encoded as =26. Note that it is always acceptable to encode characters in this form even if you don't have to.

3. The ASCII tab (0x09) and ASCII space (0x20) can be written literally except at the end of a line, where they must be escaped as =09 and =20, respectively.

4. All line breaks are replaced by carriage return–line feed pairs.

5. Each line can be no be longer than 76 characters. You can indicate that a line should be continued on the next line by adding a single equals sign at the very end of the line If so, nothing can follow this, not even an extra space. The equals sign must be the very last character on the line.

For example, suppose you're extracting text from a database that allows nulls, form feeds, and other C0 controls in the strings. You might, for instance, have a field like this:

```
"Wong, Gao Yin (ACF)"\00<GWong@acf.hhs.gov>\0C
```

(Naturally, I can't print the nonprinting control characters in this book, so they're represented above as a backslash followed by two hexadecimal bytes.)

Leaving aside for a second the fact that this field violates just about every normalization rule in the book, it could easily be encoded in quoted printable like this when exported to XML:

```
"Wong, Gao Yin (ACF)"=00=3CGWong@acf.hhs.gov=3E=0C
```

Of course, most of your data will not need to be so encoded. The advantage to quoted printable encoding is that it leaves most characters intact most of the time. The result may not be perfectly legible as ASCII, but it's normally possible to make sense out of it.

Most major environments have quoted printable encoders and decoders hiding somewhere, often in mail APIs, so you don't have to roll your own. For instance, in Java the `javax.mail.internet.MimeUtility` class from the Java Mail API, a standard extension to Java, can encode and decode quoted printable strings, as well as several other encodings. Perl has the `MIME::QuotedPrint` module. Python has a `mimetools` module with encode and decode functions. Microsoft hasn't added this functionality to the standard .NET library yet, but several third-party libraries are available that implement this algorithm. If you use these instead of writing your own (which isn't hard), you'll also need to further escape the less than, greater than, and ampersand characters because the standard encoders likely won't do this for you. (The standard decoders should have no trouble reversing the process though.)

When should you not use quoted printable? I can think of two situations.

1. When the only problematic characters are the reserved characters (less than sign, greater than sign, and ampersand). In these cases you're better off using entity references like `&lt;` or CDATA sections instead. Quoted printable becomes important when the data is likely to contain control characters like null and vertical tab.

2. When the data is pure binary rather than text, such as a JPEG image. In this case, Base64 will be smaller and no more opaque.

Base64

Base64 is an algorithm that is designed for encoding arbitrary sequences of bytes. Each group of three bytes (24 bits) is encoded as four characters taken from a subset of ASCII specifically designed to pass through various gateways and processors intact. The characters are the capital letters A–Z, the lowercase letters a–z, the digits 0–9, the plus sign (+), the forward slash (/), and the equals sign (=). None of these are likely to cause any problem for XML processors.

The downside to Base64 is that the data is completely opaque. Just because something is an ASCII character in input doesn't mean it's likely to be the same one in output. (In fact, that's almost guaranteed not to happen because Base64 encoding splits the bits of each byte across two bytes in the output.) Here's a typical small Base64 encoded file.

```
IldhbmcsIERvbmd6aGkgKEFDRikiIDxEV2FuZ0BhY2YuaGhzLmdvdj4=
```

Just looking at it gives you no clue what's hiding in the data. If the data is text, quoted printable will be more transparent. However, for nontext data, such as digital signatures, encrypted content, JPEG images, MP3 recordings, and the like, Base64 is no more opaque than the actual data and is as or more efficient than quoted printable.

Generally the same libraries and tools that know how to encode and decode quoted printable can decode Base64. It's normally just a question of passing the right encoding name to the method call. In addition, in .NET the `System.Xml.XmlTextReader` and `System.Xml.TextWriter` classes include built-in support for reading and writing Base64-encoded data.

The downside to encoding in Base64, quoted printable, or any other format is that it increases the size of the data. Base64 increases size by a third in an eight-bit encoding such as UTF-8 and by somewhat more in other encodings like UTF-16. If the data is really large you may well be better off just pointing to the original binary form with a URL as discussed in Item 16 and used in many applications such as XHTML. Alternately, rather than shipping around a single XML document you might choose to ship an archive such as a zip or jar file that contains both the XML document and the supporting binary data. However, if you do need to encode a small amount of non-XML data in a document, Base64 and quoted printable are often convenient, relatively efficient ways to do it.

Item 20 Use Namespaces for Modularity and Extensibility

Namespaces are the standard tool for mixing multiple vocabularies into a single document. They are essential for allowing software to quickly and definitively decide which elements come from which applications, even when there's no potential conflict between names in the different applications. All new XML applications should define a namespace for their elements. Even if you don't plan to integrate your vocabulary with other applications, your users might want to integrate it with theirs.

This need not be particularly onerous. The simplest case, a document that uses a single namespace, can be handled with a single default namespace declaration on the root element. You don't even need to use namespace prefixes. For example, the following document places all elements in the http://namespaces.cafeconleche.org/chess namespace.

```
<?xml version="1.0"?>
<game xmlns="http://namespaces.cafeconleche.org/chess">
  <move>f3</move>
```

```
  <move>e5</move>
  <move>g4</move>
  <move>Qh4++</move>
</game>
```

Of course, you should design all your processing so that it depends on the local name and namespace URI, rather than the namespace prefix (or lack thereof). The following document is exactly equivalent to the one above.

```
<?xml version="1.0"?>
<chess:game xmlns:chess=
        "http://namespaces.cafeconleche.org/chess">
  <chess:move>f3</chess:move>
  <chess:move>e5</chess:move>
  <chess:move>g4</chess:move>
  <chess:move>Qh4++</chess:move>
</chess game>
```

Item 21 covers this further.

Choosing a Namespace URI

The first choice to make is the URI scheme. While theoretically any URI scheme can be used, in practice only two are at all common: http and urn. An http scheme is the familiar http URL that is loaded into web browsers, printed in books, advertised on the sides of buses, and painted on building walls. A URN scheme, by contrast, identifies a Uniform Resource Name (as opposed to a Uniform Resource Locator). According to the URN specification, RFC 2141, URNs "are intended to serve as persistent, location-independent, resource identifiers."[1] Here are a few examples of URNs:

- urn:uuid:BDC6E3F0-6DA3-11d1-A2A3-00AA00C14882
- urn:publicid:-:OASIS:DTD+DocBook+XML+V4.1.2:EN
- urn:schemas-microsoft-com:xml-data
- urn:schemas-microsoft-com:datatypes
- urn:ISBN:059600292
- urn:ndw:stylesheets:xsl:docbook:1.15

---

1. R. Moats (ed.). "URN Syntax." 1997. Accessed online in June 2003 at http://www.ietf.org/rfc/rfc2141.txt.

URNs feel like a very good fit for namespace URIs. They are not resolvable, and they have no particular dependence on location. Nonetheless, many developers prefer http URLs for namespace URIs, some because they want the namespace names to be resolvable, others because they're just not familiar with URNs. Perhaps the most common reason for choosing an http URL is that URN schemes must be registered before use. Except for experimental URNs that look like urn:X-*foo*, you can't just make them up on the fly. The domain name in an http URL also has to be registered, but the process for doing so is less involved (if more expensive), and many developers already own or have access to domain names they can use.

Assuming you do choose http for the protocol, the URI should be in a domain you own and control. For example, I often use http://namespaces.cafeconleche.org/ because I own the cafeconleche.org domain. You will of course choose something else. The namespace URI does not necessarily have to point to an existing page, host, or even domain. For the long term it's sensible to put something there, especially a RDDL document. (See Item 42.) However, when you're just beginning to design an application, this is not an urgent need. Parsers do not treat namespace URIs as anything more than strings. In particular they do not resolve the URL or load any page that may be found there. You do not need to have a network connection to parse a document that uses namespaces.

All namespace URIs should be absolute. That is, http://namespaces.cafeconleche.org/chess is a good choice for a namespace name. However, /chess, /games/chess, games/chess, and chess are bad choices. The exact meaning of a relative namespace URI is unclear. Is it just the string? Does it depend on the base URI of the document, and thus can it change when the document is moved from one system to another? The W3C has not been able to decide this point and seems unlikely to do so in the future. All they've been able to agree on (and that with a lot of argument) is that relative namespace URLs are a very bad idea. Most APIs and tools just compare namespace URIs as strings, but a few may try to resolve the URI against the base URI. The results are unpredictable. Far and away the best solution is to simply make all namespace URIs absolute. This makes the namespace constant when documents are moved from one host to another. After all, do you really want the namespace of a document to change just because you saved it on your local hard drive from a remote server?

Occasionally, you'll see URI references with fragment identifiers used as namespace URIs, shown as follows.

```
<game xmlns="http://namespaces.cafeconleche.org/games#chess">
  <move>f3</move>
  <move>e5</move>
  <move>g4</move>
  <move>Qh4++</move>
</game>
```

There's nothing wrong with this. However, it does not have any particular specification-defined meaning. Namespace URIs are compared for string equality character for character. That's all. From this perspective, http://namespaces.cafeconleche.org/games#chess and http://namespaces.cafeconleche.org/games#checkers are two completely different namespaces.

Slightly more common is the pattern used by the Resource Description Framework, XML Digital Signatures, XML Encryption, and a few other applications. In these cases, the namespace URI ends in a sharp sign (#), but no fragment identifier is present. The following list gives the namespace URIs for the three vocabularies named above, respectively.

- http://www.w3.org/1999/02/22-rdf-syntax-ns#
- http://www.w3.org/2000/09/xmldsig#
- http://www.w3.org/2001/04/xmlenc#

This pattern enables more URLs to be formed by appending the appropriate fragment identifiers. For example, XML encryption appends algorithm names to identify specific algorithms.

- http://www.w3.org/2001/04/xmlenc#tripledes-cbc
- http://www.w3.org/2001/04/xmlenc#aes128-cbc
- http://www.w3.org/2001/04/xmlenc#aes256-cbc
- http://www.w3.org/2001/04/xmlenc#aes192-cbc
- http://www.w3.org/2001/04/xmlenc#rsa-1_5
- http://www.w3.org/2001/04/xmlenc#rsa-oaep-mgf1p
- http://www.w3.org/2001/04/xmlenc#dh

However, this is just a convention. Since these algorithm URLs are not used as namespace URIs, the bare names would probably work equally well. Mostly this usage is just a symptom of the W3C's mania for making all names URIs (and http URLs in particular). It doesn't hurt much, aside from added verbosity; but it doesn't have much practical value either.

Theoretically, query strings could also be used in namespace URIs, as in the following example.

```
<game
xmlns="http://namespaces.cafeconleche.org/games?name=chess">
  <move>f3</move>
  <move>e5</move>
  <move>g4</move>
  <move>Qh4++</move>
</game>
```

I've never seen this in practice and can't really imagine a reason for doing it. Query strings have meaning only when the URI is processed by an HTTP server. Since that is not normally done to a namespace URI, I suggest you not use query strings in namespace URIs.

Currently namespace URIs are limited to the ASCII character set, just as all other URIs are. (This may change when Namespaces 1.1 is released.) Non-ASCII characters such as é and ψ have to be percent escaped. Certain other characters like : and = that have particular meaning in a URI context also have to be escaped when they're used in a different way. And some characters such as <, >, and " must always be percent escaped. The namespaces and URI specifications are unclear about how such escaping is treated, including what character set non-ASCII characters are encoded in and whether namespace URIs are compared for equality before or after the escape sequences are resolved. Even such trivial differences as http://www.example.com/%7E versus http://www.example.com/%7e can be important in some environments. Some APIs and tools consider these to be the same. Others consider them to be different. Using any of these guarantees trouble. Make sure all your namespace URIs use only ASCII characters that do not have to be escaped.

For similar reasons, it's necessary to pick a case convention, even for normally case-insensitive parts of a URI such as the domain name. HTTP://WWW.EXAMPLE.COM/namespace and http://www.example.com/namespace are not the same namespace name, even if they are the same URL. Almost everybody just makes the scheme and domain name lower case.

Validation and Namespaces

DTDs, unfortunately, are not namespace aware. When writing a DTD for a document that uses namespaces, you must declare the prefixed names, as shown below.

```
<!ELEMENT chess:game (chess:move+)>
<!ELEMENT chess:move (#PCDATA)>
```

If the documents don't use a prefix, you declare the unprefixed names instead.

```
<!ELEMENT game (move+)>
<!ELEMENT move (#PCDATA)>
```

You must further declare the namespace attributes just as you would any other attribute.

```
<!ATTLIST chess:game xmlns:chess
     CDATA "http://namespaces.cafeconleche.org/chess" #FIXED>
<!ATTLIST game xmlns CDATA
     "http://namespaces.cafeconleche.org/chess" #FIXED>
```

This is rather annoying and inconvenient. Fortunately, the parameterization techniques discussed in Item 7 enable you to adjust the namespace prefix within any given document by overriding a couple of parameter entity references in the internal DTD subset.

All other schema languages are namespace aware and do validate against the namespace URI and local name rather than the prefixed name.

Aside from this small if annoying inconsistency with DTDs, namespaces are not particularly burdensome. The classes of elements defined by different namespace URIs often significantly simplify XML processing. It's like the difference between writing a system that knows only first names and one that knows both first and family names. When there are a million different people named John in the world, it really helps to know who is John Jones and who is John Finkelstein. While there are well-designed legacy XML applications such as DocBook that predate namespaces and thus don't use them, all new XML applications should use namespaces.

Item 21   Rely on Namespace URIs, Not Prefixes

Namespaces use URIs to distinguish elements and attributes. The prefix is syntax sugar, nothing more—it's the URI that counts, not the prefix. All code you write should depend on the URI, not the prefix. For example, suppose you're writing a Java program that uses the DOM API to search for XLink elements. The following code fragment is correct because it relies on the URI and the local name.

```
public boolean isSimpleLink(Element candidate) {
  if (candidate.hasAttributeNS("http://www.w3.org/1999/xlink",
      "type"); {
    return true;
  }
  return false;
}
```

However, the following code is incorrect because it assumes the prefix is xlink and does not consider the URI.

```
public boolean isSimpleLink(Element candidate) {
  if (candidate.hasAttribute("xlink:type"); {
    return true;
  }
  return false;
}
```

Sometimes the prefix will be xlink. Sometimes it won't be. For instance, the shorter xl prefix is also often used in practice.

Namespace comparison can be a little tricky. For instance, consider the following namespace URIs:

- http://www.w3.org/1999/02/22-rdf-syntax-ns#
- http://WWW.W3.ORG/1999/02/22-rdf-syntax-ns#
- http://www.w3.org/1999/02/22-rdf-syntax-ns%23
- http://www.w3.org/1999/02/22%2Drdf%2Dsyntax%2Dns#
- http://www.w3.org/1999/02/22%2drdf%2dsyntax%2dns#

Are they the same or different? If some are different, which ones? The namespaces specification is not clear, which is a very good reason for choosing namespace URIs such that these issues do not arise. That being said, the most common approach, and probably the most interoperable, is to simply compare all namespace URIs character by character, in a case-sensitive fashion, without resolving hexadecimal escape sequences such as %2D.

Some applications have certain common prefixes, and it's kind to use them when authoring. For example, XSL Formatting Objects documents al-most always use the prefix fo. Using the customary prefixes helps people recognize particular applications. This is also helpful in documentation such as this book or W3C specifications since it avoids having to place a namespace declaration on every small code fragment. For example, the XLink specification states, "Most code examples in this specification do not show an XLink namespace declaration. The xlink prefix is used throughout to stand for the declaration of the XLink namespace on elements in whose scope the so-marked attribute appears (on the same element that bears the attribute or on some ancestor element), whether or not an XLink namespace declaration is present in the example."[1] However, this is only a documentation convention. In code it's always the URI that's normative, not the prefix.

Table 21–1 lists a few of the common prefixes. However, as this table also shows, several XML applications have more than one customary prefix. Thus you can't rely on the prefix as the final identifier.

It's even possible for a customary prefix to be mapped to a noncustomary URI. For instance, the document on the next page uses the default namespace for the XSLT elements and `xsl` for the XSL-FO elements in the result tree.

Table 21–1 Customary Prefixes

Application	Namespace	Prefixes
SVG	http://www.w3.org/2000/svg	default, `svg`
XSLT	http://www.w3.org/1999/Transform	`xsl`
XSL-FO	http://www.w3.org/1999/Format	`fo`
XHTML	http://www.w3.org/1999/xhtml	default, `html`, `xhtml`
XInclude	http://www.w3.org/2001/XInclude	`xi`, `xinclude`
XLink	http://www.w3.org/1999/xlink	`xlink`, `xl`
W3C XML Schema Language schema documents	http://www.w3.org/2001/XMLSchema	default, `xsd`, `xs`
W3C XML Schema Language instance documents	http://www.w3.org/2001/XMLSchema-instance	`xsi`
RDF	http://www.w3.org/1999/02/22-rdf-syntax-ns#	default, `rdf`

---

1. W3C XML Linking Working Group. "XML Linking Language (XLink) Version 1.0." 2001. Accessed online in June 2003 at http://www.w3.org/TR/xlink/

```
<?xml version="1.0"?>
<stylesheet version="1.0"
  xmlns="http://www.w3.org/1999/XSL/Transform"
  xmlns:fo="http://www.w3.org/1999/XSL/Format">

  <template match="/">
    <xsl:root>

      <xsl:layout-master-set>

        <xsl:simple-page-master master-name="basic"
          page-width="8.5in"  page-height="11in"
          margin-top="1in"     margin-bottom="1in"
          margin-left="1in"    margin-right="1in">
          <xsl:region-before extent="3.0in"/>
          <xsl:region-body margin-top="1.0in"
                             margin-bottom="1.0in"/>
          <xsl:region-after extent="1.0in"/>
        </xsl:simple-page-master>

      </xsl:layout-master-set>

      <xsl:page-sequence master-reference="A4"
        initial-page-number="1" language="en" country="us">

        <xsl:flow flow-name="xsl-region-body">
          <apply-templates select="//section"/>
        </xsl:flow>

      </xsl:page-sequence>

    </xsl:root>
  </template>

  <template match="section">
    <xsl:block><value-of select="title"/></xsl:block>
  </template>

</stylesheet>
```

This is perverse and confusing, and I certainly recommend you don't do this. It can only confuse anyone who's reading the stylesheet. However, it is completely legal, and properly written software should have no trouble comprehending it.

In a few cases, especially involving XSLT, it may be necessary to use non-standard prefixes to avoid conflicts. For example, XHTML customarily uses the default namespace. However, XPath can't match element names in the default namespace, so when writing templates that apply to XHTML elements, it's necessary to assign them a prefix. The following template changes XHTML paragraphs into XSL-FO blocks.

```
<?xml version="1.0"?>
<stylesheet version="1.0"
  xmlns:xsl="http://www.w3.org/1999/XSL/Transform"
  xmlns:html="http://www.w3.org/1999/xhtml"
  xmlns:fo="http://www.w3.org/1999/XSL/Format">

  <xsl:template match="html:p">
    <fo:block><xsl:value-of select="."/></fo:block>
  </xsl:template>

</xsl:stylesheet>
```

Another weird case occurs when you're using XSLT to generate XSLT. In this situation you need to distinguish between the XSLT instructions and the XSLT literal result elements. Changing the prefix is not enough. You also need to change the URI. This requires using the `xsl:namespace-alias` element to assign a temporary URI for the output elements and let the processor fix up the namespace when it generates the final document. However, this is an extremely unusual thing to do. Most of the time, a little adjustment of the prefixes is all that's required.

The fundamental principle of namespaces is this: The URI matters. The prefix doesn't. Always write code that keys off of the URI, not the prefix. Namespace prefixes are just syntax sugar intended to make XML documents easier to type and read. They do not in any way change the information content of a document.

Item 22 Don't Use Namespace Prefixes in Element Content and Attribute Values

The namespaces specification is very schizophrenic about using namespace prefixes in places that aren't actually defined to be XML names. The most common offender here is attribute values. This is particularly common in schema documents and XSLT stylesheets. For instance, the XSLT template below matches XHTML `head` elements and then selects the XHTML `title` element.

```
<xsl:template match="html:head"
              xmlns:html="http://www.w3.org/1999/xhtml">
  <fo:block><xsl:value-of select="html:title"/></fo:block>
</xsl:template>
```

However, element content can also be an issue. For example, consider the following elements.

```
<feature>uuid:a088355f-2fee-4001-ba17-e9926fca3eb5</feature>
<file path="HD:documents">2003:02:21 Notice.doc</file>
<book>
  <author>John Wogglebug</author>
  <title>Plato: An Analysis</title>
</book>
<classpath>xerces.jar:xalan.jar</classpath>
```

All of these look more or less like prefixed names, but none of them is. There are also many uses of colons in data that are not XML names but still might appear so at first glance.

```
<book id="isbn:2841771431" />
<a href="http://www.w3.org/">The W3C</a>
<file path="HD:books:effectivexml" />
<a href="mailto:elharo@metalab.unc.edu">Elliotte Rusty
Harold</a>
<classpath value="/home/elharo/lib:/java/classes/."/>
<module name="XML::Parser"/>
```

And it gets even worse when you consider things like XPath expressions that may contain one or more prefixed names but are not themselves simple XML names. It is extremely difficult to tell whether a string containing a colon is or is not an XML name when used in such places. Most XML APIs including SAX, DOM, and JDOM provide only marginal support for resolving prefixes in element content. Generally, they can tell you what URI any given prefix maps to at a certain point in the document, but they cannot tell you whether a word that contains a colon is or is not a prefixed name.

XSLT and the W3C XML Schema Language both require prefixes in content, and this has caused no end of trouble for implementers. Don't follow their bad example. If you need to use namespaces in element content and/or attribute values, use the URI and the local name rather than the prefixed names. This way there will be no ambiguity.

RELAX NG and the W3C XML Schema Language provide an excellent contrast between the right way and the wrong way to fill this need. Both RELAX NG and the W3C XML Schema Language are namespace aware, and thus they need to specify the namespaces of the elements and attributes a schema declares. The W3C XML Schema Language uses prefixed names in attribute values to do this. For instance, here is a W3C XML Schema Language declaration of a `Year` element in the http://www.example.com/ namespace that has type `xsd:gYear`.

```
<xsd:element xmlns:xsd="http://www.w3.org/2001/XMLSchema"
             xmlns:ex="http://www.example.com/"
             name="ex:Year" type="xsd:gYear"/>
```

Namespace prefixes are used not only on element names but also in the values of the `name` and `type` attributes.

By contrast, RELAX NG would declare the same element like this:

```
<rng:element xmlns:rng="http://relaxng.org/ns/structure/1.0"
    name="Year" ns="http://www.example.com">
  <rng:data type="gYear"
    datatypeLibrary="http://www.w3.org/2001/
    XMLSchema-datatypes"
  />
</rng:element>
```

Here namespace prefixes are used only on the element names. The namespace of the element being declared is identified by an `ns` attribute. The type set is identified by a URI in the `datatypeLibrary` attribute that isn't even a namespace URI. There are no prefixes anywhere in the attribute values. It's not that the W3C XML Schema Language approach binds a specific prefix. You can still change the prefix in instance documents. It's merely that the RELAX NG schema is much easier to parse and manipulate. There's no implicit substructure in the attribute values that the parser can't expose. It's all laid out in attribute values and element content.

Item 23   Reuse XHTML for Generic Narrative Content

Many XML applications are intended solely for machine processing. For instance, SOAP messages are almost never seen by a person. However, most DocBook documents are edited by hand and are intended to be formatted and presented to people. In machine-oriented documents, mixed content is uncommon and order tends not to matter much. In narrative documents meant for human eyes, mixed content is extremely common and order matters a great deal. However, there's also a common middle ground of documents that are mostly intended for machine processing but may contain some portion of text meant for people.

For example, consider a bank or credit card statement. Mostly it's just a list of transactions. However, statements often also contain a significant amount of narrative for a person to read, as shown in Figure 23–1. There is nothing in this part of the statement that could not be written in standard XHTML.

For another example, imagine an invoice document. It probably contains a list of the products ordered, their prices, the delivery address, and so forth. This can all be represented in a straightforward, record-oriented fashion.

```
<?xml version="1.0"?>
<Invoice>
  <Customer>Jane's Electronics</Customer>
  <Product>
    <Name>Widget</Name>
    <SKU>324</SKU>
    <Quantity>10</Quantity>
    <Price currency="USD">2.95</Price>
  </Product>
  <Product>
    <Name>Gizmo</Name>
    <SKU>325</SKU>
    <Quantity>1</Quantity>
    <Price currency="USD">2344.95</Price>
  </Product>
  <ShipTo>
    <Street>135 Fremont Ave.</Street >
    <City>Santa Clara</City>
    <State>CA</State>
```

IMPORTANT INFORMATION ABOUT THIS ACCOUNT STATEMENT AND YOUR RIGHTS

1. <u>Review At Once:</u> Notify the Bank in writing, within 14 days after we mail or make this statement available to you, of any irregularities, or you may lose valuable rights. See the brochure "Information About Our Accounts and Services" for details about this and other time limitations regarding notice or irregularities. (This paragraph does not apply to electronic funds or wire transfers.)

2. <u>Electronic Funds Transfers Under Regulation E:</u> In case of errors or questions about your electronic funds transfer, telephone our Electronic Data Interchange Department, at (212) 555-0000, or write us at:

Electronic Data Interchange Department
Some Bank of New York
100 Square Place, New York, N.Y., 10003

If you think your statement or receipt is wrong or if you need more information about a transfer on your statement or receipt, you must notify us not later than 60 days after we send you the FIRST statement on which the error or problem appears.

    A. Tell us your name and account number.

    B. Describe the error or the transfer you are unsure about, and explain as clearly as you can why you believe there is an error or why you need more information.

    C. Tell us the dollar amount of the suspected error.

We will investigate your complaint and correct any error promptly. If we take more than 10 business days to do this we will re-credit your account for the amount you think is in error, so that you will have use of the money during the time it takes us to complete our investigation. However, for any complaint regarding a transfer initiated outside the United States or a Point of Sale (POS) ATM card transaction, the Bank may take up to 20 business days before recrediting your account.

    Confirmation of Direct Deposit: If you have arranged to have your account credited by regularly scheduled (at least once every 60 days) electronic funds transfers (for example, direct deposit of social security, pension or payroll), then to learn if the deposit was made, you can call the branch office where you maintain your account (see list below).

3. <u>Wire Transfers:</u> In case of errors or if you have questions about particular wire transfer transactions, contact our E.D.I. Department at (212) 555-0000.

4. <u>For all other inquiries:</u> Please call the branch where your account is maintained (see list below).

Important Information About Money Market Accounts

Each month you are limited to six (6) of the following types of transactions:

• pre-authorized and telephone transfers to another of your accounts at the Bank; and/or

• transfers payable to a third party that may be pre-authorized or made by your instructions over the telephone.

    Included in these six (6) transfers and/or withdrawals per month, you may make up to three (3) transfers from your account to a third party by using your ATM card (such as a POS transaction) or writing a check drawn on your Money Market Account.

    Certain transfers and withdrawals are not subject to the limits described above. You may make an unlimited number of transfers from your account to another account you have at the Bank and withdrawals payable directly to you provided these transfers or withdrawals are made in person, by mail, by messenger, or by check payable to you according to your telephone instructions.

NOTIFY THE BANK IMMEDIATELY IN WRITING TO CHANGE OR CORRECT YOUR ADDRESS

If your account is maintained at:	The telephone number is:
1000 Some Ave., Bronx, N.Y.	(212) 555-0000
500 Another Place, New York, N.Y.	(212) 555-0000
30 Square Place, New York, N.Y.	(212) 555-0000

Figure 23–1 | The Narrative Fine Print from a Typical Bank Statement

```
    <Zip>95054</Zip>
  </ShipTo>
  <Terms>Net-30</Terms>
</Invoice>
```

However, an invoice may also contain a paragraph of text thanking the customer for ordering the products, instructions for returning the product if necessary, and even ads for other products. All of these are traditional narrative text and need a more human-centered markup.

Most developers focus on the more record-like aspects of a document when designing an XML application. Developers are more comfortable with this sort of data, and its structure tends to be more closely tied to the business rules. The narrative content is often an afterthought, if it's included at all, and it's rarely very well thought out. Fortunately, even as an afterthought, it doesn't have to be hard to add sophisticated narrative structure to your documents. The trick is, instead of trying to invent a markup language that describes paragraphs, sections, title, emphasis, and so on from scratch, borrow an existing markup language. In particular, I recommend that you borrow XHTML. XHTML has a number of advantages, not least among them:

- XHTML is simple but complete. It includes many features you probably need but may not have considered, such as accessibility, language identification, standard entity references, and more.
- Many tools can process and display XHTML. For instance, you can render XHTML in your applications by using javax.swing.JEditorPane in Java, the Gecko engine in C++, the Internet Explorer engine in Windows, and many more.
- Authors are very familiar with XHTML already. Including it requires very little extra training.
- The DTD is modular, so it can be easily integrated into your application. You can pick and choose those parts you need and leave out the parts you don't.
- XHTML uses namespaces, so it's easy to distinguish your elements from the HTML elements. This isn't true of some other formats for generic narrative documents such as DocBook and TEI.
- The W3C licenses XHTML on extremely liberal terms, so you don't have to worry about intellectual property issues getting in the way of your data or software. This makes the lawyers happy.

There are two basic ways to integrate XHTML into other, more record-like documents.

1. Define a placeholder element that contains the XHTML markup (e.g., an `AccountInformation` element in a bank statement).
2. Include an entire XHTML document, starting with the root `html` element as a child of one of the domain-specific elements.

Both approaches have their advantages and disadvantages. The first often seems to flow more naturally with the document as a whole, while the second makes it much easier to extract and process the HTML using a separate process from the one that manipulates the records in the document. Perhaps the best approach is to combine them, that is, to insert a placeholder element that contains an `html` element. For example, here's a simplified bank statement that includes HTML account information.

```
<?xml version="1.0"?>
<!DOCTYPE statement PUBLIC "-//MegaBank//DTD Statement//EN"
                          "statement.dtd">
<Statement xmlns="http://namespaces.megabank.com/">
  <Bank>MegaBank</bank>
  <Account>
    <Number>00003145298</Number>
    <Type>Savings</Type>
    <Owner>John Doe</Owner>
  </Account>
  <Date>2003-30-02</Date>
  <OpeningBalance>5266.34</OpeningBalance>
  <Deposit>
    <Date>2003-02-07</Date>
    <Amount>300.00</Amount>
  </Deposit>
  <ClosingBalance>5566.34</ClosingBalance>
  <AccountInfo>
    <html xmlns="http://www.w3.org/1999/xhtml">
      <body>
        <h1>
          IMPORTANT INFORMATION ABOUT THIS ACCOUNT STATEMENT
          AND YOUR RIGHTS
        </h1>
        <ol>
          <li><strong>Review At Once:</strong>
              Notify the Bank in writing, within 14 days
              after we mail or make this statement available
              to you, of any irregularities, or you may lose
              valuable rights. See the brochure <cite>
              Information About Our Accounts and Services
              </cite> for details about this and other time
              limitations regarding notice or irregularities.
              (This paragraph does not apply to electronic
              funds or wire transfers.)
          </li>
          <li><strong>Electronic Funds Transfers Under
```

```
                    Regulation E:</strong>
            In case of...</li>
        </ol>
        ...
        </body>
      </html>
    </AccountInfo>
</statement>
```

If you want to validate documents like this (and you don't always need to do that; sometimes just the markup is enough), you'll want to reference the XHTML DTD. This is not hard. You can load it with a parameter entity reference as discussed in Item 8 and demonstrated below.

```
<!ENTITY % xhtml PUBLIC "-//W3C//DTD XHTML 1.1//EN"
                        "xhtml11.dtd">
%xhtml;
```

You then simply include the `html` element in the content model of the `AccountInfo` element.

```
<!ELEMENT AccountInfo (html)>
```

The only tricky part is ensuring that no elements in your application share names, such as `p`, `div`, `body`, or `table`, with standard HTML elements. This is probably a good idea anyway because the HTML elements are so familiar to so many people that using the same names for other things is likely to cause confusion. (Other schema languages do not have this problem because they're namespace aware, but the W3C XML Schema Language schema for XHTML has not been finished as of June 2003.)

In fact, you actually can choose from several variants of XHTML, depending on your needs. These include:

- XHTML Basic, -//W3C//DTD XHTML Basic 1.0//EN (http://www.w3.org/TR/xhtml-basic/xhtml-basic10.dtd): A minimal profile of XHTML 1.1 that includes headings, paragraphs, lists, links, basic forms, basic tables images, and meta information. This is particularly well suited for embedding narrative content in other XML applications and is usually my first choice.
- XHTML 1.1, -//W3C//DTD XHTML 1.1//EN (http://www.w3.org/TR/xhtml11/DTD/xhtml11.dtd): Complete, standard XHTML 1.1 including everything in XHTML Basic plus ruby text, image maps,

events, scripting, revision marking, complete forms, complete tables, and more. This is normally overkill for simple, embedded narrative content.

- XHTML 1.0 Transitional, -//W3C//DTD XHTML 1.0 Transitional//EN (http://www.w3.org/TR/xhtml1/DTD/xhtml1-transitional.dtd): All the standard features of traditional HTML 4.0 except for frames. This includes deprecated style elements such as `font`, `i`, and `b`. This is useful for incorporating existing legacy content. It is not as customizable as the modular form of XHTML introduced in XHTML 1.1.
- XHTML 1.0 Frameset, -//W3C//DTD XHTML 1.0 Frameset//EN (http://www.w3.org/TR/xhtml1/DTD/xhtml1-frameset.dtd): Transitional XHTML plus frames. This is rarely needed when embedding XHTML inside other XML documents.

The W3C has even published profiles of XHTML that integrate MathML, SVG, and/or VoiceXML support. If none of these suit you, you can use the modularization techniques built into XHTML 1.1 to customize your own. You can add and remove elements and attributes, select only some of the modules, and build almost exactly the language you need. For example, suppose you want to use XHTML Basic but remove forms support. You would simply redefine the `xhtml-form.module` entity to IGNORE before importing the XHTML basic driver.

```
<!ENTITY % xhtml-form.module "IGNORE" >
<!ENTITY % xhtml-basic PUBLIC "-//W3C//DTD XHTML Basic 1.0//EN"
         "http://www.w3.org/TR/xhtml-basic/xhtml-basic10.dtd" >
%xhtml-basic;
```

It is also possible to go the other way, that is, to mix your own vocabularies into XHTML. The difference is that in this case, the root element is `html`, and the main driver is HTML, not your own application. This is primarily useful for browser display, either with stylesheets or particular plug-ins. For instance, this is how SVG and MathML are added to web pages. However, this technique tends not to be as useful in custom, local applications.

You may or may not need to customize XHTML like this before mixing it with your own applications. Either way, it's a lot easier to borrow one of the XHTML DTDs and embed XHTML in your documents rather than invent an equivalent language from scratch. Reusing XHTML saves developer time, saves author time, and produces more robust and maintainable documents.

Item 24   Choose the Right Schema Language for the Job

About two years ago, the W3C XML Schema Working Group released the fruits of its labors into an eager world. The specification was titled simply "XML Schema." This has unfortunately given many people the mistaken idea that the language the group invented is the only schema language and that all others are doomed to fall by the wayside. In fact, nothing could be further from the truth. There are numerous XML schema languages available today, all with their own strengths and weaknesses. It behooves you to familiarize yourself with the different possibilities and to select the one that best fits your problem. Indeed, there's no reason you have to select only one. It's often useful to mix and match several schema languages and perform multiple layers of validation.

Four main schema languages are being actively developed and supported at the current time. Doubtless there will be more in the future but, in my opinion, today these four will most effectively achieve almost any end:

1. The W3C XML Schema Language
2. Document Type Definitions (DTDs)
3. RELAX NG
4. Schematron

Finally, some constraints are always going to require a traditional programming language such as Python, Java, or C++ to verify. I'll also explore the use of procedural code to verify constraints.

The W3C XML Schema Language

The W3C XML Schema Language (often misleadingly labeled simply "schemas") is a very powerful but very complex language. The primary feature of this language, relative to other schema languages, is data typing, especially for attribute values and simple element text. This language can state that a particular element or attribute contains an int, a date, a string, a double, a qualified name, a positive integer, and so on. Beyond the 42 simple types it defines, developers can extend the language with their own types such as money, phone number, color, and more.

Key features of this language include the following:

- Validation of element and attribute structures by complex types
- Validation of text content by simple data types

- Derivation of new types
- Validation of parent–child relationships
- Support for both ordered and unordered structures
- Namespace awareness
- Keys and key references
- Annotation of elements

The W3C XML Schema Language is most appropriate when:

- Documents contain traditional programming constructs such as database records or objects, rather than narrative documents like essays and poems.
- Data is strongly typed in ways that are not apparent from the XML markup alone.
- You need to define your own data types.
- You want to annotate elements with meta-information placed in the schema, rather than the instance document.
- The decision of which schema to apply is made by someone other than the schema author.

The W3C XML Schema Language is least appropriate when:

- Ease of schema development is a major concern.
- Performance is critical.
- Constraints are based on structures other than parent–child relationships.

There are times when the W3C XML Schema Language is the right tool, but these cases aren't nearly as common as many developers think. It is just one tool in the XML toolbox, and a rather specialized one at that. The W3C XML Schema Language is sort of like a Torx T-15 screwdriver—crucial for certain jobs but not nearly as broadly useful as Phillips or flat-head screwdrivers. With that in mind, let's look at some of the other schema tools in the XML toolbox.

Document Type Definitions

If the W3C XML Schema Language is a Torx screwdriver, then DTDs are the old reliable flathead screwdriver, not nearly as sexy but a lot more practical and a lot easier to find at the corner store. Contrary to popular belief, schemas do not replace DTDs. DTDs are an extremely well-tested, well-understood, broadly supported, compact syntax for expressing constraints on XML documents. Furthermore, DTDs can do things that none of the other schema languages can accomplish, notably entity definition. Finally, a document can have both a schema and a DTD.

Don't reject DTDs simply because they're not as hip as schemas. Indeed, if your constraints are limited to the element and attribute structure of a document and do not involve PCDATA and attribute values, a DTD can do almost anything a W3C XML Schema Language schema can do— and do it a lot more simply, robustly, and compatibly.

Key features of DTDs include the following:

- Very broad parser and library support
- Extensive support for parent–child structures
- The ability to define entities and notations
- Default values for attributes

DTDs are most appropriate when:

- Documents are narrative-like, with lots of mixed content.
- Most validation is concerned with element and attribute structure, not with the content of elements and attributes.
- You need to define entities.
- Ease of schema authoring is a primary concern.
- Document producers and document consumers can agree on the schema to use.

DTDs are least appropriate when:

- Validation is concerned with the internal structure of PCDATA and attribute values (as opposed to the external structure identified by tags).
- Data typing is desirable.
- The order of child elements doesn't matter but the number of them does.
- Element constraints are based on sibling, ancestor, or descendant relationships rather than parent–child relationships.
- The namespace prefix is not consistent across documents.
- The schema to apply is chosen by something other than the instance document itself.

In brief, DTDs work best for the sorts of documents they were originally designed for when the SGML community invented them: narrative documents intended ultimately for human consumption in which all text content is basically a string. It's not really surprising that they work less well for applications that postdate them and weren't really conceived of yet when DTDs were invented: namespaces, object serialization, database exchange, vector graphics, and other computer-focused applications with strong typing requirements. But just because DTDs don't fit these new applications perfectly is no reason to discount them for the applications they were designed for, which they fit very well.

RELAX NG

RELAX NG (pronounced "relaxing") is the real sleeper of schema languages, but it has the potential to become the most popular schema language of all. Where the W3C XML Schema Language can feel a bit intimidating at times, RELAX NG is far simpler and cleaner, perhaps because RELAX NG is primarily the product of two smart developers (James Clark and Murata Makoto) rather than a design by committee. RELAX NG can do everything DTDs can do except define entities and notations, and it can do everything the W3C Schema Language can do except define new data types. However, RELAX NG does enable you to reference different data type libraries, including the W3C's own set of XML Schema primitive types.

Key features of RELAX NG include the following:

- Extensive support for parent–child structures
- Exceptional support for order-independent structures and constraints
- External data type libraries that support various kinds of simple data types
- Namespace-aware validation
- Annotation of elements
- Great ease of writing and reading, both in XML and non-XML forms

RELAX NG is most appropriate when:

- Most validation is concerned with element and attribute structure, not with the content of elements and attributes.
- Simple data types are sufficient.
- Ease of schema authoring is a primary concern.
- Very complicated validation rules require a traditional programming language to implement; for example, a key element contains a prime number or a time element contains a value in the past.

RELAX NG is least appropriate when:

- Element constraints are based on sibling, ancestor, or descendant relationships rather than parent–child relationships.

Because RELAX NG does not come with the W3C imprimatur, it has not gained as broad a mind share as the W3C XML Schema Language. However, as more developers experiment with schemas and discover that the W3C XML Schema Language is just too baroque for their tastes, many of them are choosing RELAX NG instead. Most recently the members of the OASIS OpenOffice XML Format Technical Committee have committed to writing their schemas in RELAX NG instead of the W3C XML Schema Language. If you need something with all the expressivity of the W3C XML Schema Language but none of its complexity and verbosity, you really can't do better than RELAX NG.

Schematron

Rick Jelliffe's Schematron is a radically different approach to schema languages. Whereas other schema languages are conservative (everything not permitted is forbidden), Schematron is liberal (everything not forbidden is permitted). A Schematron schema makes assertions about the content of the document. If all assertions are true, the document is valid. Since the assertions are written in XPath, Schematron can state things that no other schema language can. Here are some examples.

- The entire document contains exactly ten paragraph elements (which may be nested inside each other).
- Every `FirstName` element is followed by a `LastName` element, regardless of the parent element.
- If the `CPU` attribute of a `Machine` element has the value `Sparc`, the value of the `OS` attribute must be either `Solaris` or `Linux`.

Key features of Schematron include the following:

- The ability to compare arbitrary nodes in the document (not limited to parent–child structures)
- Namespace awareness
- The ability to validate text, processing instructions, and even comments (not limited to elements and attributes)
- Customizable error messages

Schematron is most appropriate when:

- You need to state constraints that are simply not expressible in DTDs, the W3C XML Schema Language, or RELAX NG.
- Constraints focus on the XML structure of a document.
- You need to verify co-occurrence constraints; for example, every element that contains a `Price` child element must have an `SKU` attribute.
- You need to verify exclusions such as XHTML's requirement that no a element can contain another a element, not just as a child but as a descendant.
- You want to verify a few constraints without specifying every aspect of the markup.
- You want to allow unanticipated developments in the markup.

Schematron is least appropriate when:

- Validation is concerned with the structure of text in element content and attribute values.
- Data typing is needed.

I don't know that I would ever pick Schematron as the sole validation layer for documents. Writing a complete Schematron schema that's equivalent to even a simple DTD is very tiresome. Used in this fashion, Schematron would be far and away the most verbose and difficult of the various schema languages. However, Schematron is not normally used in this way. Instead, it is used to attach additional constraints that are impossible to state in the other languages. It is applied as an extra validation step after a document has already been validated against a DTD or some other schema. In particular, it's often used to add co-occurrence and exclusion constraints to schemas in languages such as RELAX NG and the W3C XML Schema Language that don't have them. Some tools (e.g., the Topologi Schematron Validator) will even recognize Schematron schemas hidden inside annotations in a schema written in a different language.

Java, C#, Python, and Perl

None of the common schema languages are Turing complete. Thus none of them can state and verify every possible constraint on an XML document. For example, none of them can verify that the content of a `Prime` element is in fact a prime number. However, this verification is straightforward in any reasonably powerful programming language. For example, here's a very naïve algorithm implemented in Java that accomplishes this task by dividing the number by every integer between 2 and its square root until it finds a divisor.

```java
public void isPrime(String text) {
  int test;
  try {
    test = Integer.parseInt(text);
  }
  catch (NumberFormatException ex) {
    return false;
  }

  if (test < 2) return false;
  for (int i = 2; i < Math.sqrt(test); i++) {
    if (test % i == 0) return false;
  }
  return true;
}
```

(Mathematically inclined readers should feel free to substitute a more efficient algorithm.)

For a slightly less mathematical example, consider an order form that can include multiple products.

```xml
<Order>
  <Product SKU="78X" quantity="12" price="21.95">
    Clown Hat
  </Product>
  <Product SKU="83X" quantity="1" price="144.95" discount=".10">
    Clown Car
  </Product>
  <Tax rate="7.0">27.57</Tax>
  <Shipping  method="USPS" currency='USD'>8.95</Shipping>
  <Total>430.37</Total>
</Order>
```

Before accepting the order, you want to multiply each quantity by its corresponding price, apply the discount to the items with discounts, calculate and add in the tax and shipping, and verify that it all equals the value of the `Total` element. In a traditional programming language, this is a CS101 problem. For example, using JDOM, a method might act like this:

```java
boolean orderValid(Element order) {

    try {
        Iterator products
            = order.getChildren("Product").iterator();
        double subtotal = 0;
        while (products.hasNext()) {
            Element product = (Element) products.next();
            double price = Double.parseDouble(
                product.getAttributeValue("price"));
            int quantity = Integer.parseInt(
                product.getAttributeValue("quantity"));
            subtotal += price*quantity;
        }
        Element tax = order.getChild("Tax");
        double rate = Double.parseDouble(
            tax.getAttributeValue("rate"))/100.0;
        if (Math.abs(subtotal * rate
            - Double.parseDouble(tax.getText())) >= 0.01) {
            return false;
        }
        subtotal += rate;
        Element shipping = order.getChild("Shipping");
        subtotal += Double.parseDouble(shipping.getText());
        Element total = order.getChild("Total");
        if (Math.abs(subtotal
            - Double.parseDouble(total.getText()))>=0.01) {
            return false;
        }
    }
    catch (Exception ex) {
      return false;
    }

    return true;

}
```

However, in the common schema languages, this problem is unsolvable. (RELAX NG actually allows you to plug in new data type libraries written in a traditional language like Java, Python, or C. The RELAX NG language itself can't verify these constraints without extra code like that shown here, but it does make it easier to insert your own custom code into the validation process.)

Traditional programming languages are also useful for verifying constraints that require access to external data. For example, you might want to look up the price of each item in an order in a remote database to verify that the process submitting the order hasn't gotten the price wrong. All major programming languages have libraries for talking to SQL databases. No schema languages do.

Layering Schemas

When considering the schema language that's appropriate for your needs, the following questions may help you decide.

- Do you need to constrain element and attribute structures? If so, choose DTDs, the W3C XML Schema Language, or RELAX NG.
- Do you need to define entities? If so, you'll need a DTD.
- Do you need broad compatibility with existing software and systems? Choose DTDs.
- Do you need a simple, human-authorable syntax? Choose RELAX NG.
- Do you need to annotate elements and attributes, either with types or other information? If so, the W3C XML Schema Language is powerful.
- Do you need to store the schema documents independent of the instance documents? Choose the W3C XML Schema Language, Schematron, or RELAX NG.
- Do you need co-occurrence or exclusion constraints? If so, Schematron is for you.
- Does validation require access to data from outside the document, for example, in the file system or an external database? If so, you'll need to write a custom program in your language of choice to perform the validation, but you may be able to plug this into a RELAX NG validator.

Finally, remember that none of these needs are mutually exclusive. If you answered yes to several of these questions, you may want to apply multiple schemas to a single document in sequence.

Hammers are useful tools, but you wouldn't use one to cut wood. Use the right tool for the job. The W3C XML Schema Language is a useful tool, but it's not the only tool, and it doesn't fit all applications. DTDs still work very well for traditional narrative documents such as books, transcripts, and e-mail. Schematron can make assertions no other schema language can make. RELAX NG is much easier to learn and master than the W3C XML Schema Language. All carpenters have many tools in their toolboxes. You should have many schema languages in your XML toolbox.

Item 25   Pretend There's No Such Thing as the PSVI

Schemas are an extremely useful means of checking preconditions on XML documents before processing them. While schema validation normally can't detect every possible violation of an application's constraints, it can often detect a lot of them. However, some schema languages (especially the W3C XML Schema Language) have a second, less salutary purpose. Although support is mostly experimental so far, the W3C XML Schema specifications indicate that a truly schema-aware parser should produce a post-schema validation information set (PSVI).

The concept is that the PSVI includes not only the actual content of the XML document but also annotations about that content from schemas. In particular, it defines types for elements and attributes. Thus you can know, for example, that a `Price` element has type `xsd:double`, a `CurrentStock` element has type `xsd:nonNegativeInteger`, an `expires` attribute has type `xsd:date`, and a `Weight` element has type `xsd:decimal`.

This sounds good in theory. In practice, the real world is rarely so simple. The types defined in the schema are only occasionally the correct types to be used in the local processing environment.

- A `Price` element might be declared as a double. However, to avoid round-off errors when adding and subtracting prices, it might need to be processed as a fixed point type as in Cobol or as an instance of a custom `Money` class that never has round-off errors.

- `CurrentStock` might always be non-negative (that is, greater than or equal to zero), but it might still be represented as a signed int in languages such as Java that don't have unsigned types.
- An `expires` attribute may contain a date, but the local database into which the dates are fed might represent dates as an integer containing the number of days since December 1, 1904, or the number of seconds since midnight, December 31, 1969. It might round all dates to the nearest month or the nearest week. It might even convert them to a non-Gregorian calendar.
- A `Weight` element might be declared as type `xsd:decimal`, equivalent to `BigDecimal` in Java. However, local processing might change it to a double for efficiency of calculation if the local process doesn't need the extra precision or size of the decimal type. It might also need to convert from pounds to kilograms, or ounces to grams, or grams to kilograms. The mere annotation as a decimal is insufficient to truly determine the weight.

The fact is schema-defined types just aren't all that useful. XML 1.0 also has a notion of types based purely on element and attribute names. Along with the namespace and the outer context (that is, the parents and ancestors of the element and attribute), this is normally all you need to convert XML into some local structure for further processing. If you can recognize that the `CurrentStock` element represents the number of boxes sitting in the warehouse, you normally know that it's a non-negative integer, and you know how to handle it in your code. In fact, you can handle it a lot better by understanding that it is the number of boxes sitting in the warehouse than you can merely by knowing that it's a non-negative integer.

Look at it this way: It's very rare to assign different types to the same element. What is the chance you'll have a `CurrentStock` element that is an integer in one place and a string in the next, or any other element for that matter? This does happen—for example, in a medical record, a `Duration` element might contain minutes when describing the length of a procedure and days, months, and years when describing a preexisting condition—but normally this indicates that the type is really some broader type that can handle both types, in this case perhaps an ISO 8601 duration that handles everything from years down to fractions of a second. Almost always, knowing the name, namespace, and context of an element is sufficient to deduce its nature and to do this in a far more robust and useful way than merely knowing the type. Adding the schema type really does not provide any new information.

The normal response of PSVI proponents is that the type is necessary for documentation—that it serves as some sort of contract between the producer of the data and the consumer of the data. The type tells the eventual recipient that the sender intended a particular element to be treated as a non-negative integer, or a date in the Gregorian calendar, or in some other way. A schema and its types can certainly be useful for documentation purposes. It helps to more unambiguously define what is expected, and like all extra-document context it can be used to inform the development of the process that receives the document. However, the software generally won't dispatch based on the type. It will decide what to do with elements based on the element's name, namespace, position within the document, and sometimes content. The type will most often be ignored.

Even more importantly, there is absolutely no guarantee that the type the sender assigns to a particular element is in any way, shape, or form the type the recipient needs or can process. For example, some languages don't have integer types, only decimal types. Thus they might choose to parse an integer as a floating point number. Even more likely, they may choose to treat all numbers as strings or to deserialize data into a custom class or type such as a money object. The idea that each data has a type that can satisfy all possible uses of the data in all environments is a fantasy. Regardless of what type it's assigned, different processes will treat the data differently, as befits their local needs and concerns.

Some more recent W3C specifications, especially XPath 2.0, XSLT 2.0, and XQuery, are based on the PSVI, and this has caused no end of problems. The specifications are far more complex and elaborate than they would be if they were based on basic XML 1.0 structures. They impose significant additional costs on implementers, significant enough that several developers who have implemented XPath and XSLT 1.0 have announced they won't be implementing version 2 of the specification. They also impose noticeable performance penalties on users because schema validation becomes a prerequisite for even the simplest transformation.

What exactly is bought for this extra cost? Honestly, that's hard to say. It's not clear what, if anything, can be done with XPath 2.0/XSLT 2.0/XQuery as currently designed that couldn't be done with a less typed language. It is possible to search a document for all the elements with type `int` or for all the attributes with type date, but that's rarely useful without knowing what the int or date represents. Indeed, in the XQuery Use Cases specification (May 2003, working draft), only 12 of 77 examples actually use typed data, and most of those could easily be rewritten to depend on element names rather than element types. Some developers suspect they can use strong typing information to optimize and speed up certain queries, but so far this is no more than a hypothesis without any real evidence to back it up. Indeed, the main purpose of all the static typing seems to be soothing the stomachs of the relational database vendors in the working group who are constitutionally incapable of digesting a dynamically typed language.

The PSVI also causes trouble in many of the data binding APIs such as Castor, Zeus, JAXB, and others. Here the problem is a little less explicit. These APIs start with the assumption that they can read a schema to determine the input form of the document and then deserialize it into equivalent local objects. They rely on schema types to determine which local forms the data takes: int, double, BigDecimal, and so on. There are numerous problems with this approach, which are not shared by more type-agnostic processes.

- More documents don't have schemas than do. Limiting yourself only to documents with schemas cuts way down on what you can usefully process.
- Documents that have schemas don't always have schemas in the right language. Most data binding APIs such as JAXB are based around the W3C XML Schema Language. Most actual schemas are DTDs. A few tools can handle DTDs, but what do you do when the schema language is RELAX NG or something still more obscure?
- Documents that do have schemas aren't always valid. Just because some expected content is missing doesn't mean there isn't useful information still in the document. It's even more likely that extra, unexpected content will not get in the way of your processing. However, because most data binding tools take validity as a prerequisite, they throw up their hands in defeat at the first sign of trouble. Type-agnostic processes soldier on.
- Many data binding tools make assumptions about types, particularly complex types, that simply aren't true of many, perhaps most, XML documents. For instance, they assume order doesn't matter, mixed content doesn't exist, elements aren't repeated (the normalization fallacy), and more. In essence, they're trying to fit XML into object or

relational structures rather than building objects or tables around XML. Too often when somebody talks about strong typing in XML, they really mean limiting XML to just a few types they happen to be familiar with that work well in their environment. They aren't considering approaching XML on its own terms.

The PSVI is a useful theory for talking about schema languages and what they mean. However, its practice remains to be worked out. For the time being, simple validation is the most you can or should ask of a schema.

Item 26 Version Documents, Schemas, and Stylesheets

XML applications evolve over time just like traditional software applications. It's almost inevitable that some months after releasing an application, you'll have a better understanding of the domain your documents represent. You'll undoubtedly discover mistakes and inefficiencies in the original design. Requirements will shift and grow and vanish. Laws, regulations, and business practices can all change in ways that require you to modify XML applications. XML may not be a programming language, but XML applications are subject to all the same software engineering headaches associated with programs written in Java, C++, Cobol, and other languages. Consequently, it's important to use the same practices to track the components of your XML systems as you would any other equivalently complex piece of software. Use version control systems like CVS for your schemas and stylesheets, and follow the same release naming and numbering conventions as you would for a program written in Java, C++, or any other language.

Within the XML documents, schemas, and stylesheets themselves, it's generally a good idea to identify the version of the application they adhere to. XML 1.0 itself recognized its likely need to evolve and included a version number in its XML declaration so that parsers could recognize what version of XML was in use. So far that hasn't been needed, but it probably will be soon.

You should do the same in your own documents. Each XML application should include a version element or attribute that can contain a reasonable version number. Typically this would be placed on the root element, as shown here.

```
<?xml version="1.0"?>
<Statement xmlns="http://namespaces.megabank.com/" version="1.0">
  ...
</Statement>
```

However, in cases where a document combines elements from multiple applications and namespaces, you should probably put the version attribute on each top-most element from a particular vocabulary. For example, the following statement uses the `Statement` vocabulary, an `Address` vocabulary, and XHTML, all with separate versions.

```
<Statement xmlns="http://namespaces.megabank.com/" version="1.0">
  <Bank>
    <Logo href="logo.jpg" height="125" width="125"/>
    <Name>MegaBank</Name>
    <Motto>We Really Pretend to Care</Motto>
    <Branch>
      <Address xmlns="http://www.example.com/addresses/"
               version="1.2">
        <Street>666 Fifth Ave.</Street>
        <City>New York</City>
        <State>NY</State>
        <PostalCode>10010</PostalCode>
        <Country>USA</Country>
      </Address>
    </Branch>
  </Bank>
  <Account>
    <Number>00003145298</Number>
    <Type>Savings</Type>
    <Owner>John Doe</Owner>
    <Address xmlns="http://www.example.com/addresses/"
             version="1.2">
      <Street>123 Peon Way</Street>
      <Apt>28Z</Apt>
      <City>Brooklyn</City>
      <State>NY</State>
      <PostalCode>11239</PostalCode>
      <Country>USA</Country>
    </Address>
  </Account>
```

```
  <Date>2003-30-02</Date>
  <AccountActivity>

    ...

  </AccountActivity>
  <Legal version="1.0 Transitional">
    <html xmlns="http://www.w3.org/1999/xhtml/">
      <body style="font-size: xx-small">

        ...

      </body>
    </html>
  </Legal>
</Statement>
```

There's generally no need to repeat the version on each element.

Most of the time, a simple numeric versioning system as used in most software (0.1, 0.2, 0.9, 1.1, 2.0, and so on) works well enough. This should normally be treated as a string because it may contain letters (e.g., 1.0a1, 1.0b2) or may not exactly fit as a decimal (e.g., 1.0.1, 1.5.3). There are a number of related conventions for how to version software. Any of them work as long as you're consistent.

Other options are possible. For example, some developers prefer to use the date when a particular application was released.

```
<?xml version="1.0"?>
<Statement xmlns="http://namespaces.megabank.com/"
           version="20020824">

  ...

</Statement>
```

Use whatever form works best for you, but do use something.

Instead of an attribute, some applications use the public ID in the document type declaration. For example, XHTML documents can begin in any of the following ways, all of which identify different variations and profiles of XHTML. (See Item 23.)

```
<!DOCTYPE html PUBLIC "-//W3C//DTD XHTML Basic 1.0//EN"
    "http://www.w3.org/TR/xhtml-basic/xhtml-basic10.dtd">
<!DOCTYPE html PUBLIC "-//W3C//DTD XHTML 1.1//EN"
    "http://www.w3.org/TR/xhtml11/DTD/xhtml11.dtd">
<!DOCTYPE html PUBLIC "-//W3C//DTD XHTML 1.0 Transitional//EN"
```

```
    "http://www.w3.org/TR/xhtml1/DTD/xhtml1-transitional.dtd">
<!DOCTYPE html PUBLIC "-//W3C//DTD XHTML 1.0 Frameset//EN"
    "http://www.w3.org/TR/xhtml1/DTD/xhtml1-frameset.dtd">
<!DOCTYPE html PUBLIC "-//W3C//DTD XHTML 2.0//EN" "xhtml20.dtd">
<!DOCTYPE html PUBLIC
    "-//W3C//DTD XHTML 1.1 plus MathML 2.0 plus SVG 1.1//EN"
    "http://www.w3.org/2002/04/xhtml-math-svg/xhtml-math-svg.dtd"
>
```

This works well enough as long as you expect documents to carry document type declarations and to be fairly independent. However, it's much more problematic when you begin mixing and matching several DTDs into the same document. You need to define (and applications need to recognize) new public IDs for each separate combination. Furthermore, including a document type declaration may convince some tools that they actually have to read and process the DTD in order to handle the document. Worse yet, not all APIs provide reliable access to the public ID. Version attributes are much more reliable and portable and much less fraught with unintended side effects.

One thing you should probably *not* do is change the namespace URI with each new version. Too much other software depends on the namespace for proper operation. Changing it can unnecessarily break all these applications, many or most of which will function properly with the new version. Unless the changes in the new version of the application are so radical that essentially an entire new language has been invented, keep the namespace URI constant.

You should also identify the version in use in the ancillary documents for the application: schemas, stylesheets, documentation, and so on. Here you need to be careful not to confuse the version of the XML vocabulary in which the document is written and the version of the XML vocabulary for which the document is intended. For example, here's an XSLT stylesheet that's written in XSLT 1.0 but processes DocBook 4.1.2.

```
<?xml version="1.0" encoding="US-ASCII"?>
<xsl:stylesheet
xmlns:xsl="http://www.w3.org/1999/XSL/Transform"
                version="1.0">

  <rdf:RDF
    xmlns:rdf="http://www.w3.org/1999/02/22-rdf-syntax-ns#"
```

```
    xmlns:dc="http://purl.org/dc/elements/1.1/">
    <rdf:Description about="http://ibiblio.org/xml/">
      <dc:title>docbook.xsl</dc:title>
      <dc:date>2002-04-23</dc:date>
      <dc:relation>
        -//OASIS//DTD DocBook XML V4.1.2//EN
      </dc:relation>
    </rdf:Description>
  </rdf:RDF>

  <!-- rest of stylesheet... -->

</xsl:stylesheet>
```

In this example, I placed the version information in a top-level element from a non-XSLT namespace, which an XSLT processor is guaranteed to ignore. I also identified the version of DocBook the stylesheet applies to using a formal public identifier. I got a little fancy here (possibly too fancy) and used RDF and the Dublin Core, but any non-XSLT namespace would suffice.

One of my favorite stylesheet tricks is to put the version information in global variables. This allows it to be referenced from the stylesheet itself so it can be moved to the output. Here we use two variables, one for the version of DocBook in use and one for the version of the stylesheet itself.

```
<xsl:variable name="stylesheet-version" value="1.73"/>
<xsl:variable name="application-version" value="1.1.2"/>

<xsl:template name="VersionInfo">
  Output produced by the MegaBank Statement Stylesheet
  <xsl:value-of select="$stylesheet-version"/>
  for  MegaBank Statement
  <xsl:value-of select="$application-version"/>
</xsl:template>
```

CSS stylesheets present much less opportunity to embed version information. Here you essentially must use a comment, as demonstrated below.

```
/*  MegaBank Statement CSS stylesheets  1.73 for MBSML 1.1.2 */
book { display: block; font-size: 12pt;
       font-family: Times, serif }
/* ... */
```

DTDs are similarly limited. They provide no formal way to identify the version of the DTD. Normally a comment suffices.

```
<!-- MegaBank Account Statement DTD, Version 1.1.2 -->
```

See Item 5 for more suggestions about how to comment a DTD.

The W3C XML Schema Language, by contrast, provides an `xsd:annotation` element that is perfect for storing version information and other meta-information about the schema. Generally, its `xsd:documentation` child is used for human-readable metadata and its `xsd:appInfo` child is used for machine-processable metadata. These may contain any elements from any vocabulary other than the W3C XML Schema Language itself. For example, the following schema has a top-level `xsd:annotation` element providing both RDF and human-readable metadata about the schema.

```
<xsd:schema xmlns:xsd="http://www.w3.org/2001/XMLSchema">

  <xsd:annotation>
    <xsd:appInfo>
      <rdf:RDF
        xmlns:rdf="http://www.w3.org/1999/02/22-rdf-syntax-ns#"
        xmlns:dc="http://purl.org/dc/elements/1.1/">
        <rdf:Description about="http://ibiblio.org/xml/">
          <dc:title>docbook.xsd</dc:title>
          <dc:date>2002-04-23</dc:date>
          <dc:relation>
             -//OASIS//DTD DocBook XML V4.2//EN
          </dc:relation>
        </rdf:Description>
      </rdf:RDF>
    </xsd:appInfo>

    <xsd:documentation>
      Schema version 1.5 for DocBook XML 4.1.2
    </xsd:documentation>

    <!-- rest of schema... -->
  </xsd:annotation>

</xsd:schema>
```

Schema processors will normally ignore `xsd:annotation` elements, but other processes reading the schema can easily extract the relevant metadata, including the version information.

Other components of an XML-based system, such as processing software, RDDL documentation, schemas in other languages like RELAX NG, and so forth, can be handled similarly. The main thing to remember is that your applications will change, whether you expect them to or not. It only makes sense to be ready for them to do so.

Item 27   Mark Up According to Meaning

One of the most fundamental principles of XML design is the separation of presentation and content. The names of all tags and attributes should reflect the information they contain rather than how they'll be presented to an end user. This is sometimes called *semantic markup*. Semantic markup has a number of advantages compared to more traditional presentational markup as practiced in HTML, TeX, and other languages.

- Semantic markup provides much greater assistance to software that does anything other than present the content to an end user. It provides more reliable hooks to decipher the meaning of the data.
- Semantic markup makes it much easier to attach alternate stylesheets and presentations to the document. This allows the content to more easily be displayed in diverse environments, including cell phones, Web TVs, billboards, printed materials, screen readers, Braille printers, and things you haven't even dreamed of.
- Semantic markup is much easier for developers to decipher by reading the raw code.
- Semantic markup is less likely to conflict with other XML applications with which it may need to be integrated.

However, there is one thing semantic markup does not do:

- It does not magically give computers the ability to understand the content of documents, as some of the more excessive XML hype has occasionally claimed.

What semantic markup *does* do is provide stronger, more accessible hooks to which programs with localized knowledge of the domain and element names can more easily connect.

Presentation is an important use for many XML documents, but it is only one use. It should not overshadow all other uses to which the data may be put. If the formatting outweighs the data's own structure, it can establish connections that aren't really there while hiding those that are. For example, consider italics. These are customarily used to indicate the following:

- Importance (*Do not forget your gloves.*)
- Titles of books and magazines (*Processing XML with Java, Software Development*)
- Foreign words (*bonjour, ein, zvei, drei*)
- Names of vehicles (*Challenger, Queen Elizabeth II*)
- Words that reproduce sounds (*hmm, doh!*)

If the markup indicates which words are italicized rather than what the types of the words are, it becomes impossible to easily tell whether a given italicized phrase is a citation, a particularly important point, a word from another language, an onomatopoetic invention, or something else. Yes, a human can almost always figure out which is which without any ambiguity and with very low chances of error. However, software just isn't as smart as people are, and it needs the extra help well-defined semantic markup gives it.

For example, suppose you're marking up a mutual fund prospectus. This is basically a narrative document intended for people to read. It may have very precise formatting requirements, perhaps established by law or securities regulations. Nonetheless, the markup should be designed to reflect the unique meaning and jargon of the mutual fund industry. For example, you could write it in XHTML or DocBook, as shown in Example 27–1.

Example 27–1 | A Partial Mutual Fund Prospectus in XHTML

```
<html xmlns="http://www.3.org/1999/xhtml">
  <head>
    <title>California Gold Rush Fund</title>
  </head>
  <body>

<h1>Fund Summary</h1>
```

```
<p>
This is a money market fund that seeks to preserve
the value of your investment at $1.00 per share.
However, the fund is not a bank and investments
in the fund are not insured or guaranteed by the Federal
Deposit Insurance Corporation or any other government agency.
It is possible to lose money by investing in the fund.
</p>

<h2>Investment Summary</h2>
<h3>Investment Objective</h3>

<p>The California Gold Rush Fund seeks
maximum current income exempt from both
federal and California state income tax.
</p>
<h3>Principal Investment Strategies</h3>

<p>The investment strategies of this fund include:</p>

<ul>
<li>Investing in municipal money market securities of California
    localities.</li>
<li>Investing at least 75% of assets in municipal securities
    whose interest is exempt from both federal and California
    state income tax.</li>
</ul>

<h3>Principal Investment Risks</h3>

<p>The California Gold Rush Fund
  is subject to the following principal investment risks:
</p>

<ul>
  <li>Legislative changes make tax-free munis less
      attractive.</li>
  <li>Orange County declares bankruptcy (again).</li>
  <li>California sinks into the ocean.</li>
</ul>

  </body>
</html>
```

However, it is much preferred to use a specific vocabulary, as shown in Example 27–2.

Example 27–2 | A Partial Mutual Fund Prospectus Using Semantic Markup

```
<Prospectus xmlns="http://www.bigfundco/prospectus/">
  <Name>California Gold Rush Fund</Name>
  <Summary>

    This is a money market fund that seeks to preserve
    the value of your investment at $1.00 per share.
    However, the fund is not a bank and investments
    in the fund are not insured or guaranteed by the Federal
    Deposit Insurance Corporation or any other government
    agency. It is possible to lose money by investing in
    the fund.

    <InvestmentSummary>
      <Objective>
      The California Gold Rush Fund seeks
      maximum current income exempt from both
      federal and California state income tax.
      </Objective>
    <Strategies>

      <Strategy>
        Investing in municipal money market securities of
        California localities.
      </Strategy>
      <Strategy>
        Investing at least 75% of assets in municipal
        securities whose interest is exempt from both federal
        and California state income tax.
      </Strategy>
    </Strategies>

    <Risks>
        <Risk>Legislative changes make tax-free munis less
              attractive.</Risk>
        <Risk>Orange County declares bankruptcy (again). </Risk>
        <Risk>California sinks into the ocean.</Risk>
    </Risks>
```

```
    </InvestmentSummary>
  </Summary>
</Prospectus>
```

This enables various processes ranging from print formatters to SEC enforcement programs to verify that all requirements are satisfied and to easily extract that subset of the information in which each process is interested. It is much harder to extract the securities meaning out of a more presentational format such as XHTML or DocBook than it is to convert semantic markup to presentational markup as necessary.

Arguably, the semantically marked-up version contains more information than the presentational version. It is always possible to go from a document with more information to one with less. In essence, this is what an XSLT stylesheet that converted the second example into the first would do. However, going from a document with little information to one with more is far more difficult. It is not impossible, mind you. However, some external context would be necessary to provide the additional information, as would a lot more intelligence than most software programs have. Unlike some people in the markup community, I do believe that one day we will have computers that are smart enough to read a presentationally marked-up document such as Example 27–1 and infer all the necessary semantics, and I even believe this will happen within the next 20 years. However, it's clear we're not there yet, so in the meantime we smart humans have to help out the poor dumb computers by being more explicit about what we mean in our markup.

Do not, however, get sucked in by the XML hype that says just because you've used semantic markup that systems will automatically understand what you've done. A computer no more understands that a `Risk` element indicates a probability of a disadvantageous occurrence than a fish understands that a baited hook is more than a tasty meal. It is still necessary for software code to be written that keys off the semantic markup to take appropriate actions. However, it is much easier to write this code to operate on a neatly semantic document than to write code that screen-scrapes HTML.

What's semantic and what's purely presentational varies depending on what the XML application is describing. Formatting languages like XSL-FO are the exceptions that prove the rule. Although superficially they appear to be entirely nothing but presentation, in fact they are quite semantic. It's just that the domain they describe is the domain of page layout. The semantics are the semantics that would be familiar to any experienced printer or desktop publisher: widows, orphans, font families, columns, and so on. Most importantly, it is never intended that humans would author XSL-FO directly, even using GUI tools like FrameMaker. Instead, humans author in a markup vocabulary that's much closer to the content's semantics. Then an XSLT stylesheet is applied to transform the document into the expected semantics for page layout.

Whatever the semantics are, the markup should reflect those semantics. The element and attribute names should be words that identify what those elements and attributes contain. They should say what the elements and attributes are rather than what they look like.

3 | Semantics

XML documents by themselves simply *are*. They don't *do* anything. To become useful, a document must be processed by some piece of software that interprets the XML structures in some way, such as formatting and displaying it to a person, placing an order with a store, operating a machine, or otherwise interfacing between the computer and the real world. It is in this processing that XML documents achieve meaning and become more than just a sequence of bytes or characters. The information in the XML document stops being purely structural and becomes semantic.

This part discusses the various APIs, tools, and languages available for processing XML. You'll learn how to choose the appropriate APIs and tools for different kinds of jobs. While most of the major APIs can theoretically handle anything you throw at them, in practice some APIs are much better suited to certain types of processing than others are. It pays greatly to have a variety of tools in your toolbox and to pick the right one for the task at hand.

Item 28   Use Only What You Need

The complete family of XML specifications has grown so large that it's approaching, and in some cases exceeding, the complexity of the SGML specification it effectively replaced. While XML 1.0 is fairly straightforward and well supported, the complete family of XML + DTDs + Namespaces + XPath + Schemas + XLinks + XPointers + XInclude + Infoset + PSVI + XML 1.1 + Namespaces 1.1 + Kitchen Sink is beginning to show signs of the same interoperability issues that plagued SGML. Most tools support some subset of these technologies. Others support a different, intersecting subset. Few if any tools support all of it.

Don't buy into the hype and rumor. Do not feel obligated to include every last member of the XML family in your application. You don't need to use all or even most of this to take advantage of XML. The only parts that are really core are XML 1.0 and Namespaces. Everything else is an option you can use or not as seems appropriate for your application. Even namespaces can be ignored in a pinch. Though I would not go so far as to write markup that was namespace malformed (e.g., that used multiple colons in element names), you can certainly write regular XML 1.0 that ignores namespaces.

Most of the different specifications have their uses. You should absolutely use any of them that help you. Just don't think you have to use all of them. As a rough first approximation, here's a list of which technologies you should consider using when.

- *Well-formed XML:* Well-formedness is the absolute minimum requirement for any XML-based system. This is the only thing you cannot compromise on. If a document is not well-formed, it is not XML. Do not accept or require tools that support anything less than full well-formedness checking.

  The RSS community has made this mistake by de facto allowing programs that accept different, non-well-formed variants of XML, and as a result they are already starting to encounter the same interoperability issues that plagued HTML. Different RSS applications can read different RSS sites. While there's a subset of sites all RSS tools can process, no tool that can handle all of them. Don't let this happen to your application. Insist on 100% pure well-formed XML.

- *Namespaces:* Namespaces are important whenever you expect your vocabulary to either include or be included in other XML vocabularies. They are also very important for public XML applications since, properly used, they indicate to developers who is responsible for any given document they may encounter. Namespaces can be omitted from purely local systems that you don't intend for anyone else to look at or manipulate, such as an in-house application's file format. Nonetheless, it really doesn't hurt to use namespaces, and they do make applications much more robust and extensible in the face of unexpected developments and uses. For the most part, un-namespaced applications like DocBook and XML-RPC are relics of the year or so between the release of XML 1.0 and the release of Namespaces in XML. New applications should use namespaces. (See Item 20.)

- *DTDs:* DTDs can be helpful. They let you know whether or not any given document adheres to many of the rules of its specification, and they also serve as a useful formal vocabulary for specifying what is and is not allowed, much like a BNF grammar does. However, there are many situations in which they are not appropriate. They tend to limit extensibility. In particular, they don't work well when documents contain lots of unanticipated markup, as in XSLT stylesheets. And since the document itself specifies the DTD it should be validated against, rather than the validating process, DTDs are not a foolproof solution for detecting invalid data. Much useful work can be done without valid documents. I prefer to use DTDs for specification and for simple error checking, but not to rely on them for more important operations.

- *Infoset:* The XML Information Set began its life as a common data model for XML specifications such as XPath and DOM. However, the working group soon discovered that it was too late to define such a thing. The syntax horse had left the barn. Now the Infoset is nothing more than a collection of definitions for specifications that choose to use them. Using the same names for the same things is a good thing, but don't try to make the Infoset more than this. In particular, avoid the common mistake of believing that an Infoset is somehow more real than the XML document it's derived from. The Infoset is not the true Platonic form of an XML document. XML is Unicode in angle brackets, nothing else. There are no alternate syntaxes. If you can define your processing on Unicode with angle brackets, that's all you need to do.

- *PSVI:* As Item 25 discusses in more detail, the Post Schema Validation Infoset is even further away from Unicode in angle brackets than the regular Infoset. The PSVI is not XML. Using it instead of XML introduces a number of interoperability and performance hurdles applications must cross to be useful. Design your applications to work with real XML documents, not ethereal information sets, post-schema or otherwise.

- *XML 1.1:* As Item 3 addresses in more detail, XML 1.1 is useful if and only if you are a native speaker of Amharic, Mongolian, Burmese, Cambodian, or a few other languages. All other users can and should ignore it.

- *Schemas:* Like DTDs, schemas can be helpful for specification of a language. They're also useful for input checking through validation, more so than DTDs because the process doing the validation gets to choose which schema to apply. (See Item 37.) However, the W3C XML Schema Language is not the only one available and often is not the best choice. (See Item 24.)

Furthermore, even if you do choose to write schemas in the W3C XML Schema Language, you must be careful not to assume documents are valid or actually adhere to the schema. Do not capriciously reject invalid documents. Documents often contain useful information, despite being invalid, especially if the part that makes the document invalid has little to do with the information you're trying to extract. In many cases, processes can avoid the overhead of full-fledged schema validation by simply requesting the information they want from a document, perhaps by using XPath (see Item 35), and then attempting to convert it to the form they need. If the conversion succeeds without error, the document is valid enough for that process's current needs.

- *Simple XLinks:* Simple XLinks are a reasonably straightforward syntax for basic blue underlined things you click on to jump to another page. They can also be used for unidirectional links with other semantics. RDDL (see Item 42) uses them like this. If this is all your application requires, you should use simple XLinks. However, many applications need something more sophisticated that requires them to invent their own vocabulary for linking, and many more don't need links at all. XLink is one of the easier W3C specifications to ignore.

- *Extended XLinks:* Extended XLinks provide multidirectional, multi-ended connections between resources in which both the link ends and link connections can be annotated in a variety of ways and in which the links are not necessarily part of the resources they connect. If that sounds like gibberish to you, you're not alone. Extended XLinks have really failed to catch fire. I suspect someone, somewhere is using them for something, but I don't know who; and tool support is almost nonexistent. Almost every developer whose application needs linking beyond what simple XLinks provide has invented a custom syntax and semantics. You should probably do the same. Extended XLinks can be safely ignored.

- *XPointer:* XPointer is a URL fragment identifier syntax for XML documents based on XPath. It's referenced by a few other specifications including XLink and XInclude. However, it has some severe human-factor problems that have stymied its development. The largest part of XPointer, the `xpointer()` scheme, did not become a recommendation before the working group's charter expired, and it now seems likely that the W3C has neither the will nor the inclination to continue its development. If you need some means of pointing into an XML document, I suggest sticking with pure XPath instead.

- *XInclude:* XInclude is a very useful technology for building large documents like books out of smaller documents like chapters. However, it does not normally need to be considered in application design. Instead, each document is normally validated and processed after the inclusions are resolved. Its use (or nonuse) is pretty much transparent to other tools in the processing chain. (See Item 30.)

- *SVG:* SVG is wonderful when you need to include two-dimensional line art in a document. If you're doing this, use it. If you're not, ignore it.

- *MathML:* MathML is useful when you're including equations in documents. If you're doing that, use it. If you're not, ignore it.

- *RDF and OWL:* There seems to be a lot more smoke than fire in the efforts to apply machine-readable semantics to XML through technologies like the Resource Description Framework (RDF) and the Web Ontology Language (OWL). However, despite the tremendous amount of brain power that has been applied to these specifications, I've yet to see any concrete results. There are a few RDF-savvy applications in the world, such as RSS 1.0 and MusicBrainz, but these don't seem to do anything that couldn't be done much more simply with plain-vanilla XML with appropriately chosen tag names. (See Item 27.) It's not clear what, if anything, RDF and its family bring to the party. I'm beginning to suspect there's no *there* there. Until it's demonstrated that RDF enables anything useful that can't be accomplished with plain-vanilla XML, I suggest you simply ignore these.

- *CSS:* CSS is useful for displaying XML documents in web browsers. Any XML document that will be shown to people in a web browser can benefit from a CSS stylesheet. However, it's inadequate for any other use, including high-quality printing. The vast majority of XML documents are not displayed in web browsers and have nothing to gain from CSS.

- *XSLT and XSL-FO:* XSLT and XSL-FO have the advantage of being completely separate from the documents they process. It's rare to even mention them in an application specification whether you intend to use them or not. Whether or not an XSLT stylesheet will be applied to an XML document makes little difference to the document itself. It does not change the markup or design of the application in any way. If anything, the only common effect is indirect:

Because you know you can always apply XSLT processing to a document to generate XSL-FO output, you can leave out all presentational information from the vocabularies you design.

- *XQuery:* Like XSLT, XQuery is a language for processing XML. Also like XSLT, the needs of XQuery really don't affect application design to any significant extent any more than the needs of C# or Python do. XQuery is simply another language with which you can process XML documents in a variety of applications. It does not become a part of the applications themselves. If you like the XQuery language, use it to process XML, but don't feel you have to learn it or use it if you don't want to.

To some extent the different specifications do depend on each other. Figure 28–1 charts the dependencies. It's normally possible to ignore any functionality that's above the layer you care about. In some cases, it's even possible to ignore the lower layers. For example, although XPath 2.0 is built on the PSVI, and XSLT 2.0 is built on XPath 2.0, XSLT 2.0 still works on documents that don't have a schema. Its functionality will just be somewhat more limited. (You won't be able to take advantage of schema type information in your stylesheets.)

Never feel obligated to use specifications that don't fit your needs. Item 24 suggests that you consider schema languages other than the W3C's official choice. The same applies in other domains as well. Some developers are still doing very effective work with DSSSL instead of XSLT and XSL-FO. The W3C's own XHTML working group rejected XLink in favor of a simpler, homegrown linking syntax. Going your own way does mean you'll have to develop processing tools and techniques that you could otherwise borrow from existing work. You certainly shouldn't reject standard vocabularies purely out of a Not-Invented-Here syndrome. However, sometimes the extra overhead of a technology that does more than you need can cost more than designing a simpler technology yourself from scratch. The ultimate evaluation needs to be made on a case-by-case basis that fits both the requirements of the problem and the skills of the available developers.

For example, let's once again revisit the question of a bank account statement. What technologies would it be built on, and what would it ignore? Well-formed XML is where you start, but it's probably not where you stop. Almost by default the bank statement should have a namespace, especially since we earlier established that it would be useful to merge in

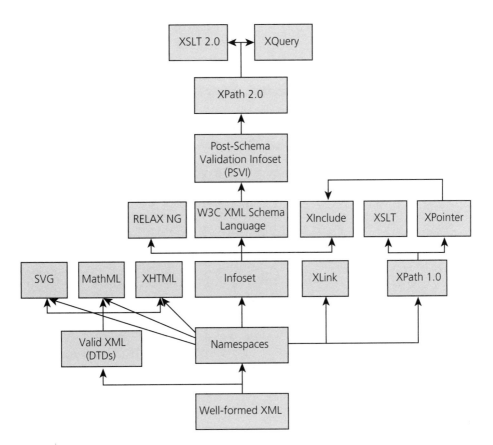

Figure 28–1 | Dependencies between XML Specifications

some basic HTML for the narrative parts of the statements, and maybe even some SVG if the statements contain logos or other art.

The next question is whether the application needs a schema and, if so, in what language you should write it. Some schema would be useful to document the agreed-upon format. The W3C XML Schema Language is probably a good fit here. Further validation of the content would require extensive mathematics and verification against a remote database, so there's not a lot of reason to add additional schema languages to this task. A 3GL like Java is more appropriate. On the other hand, although I would write a schema for documentation purposes, I would not ship it with every instance of this format using an `xsi:schemaLocation` attribute. Instead, I'd place all the information in the instance document and leave off the schema itself. This will make client-side processing much simpler.

Any recipient who really does care about the schema can always load and apply it separately, but most recipients won't need to do this, so why bother them with it?

Documents will be mostly machine processed and contain ASCII text, so there's likely no real need for entity references, and thus a DTD would probably only duplicate what the schema already says. XSLT and XSL-FO could be used to generate and print the statements mailed to account holders, but this need not be part of the application's design. There's little call for hypertext in such printed documents, so there's no need to use XLink. What little may be necessary if the statements are available online (e.g., a link to the bank's privacy policy) can probably be handled by embedding XHTML. XHTML also works well for the legal notice on the back page as discussed in Item 23.

Unnecessary and really not worth considering are RDF, OWL, the PSVI, and other more advanced specifications that seem far more interesting to computer scientists than to working programmers. None of these fit into the problem, so leave them out. XSLT, XPath, XQuery, DOM, SAX, and other means of reading and processing XML documents can all be used. However, they do not need to be specially considered when designing or documenting the format. These are tools used for processing, not something built into the specification itself.

Of course, this is just one application. Your own applications will have different purposes and different needs. Pick the XML tools and technologies that help you get your job done, and ignore the rest, even if that means you aren't using the latest hyped release from the W3C. You know what you need better than some W3C committee does.

Item 29   Always Use a Parser

XML documents are just too rich in syntax sugar to be processed by anything short of a full-blown XML parser. I've seen many hackish systems held together by string and bailing wire based on regular expressions, grep, sed, raw stream processing, and other tools. These are extremely brittle and rarely able to handle the full panoply of documents they encounter. Problems include:

- Detecting the encoding, including handling multibyte character sets
- Comments that contain tags

- Processing instructions that contain tags
- CDATA sections
- Unexpected placement of spaces and line breaks within tags
- Default attribute values applied from the internal DTD subset
- Character references like ` ` and ` `
- Predefined entity references such as `&amp;` and `&gt;`
- Malformedness errors
- Empty-element tags
- Internal DTD subsets that define default attribute values

These all have little to nothing to do with the semantic content or structure of a document. They have a great deal to do with syntax. A parser knows how to resolve all of these into the actual intended content. Very few other processes do. In fact, if you were to write your own program that handled all of this correctly, you'd be very close to inventing your own XML parser. The fact is, nothing short of a real XML parser can truly handle XML. Any program you write to process XML documents needs to sit on top of a real XML parser.

There are two main reasons developers invent their own systems based on regular expressions or other tools instead of using an XML parser.

1. They're simply not familiar with parsers and their APIs.
2. They find parsing to be too slow.

If it's simply a question of developer familiarity, the solution is simple. Learn to use SAX, DOM, JDOM, or some other API that sits on top of a parser. Numerous books can help you, including my own *Processing XML with Java* (Boston, MA: Addison-Wesley, 2002).[1]

The question of performance is more fundamental. However, fortunately it's often a canard. Before resorting to brittle non-XML tools for processing data, measure the real speed of the parser-based equivalent. Often parsing is not the bottleneck. Even if it is, the parser-based program may still be fast enough for your needs. If it isn't, you can often improve performance by moving to a different parser. For instance, Piccolo is often noticeably faster than Xerces, though it's not quite as feature rich. The slowdown may be the parser's fault but not the API's. A different parser with the same API may well do better. If it is the API's fault, you may be

---

1. See http://www.cafeconleche.org/books/xmljava/ for more information.

able to switch to a different API that performs better on your class of documents. (Items 32 and 33 discuss which APIs are appropriate for which tasks.) Finally, you may be able to live without some optional features like external entity resolution and validation that increase the cost of parsing.

However, let's assume that it is indeed the parser's fault. You're using the fastest API and parser available, and you still can't get the performance you want. Is it then acceptable to write a quick and dirty program that saves time by skipping a lot of mandated well-formedness checks and not processing all the syntax sugar? Is it acceptable to write your own mini-parser that properly handles only a subset of XML? I think the answer is no, it is not acceptable. I tend to side with Bertrand Meyer here. Although not specifically addressing XML, his more general point is correct:

> Necessary as tradeoffs between quality factors may be, one factor stands out from the rest: correctness. There is never any justification for compromising correctness for the sake of other concerns such as efficiency. If the software does not perform its function, the rest is useless.[2]

Developers think they can get away with compromising correctness because they assume they know the input format. They know the documents will always be well formed. They know all the element names in advance. They know the documents don't use CDATA sections, document type declarations, or processing instructions. Sometimes, as in SOAP, this is even required by the specification.

Nonetheless, relying on such assumptions is dangerous. In a heterogeneous, distributed, network environment, it's insane. Sooner or later (and more likely sooner) these assumptions will be violated. SOAP messages are sent with processing instructions, the specification not withstanding. Authors do use character and entity references even when they're told not to. Programmers put in document type declarations for testing and then forget to take them out in production. An upgraded library may begin inserting character and entity references whereas before it used literal characters. Any syntax that can be used will be used, and programs need to be ready for this.

Often developers object that they're only using the XML documents internally, on their intranets. These are never passed through the firewall.

---

2. Meyer, Bertrand. *Object-Oriented Software Construction*, 2nd ed. Upper Saddle River, NJ: Prentice Hall, 1997, p. 15.

Thus they have absolute confidence that the documents will always adhere to the constraints their homegrown systems require. These developers have been fortunate enough never to work with Wally or have a pointy-haired boss, but sooner or later we all have to deal with Wally. Assume nothing! Verify everything, even if you're only on an intranet. Sooner or later somebody or something is going to violate your assumptions.

At the absolute extreme, documents are passed between two well-tested and debugged computer processes on the same computer that never talk to anybody else. The output of one process is tied very closely to the input of the other. No human ever intervenes and the code is never changed; or if it is changed, it's only changed in sync with the other system. In this case, it seems perfectly reasonable to make additional assumptions about the format of the data being read. For instance, if you know the sending process never generates comments, you don't need to write the code to handle them. Indeed, if there were such processes in the real world, this might be true. However, in practice nothing is ever so clean. It may not happen today, it may not happen next week, it may not happen before you jump ship to a company with fewer pointy-haired bosses, but sooner or later the sending process is going to change the documents it sends. Perhaps this will happen because the new programmer who took your place is modifying the system but managed to misplace all the detailed documentation you left behind. (And if you aren't the sort of programmer who leaves behind documentation, they have an even bigger problem.) It may happen after a library is upgraded, and the new version uses entity references instead of character references or just puts in a comment identifying itself as the generator of the XML document. It may even happen because some programmer is using telnet to manually insert documents into the system to figure out what it does. Do you want to tell your CIO that because your program didn't use an XML parser, it missed a well-formedness error in the input data and consequently the database running all the stores in the tri-state area was corrupted and crashed at 1:22 P.M. on Christmas Eve?

Hopefully by now you're convinced that you just can't do better than a real XML parser. But what should you do if your systems are still too slow? I suppose you could always throw hardware and memory at the problem. Sometimes that's enough. However, you may reach a point where you have to admit that XML is not the right approach for your system. If you really do have an unfixable performance problem, you might need to consider using a simpler format that requires less work from the parser, such as tab-delimited text. This loses many of the well-known benefits of XML, but if you're considering throwing away XML syntax and well-formedness rules to gain speed, you've lost those already. What you're processing may look like XML, but it isn't, not really. However, this doesn't happen often. Most systems can optimize the XML parsing to the point where it is no longer a crippling deficiency.

Item 30   Layer Functionality

There are two things that experienced developers often see as lacking in XML: strong typing and a processing model. However, it turns out that the omission of both of these is a key component of XML's extensibility. Provided only that well-formedness can be maintained, local processes can much better fit XML to their needs because they aren't forced into a fixed group of types or a fixed processing model. Item 25 addressed the problems with strong typing. Now let's look at the processing non-model.

XML processing is typically implemented as a chain of operations in which the output from one step becomes input to the next step. Each step performs a single task; for example, validation, schema validation, XInclude resolution, normalization, tree building, canonicalization, and so on. The input to each process is one or more complete XML documents; the output from each process is usually a complete XML document. A process doesn't care how an XML document was created or what its history was before the process received it. Most importantly, each process performs exactly one operation. There is no one order in which these operations take place. SAX filters lend themselves particularly well to this pattern, but it can be implemented on top of DOM, streams of Unicode characters, strings, or combinations of several APIs as well. How the XML document is represented is not as important as the fact that it is an XML document.

Many processes produce an XML document as output (e.g., XInclusion, DTD processing to resolve entities and apply default attribute values). These can be used as direct input for other processes. Other processes produce documents or document fragments (e.g., XSLT, XQuery). Others produce a Boolean result that can be used to determine whether or how to continue processing (e.g., DTD validation, schema validation). Finally, some processes produce a non-XML output that possibly terminates the processing, at least insofar as the XML chain is concerned (e.g., conversion of XSL-FO to PDF).

For example, I wrote my last book, *Processing XML with Java* (Boston, MA: Addison-Wesley, 2002), in pure XML. Its processing chain looked like this.

1. Resolve XInclude elements to produce a single complete book file containing all the chapters and examples.
2. Validate the complete book (optional).
3. Apply an XSLT stylesheet to split the entire book into chapters.
4. Apply an XSLT stylesheet to each of those chapters to produce an XSL-FO file for each chapter.
5. Run FOP across each of those XSL-FO files to produce PDFs for each chapter.

The key to this process is that each step is independent of all the others. Although I run them in a certain order that makes sense for me, you could choose a different order that produces the effects you want. For example, if I perform validation at all, I perform it after the XInclude elements are resolved because the DTD I'm using (DocBook) doesn't permit any XInclude elements. However, if the DTD you're using does allow XInclude elements, you might want to validate before the XInclusion is performed. You might even want to do both, and if your application uses schemas instead of DTDs, you might want to use different DTDs for before and after validation. In fact, you can validate at other steps in the process as well (e.g., each individual chapter).

For another example, you might perform XInclusion after the XSLT processing instead of before it if your XSLT stylesheet generated XInclude elements that needed to be resolved. You could even resolve the XIncludes, apply an XSLT stylesheet that inserted new XIncludes, and then resolve the XIncludes again. Many complicated transformations, such as this one, are most easily implemented as a sequence of transformations in which the output of one process becomes the input to the next.

You can also split the processing chain into a tree, performing multiple operations on a single document to generate multiple outputs. For example, the actual process I used has a few more steps, all of which begin with the complete, validated, XInclude-resolved document and produce a variety of outputs, as shown in Figure 30–1. Although slightly less common, it's also possible for a process such as XSLT or XInclude to combine

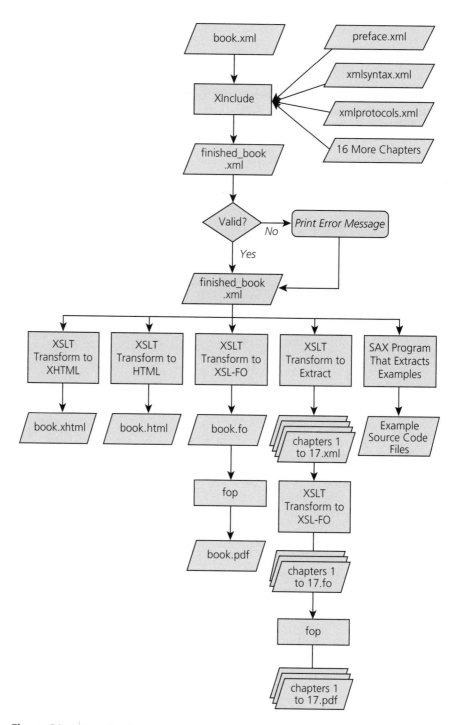

Figure 30–1 | One Possible Processing Sequence for XML

multiple documents or generate several output documents. However, the input is always well-formed XML, and the output is always well-formed XML.

Not all the operations produce XML. For instance, the transformation to HTML produces a normally malformed document, and the PDF files generated by FOP aren't even close to XML. However, these are terminal operations. Additional processing may take place (for instance, the HTML document might be uploaded to a server; the PDF can be printed), but this is completely outside the scope of XML. Indeed, to some extent all this processing is outside the scope of XML. Each member of the XML family of specifications defines either one kind of XML document or a process that can be applied to XML documents. However, the specifications never say anything about the order or sequence in which these processes are applied to these documents. That's always a decision to be made in each local processing environment. There is no one right processing chain for XML. The exact sequence of operations is a local decision. The combination I've outlined here is just one possibility that I use. You're free to use any sequence that helps you get your work done.

One of the key ideas of this layered approach is to disentangle the confusion that sometimes arises about which processes happen when. For instance, one frequent question is whether validation happens before or after XInclusion. The answer is, "It depends." This is a local decision. It can be before, after, or both, depending on local needs. You can pass the validator a document that contains `xi:include` elements or one in which those elements have been replaced by the content they point to. Either or both are acceptable.

However, you must remember that none of these tasks happen automatically, at least not in a clean chain. Each such task has to be explicitly requested. More importantly, each task does one thing. When you pass a document containing `xi:include` elements to a validator, the validator does not replace the `xi:include` elements with the documents they point to. If you want that to happen, you must pass the original document to an XInclude resolver first, and then pass the output of the XInclude process to the validator. The necessary result of DTD validation is defined by the XML specification. It does not allow any room for resolution of XIncludes. Similarly, the necessary result of schema validation is defined by the XML Schema specification. It also does not allow resolution of XIncludes. Either or both can work on a document that was created by resolving the XIncludes in another document, but the validators themselves do not resolve XIncludes. They treat `xi:include` elements the same as they do any other element.

Similar statements can be made for other possible processes such as transformation with a stylesheet or XQuery search. In all cases, a document is fed into the process, which performs the single function it's designed to perform. You can then operate on the output document with the same or different process, but always one process at a time. As long as the processes don't run in parallel, there's rarely any confusion about what should happen. However, as soon as engines for one process (e.g., XSLT) begin taking upon themselves the need to perform additional simultaneous processes (e.g., XInclusion) the actual and proper output becomes impossible to predict. Different engines produce different outputs from the same input document, and it's impossible to tell which, if any of them, are correct. Interoperability is possible only as long as each tool restricts itself to its own domain. That's why it's important to implement your own processing chain as a sequence of black boxes in which the output of one is connected to the input of the next, rather than as a single black box that does everything at once.

Item 31 Program to Standard APIs

Parsers, DOM implementations, XSLT engines, and other XML-related tools vary widely in speed, efficiency, specification conformance, and bugginess. Sometimes these are innate characteristics of the code and the skill of the programmers who wrote it. Other times the relative quality depends on the environment. For instance, early versions of the Xerces XML parser for Java, written by IBM, tended to perform very well on IBM's Java virtual machine and very poorly on Sun's Java virtual machine, while the Crimson parser written by the Sun team had almost precisely opposite performance characteristics. Still other times the relative performance of tools depends on the documents they process. For instance, some DOM implementations are tuned for relatively small document sizes while others are tuned for very large documents. Benchmarks based primarily on large or small documents can come to very different conclusions about the same tools.

One of the best ways to improve performance is to try out different libraries on your code and pick the one that performs the best for your documents in your environment. However, this only works if you haven't tied yourself too closely to one parser's API. In SAX2 and DOM3 it's normally possible to write completely parser-independent code. Do so. For Java, JAXP extends this capability to DOM2. Always prefer implementation-independent APIs like DOM and SAX to parser-dependent APIs like the Xerces Native Interface or ElectricXML.

A few APIs such as XOM and JDOM fall somewhere in the middle. They allow you to choose a different parser but not a different implementation of their core classes. If parsing is the bottleneck, this can be helpful. However, if the bottleneck lies elsewhere, for instance, in an inefficient use of string buffers that bedeviled one JDOM beta, you're pretty much stuck with it.

Unfortunately, not all standard APIs are as complete as you might wish, so you may sometimes need to tie yourself to a specific implementation. If this proves necessary, try to clearly delineate the implementation-dependent parts of your code, and keep those parts as small as possible.

Now let's investigate the details of writing implementation-independent code with different APIs and tools.

SAX

SAX enables you to write code that is completely independent of the underlying parser. The major issue is that you use the `XMLReaderFactory.createXMLReader()` method to construct new instances of the `XML Reader` interface rather than calling the constructor directly. For example, here is the correct way to load a SAX2 parser.

```
XMLReader parser = XMLReaderFactory.createXMLReader();
```

Below is the wrong way to load a SAX parser.

```
XMLReader parser = new org.apache.xerces.parsers.SAXParser();
```

The first statement loads the parser named by the `org.xml.sax.driver` system property. This is easy to adjust at runtime. The second statement always loads Xerces and can't be changed without recompiling. Both statements may actually create the same object, but the first leaves open the possibility of using a different parser without even recompiling the code.

You can hard-code the parser you want as a string if you really want to rely on a specific parser.

```
XMLReader parser = XMLReaderFactory.createXMLReader(
  "org.apache.xerces.parsers.SAXParser");
```

Ideally, however, the string containing the fully packaged qualified class name should be part of a resource bundle or other configuration file separate from the code itself so it can be modified without recompiling.

Note *This doesn't work quite as well in other languages as it does in Java. For instance, C and C++ bind early rather than late, so you probably need to recompile to switch to a different parser. Furthermore, although SAX is fairly common in C and C++ parsers, there is no official standard for it, so there are often subtle differences between implementations. Code editing may be required. Languages like Python and Perl fall somewhere in between Java and C++ in terms of ease of switching parsers. This doesn't reflect any fundamental limitations in these languages, just that the programmers who wrote the first parsers and defined SAX preferred to work in Java. Nonetheless, even if you're not working in Java, you should still endeavor to write code that's as parser independent as possible in order to minimize the amount of work you have to do when swapping out one parser for another.*

Furthermore, unless you have very good reasons to limit the choice of parser, you should always provide a fallback to the default parser if you fail to load a specific parser by name. Exactly which parsers are available can vary a lot from environment to environment, especially in Java 1.3 and earlier. For example, the following code falls back on the default parser if Xerces isn't in the classpath.

```
XMLReader parser;
try {
  parser =
    XMLReaderFactory.createXMLReader(
      "org.apache.xerces.parsers.SAXParser");
}
catch (SAXException ex) { // Xerces not found
  parser = XMLReaderFactory.createXMLReader();
}
```

As long as you stick to the core classes in the `org.xml.sax` and `org.xml.sax.helpers` packages, your code should be reasonably portable to any parser that implements SAX2. And although technically optional, every SAX2 parser I've ever encountered also implements the optional interfaces in the `org.xml.sax.ext` packages, that is, `LexicalHandler` and `DeclHandler`.

One area in which SAX parsers do differ is support for various features and properties. Although SAX2 defines over a dozen standard features and properties, only two must be implemented by all conformant processors (`http://xml.org/sax/features/namespaces` and `http://xml.org/sax/features/namespace-prefixes`). The others are all optional, and some parsers do omit them. If you attempt to set or read a feature or property that the parser does not understand, it will throw a `SAXNotRecognizedException`. If it recognizes the feature or property name but cannot set that feature or property to the requested value, it will throw a `SAXNotSupportedException`. Both are subclasses of `SAXException`. Be sure to catch these and respond appropriately.

Sometimes, the feature or property is optional for processing, and you can just ignore a failure to set it. For example, if you attempt to set a `LexicalHandler` object and fail, you may not be able to round-trip the document. However, you'll still get all the information you really care about.

```
try {
  parser.setProperty(
    "http://xml.org/sax/properties/lexical-handler",
    new MyLexicalHandler());
}
catch (SAXNotRecognizedException ex) {
  // no big deal; continue normal processing
}
```

Other times you may want to give up completely. For example, if your code depends on interning of names for proper operations—for instance, it compares element names using the `==` operator—you'll want to make sure that the `http://xml.org/sax/features/string-interning` property is true and not continue if it isn't.

```
try {
  parser.setFeature(
    "http://xml.org/sax/features/string-interning", true);
}
catch (SAXException ex) {
  throw new RuntimeException(
    "Could not find a parser that supports string interning");
}
```

Still other times you may want to take some intermediate course. For example, if the parser doesn't support validation, you might try to load a different parser that does.

```
XMLReader parser = XMLReaderFactory.createXMLReader();
try {
  parser.setFeature(
    "http://xml.org/sax/features/validation", true);
}
catch (SAXNotRecognizedException ex) {
  try { // Load a parser that is known to validate
    parser = XMLReaderFactory.createXMLReader(
      "org.apache.xerces.parsers.SAXParser");

parser.setFeature("http://xml.org/sax/features/validation",
                  true);
  }
  catch (SAXException se) {
    // Xerces is not in the classpath
    throw new RuntimeException(
      "Could not find a validating parser");
  }
}
// continue with parsing and validating...
```

In all cases, however, you should not assume that you can actually set the feature or property you're trying to set. Be prepared for the attempt to fail, and respond accordingly. This will help your code either work properly or fail gracefully no matter which parser is used.

Another area in which parsers differ is support for SAX 2.0.1. This minor upgrade to SAX adds `Locator2`, `Attributes2`, and `EntityResolver2` interfaces that fill a few small holes in SAX 2.0. These interfaces are not yet broadly supported (and arguably cannot be supported in a JAXP-compliant environment). Thus, you need to be more careful when using them. However, you can test for availability before using them by using `instanceof`. For example, the following code prints the encoding if and only if the `Locator` passed to `setDocumentLocator()` is a `Locator2` object.

```
public void setDocumentLocator(Locator locator) {
  if (locator instanceof Locator2) {
```

```
    Locator2 locator2 = (Locator2) locator;
    System.out.println("Encoding is " +
locator2.getEncoding());
  }
}
```

Alternatively, you can simply check the values of the `http://xml.org/sax/features/use-locator2`, `http://xml.org/sax/features/use-attributes2`, and `http://xml.org/sax/features/use-entity-resolver2` features. If the parser supports these SAX 2.0.1 classes, these features will have the value true. However, if it does not support them, reading these URLs will probably throw a `SAXNotRecognizedException` rather than returning false. This makes them a little more cumbersome than simply using `instanceof`.

DOM

DOM Level 3 should finally make it possible to write completely implementation-independent DOM code, at least in Java. However, in DOM Level 2 some crucial parts of DOM require parser-dependent code, and in other languages this is likely to remain true in DOM Level 3. In particular, DOM2 defines no way to:

- Construct an instance of the `DOMImplementation` interface
- Parse a document from a stream

Everything else can be done with pure DOM, but these two operations require implementation-specific classes. For example, Xerces loads its `DOMImplementation` using a nonstandard static method in the `org.apache.xerces.dom.DOMImplementationImpl` class.

```
DOMImplementation impl
  = DOMImplementationImpl.getDOMImplementation();
```

Parsing a document into a DOM tree with Xerces requires instantiating a nonstandard `DOMParser` class through its constructor as shown below.

```
DOMParser parser = new DOMParser();
parser.parse("http://www.example.com/");
Document doc = parser.getDocument();
```

Other DOM implementations such as Crimson, GNU JAXP, and Oracle use different classes and patterns.

In Java, JAXP provides a partial solution for those DOM implementations that implement JAXP (which is most of the major DOM implementations for Java nowadays). The `javax.xml.parsers.DOMBuilderFactory` class can load a `javax.xml.parsers.DOMBuilder` object. This DOM Builder object can parse a document or locate a `DOMImplementation` object.

```
DocumentBuilderFactory builderFactory
  = DocumentBuilderFactory.newInstance();
DocumentBuilder parser = builderFactory.newDocumentBuilder();
DOMImplementation impl = parser.getDOMImplementation();
Document doc = parser.parse("http://www.example.com");
```

The exact implementation is read from the `javax.xml.parsers.DocumentBuilderFactory` Java system property. If this property is not set, JAXP looks in the `lib/jaxp.properties` properties file in the JRE directory. If that fails to locate a parser, next JAXP looks for a `META- INF/services/javax.xml.parsers.DocumentBuilderFactory` file in all the JAR files in the classpath. Finally, if that fails, `DocumentBuilder Factory.newInstance()` returns a default implementation.

As with SAX parsers, you do have to worry a little about exactly which features the underlying implementation supports. However, for most applications the basic features shared by all conformant implementations suffice.

The second step in writing implementation-independent DOM code is making sure you use only standard DOM methods. Many DOM implementations including Xerces provide extra, useful methods in their implementation classes. Sometimes these methods can be very helpful and even let you do things that simply cannot be done via standard methods, such as adding a document type declaration to a document. However, using any of these methods ties your code to that one implementation, binding it far more tightly than just how you load the parser or the implementation. Implementation-specific methods can infect the entire design of your code, requiring you to completely redesign a program in order to move it to another implementation, rather than simply changing a few lines here or there. Think very carefully about whether you're willing to lock yourself into a single implementation before doing this.

By far the worst offender here is the Microsoft DOM implementation in MSXML and .NET. While MSXML supports all the standard parts of

DOM, it also includes many, many nonstandard extensions. Worse yet, very little third-party documentation and almost no official Microsoft documentation bothers to note the difference between the standard parts and the Microsoft extensions. Most tutorials and sample code make very heavy use of the Microsoft extensions, even to the point where there's almost no standard DOM code left. (By contrast, the documentation for Xerces-J focuses almost exclusively on the standard DOM interfaces. The documentation for the nonstandard extensions is relatively hidden, and few books discuss it. It is meant primarily for "maintainers and developers of the Xerces2 reference implementation," not for end users, and its existence is an open secret for the initiated.) In particular, be wary of the following fields and methods, which are very common in programs that use the MSXML DOM:

- `IXMLDOMNode`, `IXMLDOMNodeList`, `IXMLDOMAttribute`, `IXMLDOMComment`, `IXMLDOMDocument`, `IXMLDOMElement`, `IXMLDOMText`, and so on
- `innerXml`, `outerXml`, and `xml`
- `innerText`, `outerText`, and `text`
- `transformNode`
- `transformNodeToObject`
- `SelectSingleNode`
- `SelectNodes`
- `definition`
- `dataType`
- `baseName`
- `nodeTypedValue`
- `nodeTypeString`

These are all nonstandard Microsoft extensions to DOM, and using any of them effectively ties your program to MSXML such that it cannot be easily ported to other implementations.

One final thing to keep in mind: Although with care you can swap one DOM implementation for another, you cannot generally mix and match different DOM implementations in the same program. For example, you cannot add a GNU JAXP `Element` object to a Xerces `Document` object. Internally, all DOM implementations I've encountered do make intimate use of the detailed implementation classes, rather than limiting themselves to the public interfaces. This may be necessary and even desirable for the implementation internals, but it is not an excuse for doing the same in the public code that lives above the interface.

JDOM

There's only one implementation of JDOM, and JDOM is designed around classes rather than interfaces. Thus, some of the same issues that arise with DOM and SAX don't apply here. It has always been intended that you use the classes directly in JDOM. However, JDOM does not include its own parser. Instead it relies on an underlying SAX parser. By default JDOM ships with and uses Xerces, but this can be changed. Simply pass the fully packaged qualified name of the SAX `XMLReader` implementation class you want to use to the `SAXBuilder` constructor, as shown below.

```
SAXBuilder parser
= new SAXBuilder("com.bluecast.xml.Piccolo");
```

This may speed up parsing a little and save some memory (Piccolo is quite a bit more efficient than Xerces). However, any improvement is limited to the actual parsing of the document. Everything after that—including building, manipulating, and serializing the object tree—takes place with the same JDOM classes no matter which parser you used initially.

Whichever API you choose, try to stick to its well-documented parts. To the extent possible, use only those methods and classes that are part of the standard API. That way, if you do encounter performance problems or outright bugs, you'll have the opportunity to easily fix the problem by switching to a better implementation rather than having to adjust your processing to avoid the issues.

Item 32   Choose SAX for Computer Efficiency

For most applications, performing the XML processing with SAX will result in by far the fastest program. It will certainly allow the program to use much less memory than the DOM or JDOM equivalent. If maximum speed or minimum size is your primary concern, choose SAX.

What makes SAX so fast and so memory efficient is that it's effectively stateless. As the parser parses, it has an extremely local view of the XML document. It really doesn't need to concern itself with anything more than the current tag, text string, comment, or processing instruction. For purposes of well-formedness checking, a SAX parser has to hold on to a stack of ancestor elements so it can verify that each end-tag matches its corresponding start-tag. Beyond that, it really doesn't need any state at all. Since SAX stores such a small part of a typical XML document at any one time, it can easily process multigigabyte files. SAX happily parses even those supersized documents that make the most memory-efficient DOM parsers on the beefiest machines fall down in tears.

Note *There are a few internal limits on SAX. Although it has no fundamental limits on document size or the content of a text node, certain other constructs can be too large for it to handle. In particular, SAX represents the following XML constructs as single strings:*

- *Element and attribute names*
- *Attribute values*
- *Processing instruction targets*
- *Processing instruction data*
- *Entity names*
- *Comments*

If any of these exceed the maximum length of a string (about 2.1GB in Java) or, more likely, the available memory on the local machine, the parser will likely crash or at best provide only part of the content. In practice, however, I've never encountered a document that caused this. I have seen documents where the text content of elements was too large for a single string, and wisely SAX does not require these to be reported with a single string. A SAX parser can split these into pieces and report one manageable piece at a time.

SAX parsers are fast because they do very little work. A SAX parser only has to do four things.

1. Read the raw bytes of data.
2. Convert the bytes to Unicode text.
3. Verify its well-formedness.
4. Pass the text to the client application.

A DOM parser, by contrast, has to do all of this plus one extra step: It has to build a potentially very complex and very large object representing the XML document. (See Item 33.)

Even more importantly for practical applications, SAX parsers and SAX applications are *streaming*. That is, a SAX parser informs the client application of some of the data in the document before the parser has finished reading the entire document. The client application can then act on that content before the rest of the data is available.

For example, consider a program that receives a list of stock quotes over the Internet formatted roughly as follows.

```
<Ticker>
  <Quote>
    <Symbol>AAPL</Symbol>
    <Price>14.35</Price>
  </Quote>
  <Quote>
    <Symbol>AMZN</Symbol>
    <Price>21.34</Price>
  </Quote>
  <!-- several thousand more ... -->
</Ticker>
```

The program can respond to each quote immediately, before the next quote is received and parsed. Provided the relevant data comes in nice localized chunks, this approach works very well. However, streaming is not suitable for all applications. In the stock quote example, the program might wish to make comparisons between the prices of the different stocks in the document before making its buy and sell decisions. In this case, it needs to wait until all the data is available.

Another potential downside to streaming processing is the need to roll back in the event of a well-formedness error. A program may correctly process 1000 `quote` elements, but if it then encounters a missing end-tag on the 1001st, you might want to discard all the processing that's been done on the document. In this case, you need to make sure that the preliminary processing does not do anything irreversible such as placing a buy or sell order. However, you might still be able to prepare the orders so they can be sent immediately as soon as the end of the document is detected and full well-formedness has been verified.

Then again, maybe it's OK to send the initial orders. A malformedness error in the 1001st `quote` element doesn't mean that the first 1000 elements were bad. It's much more likely that their data was correct but that a network glitch corrupted data in the 1001st element. XML does not allow you to process data that appears after the first well-formedness error in a document, but you are allowed to process data that appears before it.

There are times when this is clearly not the case, however. Consider XSLT for example. The template for any node in the document can reference any other node that comes either before or after it. The entire document needs to be parsed in memory before transformation can begin. Even in this case, however, it can still be faster to build the program's own data structures while parsing rather than waiting until the parsing is complete. Similarly, you save a lot of memory by not building two data structures to represent the same document, the one the parser produces and the one the XSLT processor requires. This does depend to some extent on the design of the XSLT processor. A processor that operated directly on a DOM `Document` object rather than using its own data structures and classes would not be noticeably slower or less efficient than one that built custom data structures directly from SAX events.

Sometimes, though, SAX makes processing faster even when you do want to read the entire document before acting on it. Consider the case where, rather than using an XML data structure such as DOM objects, you use classes and data structures more suited to the problem at hand. For example, the SAX parser reading the stock quote data might well be feeding it into objects that are instantiated from the following class.

```
public class Quote {
    private String symbol;
    private double price;

    // constructors, methods, and so forth...
}
```

A SAX program can build one `Quote` object for each `Quote` element in the input document as soon as it sees the element. When the document has been fully processed, the internal data structures are ready to go. However, using DOM, after the document has been parsed, the program still needs to walk the tree and construct the objects you actually want. If the local processing and construction of these objects is relatively fast compared to the time needed to receive the next `Quote` element from the network (and generally it is), the SAX program may be quite a bit faster than the DOM equivalent.

Given that SAX-based programs are almost always faster and more memory-efficient than DOM- or JDOM-based ones, the obvious question is why would anybody ever use a tree API in the first place. The answer is that sometimes it's simply easier to write the program using a tree-oriented

API. While SAX maximizes computer efficiency, it's not always a maximum use of programmer efficiency. In my experience, most developers are much more comfortable with the pull style of DOM programs than the push style of SAX programs. Even switching to a pull-based, streaming API such as XMLPULL or StAX still requires you to respond to the data in the document where it appears rather than where you need it. The random access possible in a tree-based API can be very useful.

The second reason you might choose a tree-based API like DOM instead of SAX is that SAX is pretty much a read-only API. It can take the data in from an XML document, but it can't write the document back out again, nor does it give you any hooks for managing the document in memory. In practice, most programs that need to handle XML are primarily concerned with reading it. They convert the XML document into some custom data structure that's convenient for them and then manipulate that unique data structure. However, if instead you want to manipulate a data structure that's very close to the XML document and possibly export the modified XML document to text once again, APIs like DOM and JDOM provide a lot more support than SAX.

The key to most significant SAX programs is this data structure you build in memory as the document is read. It's rare that any one call to a SAX `ContentHandler` method like `startElement()` or `text()` actually gives you all the information you need when you need it. You almost always have to store this information somewhere until more data becomes available. It's only by combining the data passed to several methods that you get something you can work with. However, depending on the nature of the problem, the data structures can be more or less complex. Generally, the flatter the document structure and the more local the processing, the simpler the data structures are and the easier it is to make SAX work.

The stock quote document is a good example of the sort of problems for which SAX processing is straightforward. No elements are more than three deep from the root. No elements contain other elements of the same type. Internally, the data is not stored as XML. Instead it's stored as `Quote` elements. Each `Quote` element is pretty much complete unto itself without implicit or explicit linkages to other elements in the document. The overall structure is very flat, very predictable, and very simple. Finally, the program may well not export any XML.

By contrast, writing an XSLT processor is an example of a problem that is not well suited to SAX event-based processing. The data structures you need to store in memory are generally as complex as the document itself is. These data structures can be extremely nonflat and recursive. Processing the second element in the document may require access to the seventeenth, thirty-second, and/or last element in the document. The whole point of an XSL transformation is to create a new XML document that is normally then written onto a stream or into a file. This is about as extreme an example of a case where a tree-based API like DOM is necessary as I can imagine. At most, you would use SAX to build your own tree model on which the XSLT processor operated. You would not attempt to transform SAX events immediately as they're passed into the `Content Handler`.

Summing up, you should choose to do your XML processing with SAX under the following conditions.

- Speed matters.
- Memory footprint matters.
- You want to process small, contiguous chunks of the document at one time.
- The program's internal data structures represent something other than the XML document itself.
- You need to parse documents but not write them back out again.

The more of these characteristics a problem exhibits, the better SAX fits it.

Item 33   Choose DOM for Standards Support

While SAX programs are almost always faster and more memory efficient than the DOM equivalents, performance is not a god to be worshiped above all others. There are many times when using DOM makes sense. In particular, for many classes of applications, programmers will find DOM much easier to work with. If shaving off 10% of execution time or 90% of space matters less to you than saving 10% of development time, you need to consider whether DOM might better fit the problem at hand than SAX.

In particular, the following characteristics indicate that a problem might be profitably addressed by DOM.

- The documents are small relative to the available memory; roughly 10% of the heap size or less.

- Processing requires random access to widely separated parts of the tree. For instance, you need access to the last elements in the document before you can figure out what to do with the first elements.
- The program needs to navigate backward and up in the tree, as well as forward and down.
- The program needs to access all the data in the document, not just a subset of it. The program's own data structures essentially reproduce the complexity of the XML document.
- The developers find working with a tree structure to be easier and more natural than working with an event sequence.
- The program has to be portable across languages. (I can't honestly say I've ever encountered this requirement in practice, but this need explains a lot of the weirdness in DOM.)

All of these requirements are fuzzy. If speed matters more to you than product development time or memory usage, you may choose to use SAX even for a system that uses data structures as complex as the XML document itself and requires random access to the tree. The only criterion that's really carved in stone is memory. If the program needs to process documents that are large compared to the available memory, you really have to use a streaming API such as SAX. Otherwise, a lot depends on your comfort level and the need for each characteristic.

If my recommendation for DOM sounds a lot more reticent than that for SAX, there's a good reason. DOM can be just plain weird. It is very much like the proverbial horse designed by committee, and, to be perfectly honest, camels don't smell as bad as DOM. DOM is packed with gotchas. Here's a representative sampling of just a few.

- DOM requires code to specify namespace URIs when creating new `Element` and `Attr` objects and to add `xmlns` and `xmlns:prefix` attributes to elements where necessary. This is not an either/or. You must do them both, and DOM makes no efforts to make sure they don't accidentally conflict with each other.
- Nodes cannot be moved from one document to another.
- There are separate methods to add an `Attr` object to an `Element` object depending on whether or not the attribute is in a namespace.
- Every node class has a `getValue()` method, but more often than not this just returns null.
- Every node has `namespaceURI` and `localName` properties, even nodes like comments and text nodes that have neither names nor namespace URIs.

- Types are represented by integer constants rather than by classes.
- The document type declaration can be set only when the document is created; from thereon it is read-only.

I could go on—I haven't even begun to consider issues like naming conventions and the use of short constants that may make sense to programmers in some languages but not others—but I'll restrain myself. DOM is such an incredibly baroque API that most experienced XML developers turn to it only as a last resort.

Most of the reasons to use DOM are really reasons to use a tree-based API that holds the document in memory. There's no particular reason this has to be DOM instead of JDOM, XOM, dom4j, or any of the numerous other tree-based APIs. Microsoft implements DOM in MSXML but has added so many additional nonstandard methods that the resulting API really isn't DOM at all. (See Item 31.) Indeed the proliferation of alternate tree-based object models for XML is a symptom of the widespread dissatisfaction with DOM in the developer community. By way of contrast, the much cleaner SAX API has the field of push parsing XML almost completely to itself. There are a few rough spots in SAX, but none of them have itched developers enough to make them replace it. By contrast, DOM makes developers itch worse than the fleas of a thousand camels.

Considered relative to other tree-based APIs, where does DOM stand out? I've talked about its unique weaknesses. What, if any, are its unique strengths? Believe it or not, there are a few that occasionally suggest or even mandate its use.

- You want the option to change implementations to find the one that performs best on your workload. DOM is the only tree-based API that is independently implemented by many vendors.
- You need to interface with APIs and libraries that expect to receive DOM objects. DOM predates all the efforts to replace it, so it is much more broadly supported than alternative APIs.
- Company rules, government regulations, or contractual obligations require you to use standard APIs where available. DOM is a W3C recommendation. None of the competing APIs are any form of ISO, OASIS, IETF, IEEE, or W3C standard.

In brief, DOM is more standard and more broadly supported than other APIs, and this may be important in situations where you need to exchange code with diverse programmers. However, it is not the cleanest, most efficient, fastest, nor most productive API you can use to process XML.

Item 34   Read the Complete DTD

One of the innovations of XML was making validity optional. Many XML documents do not have DTDs at all. Even if a document has a DTD, there is no guarantee that the document is valid with respect to its DTD. Invalid, merely well-formed documents can be usefully processed. In fact, even if the document has a DTD the processor may choose to ignore it, and that's where a potential problem arises, because DTDs do more than merely determine whether or not a document is valid. They also make contributions to the document's information set (infoset) in several ways.

- They define entity references such as `&copy;` and `&signature;`.
- They provide default values for attributes.
- They declare notations.
- They declare unparsed entities.

The last two points aren't very important in practice (see Item 16), but the first two can be crucial. If a program fails to read the DTD, it may not have a complete picture of the document's information. For example, consider the following simple SVG document.

```
<?xml version="1.0" standalone="no"?>
<!DOCTYPE svg PUBLIC "-//W3C//DTD SVG 1.1//EN"
  "http://www.w3.org/Graphics/SVG/1.1/DTD/svg11.dtd">
<svg width="5cm" height="4cm" version="1.1">
    <rect x="1.5cm" y="1.5cm" width="2cm" height="1cm"/>
</svg>
```

The namespace declaration seems to be missing. However, the SVG DTD provides this through a default attribute value. A program that does not read the DTD cannot correctly process this document. It will not find any elements in the SVG namespace.

The situation is even worse if the document uses namespace prefixes. For example, consider the document below.

```
<?xml version="1.0" standalone="no"?>
<!DOCTYPE svg PUBLIC "-//W3C//DTD SVG 1.1//EN"
  "http://www.w3.org/Graphics/SVG/1.1/DTD/svg11.dtd" [
  <!ENTITY % NS.prefixed "INCLUDE" >
  <!ENTITY % SVG.prefix "svg" >
]>
```

```
<svg:svg width="5cm" height="4cm" version="1.1">`
    <svg:rect x="1.5cm" y="1.5cm" width="2cm" height="1cm"/>
</svg:svg>
```

Unless the parser reads the external DTD subset, it will conclude that this document is namespace malformed, throwing a potentially fatal error.

Problems can arise even without considering namespaces. Other attributes can be crucial too. For example, if an `xlink:type` attribute of a `link` element is defaulted from the DTD, a browser that doesn't read the DTD won't recognize the element as an XLink. Or consider a typical DocBook `programlisting` element like this one.

```
<programlisting>if (x == 3.5) {
  doSomething();
}</programlisting>
```

A browser that hasn't read the DocBook DTD won't know that it has `xml:space="preserve"` and `format="linespecific"` attributes, both crucial pieces of information for correct formatting.

Proper handling of entities also mandates processing the full DTD. Consider the following document.

```
<?xml version="1.0"?>
<!DOCTYPE Surgery SYSTEM "surgery.dtd">
<Surgery>
  <Procedure>Thigh Liposuction</Procedure>
  <Step>Set vacuum meter to the amount of fat to be removed,
        not more than twelve ounces per procedure.</Step>
  &preop;
  <Step>Make one inch vertical incision six inches above
        knee.</Step>
  <Step>Insert suction tube.</Step>
  <Step>Suck out fat until the vacuum automatically shuts
        off.</Step>
  <Step>Remove suction tube from patient.</Step>
  <Step>Sew up incision.</Step>
  <Disclaimer>
     I am not a doctor. These instructions are not real.
     Do not try this at home.
  </Disclaimer>
</Surgery>
```

Suppose that, when resolved, the &preop; entity points to the document fragment below.

```
<Step>Verify patient has not eaten for at least 12 hours.</Step>
<Step>Set mix to 65% oxygen, 35% ether.</Step>
<Step>Turn on oxygen.</Step>
<Step>Turn on ether.</Step>
<Step>Verify that oxygen is flowing.</Step>
<Step>Place mask on patient.</Step>
<Step>Ask patient to begin counting backwards from 100.</Step>
<Step>Verify patient is asleep.</Step>
```

I wouldn't want to be the patient on the table if these instructions were read by a parser that did not resolve entities.

I am not suggesting that you write documents that depend on the DTD, especially the external DTD subset, in these fashions. In fact, Item 18 recommends exactly the opposite. However, documents like these examples do exist and will continue to exist in the real world. They cannot be avoided. Not producing documents like these is being conservative in what you send. Reading such documents correctly is being liberal in what you accept. Both are important principles for robust software.

It is not necessary to validate in order to read the DTD. Although a fully validating parser will always read the complete DTD, apply all default attribute values, and resolve all entity references, you do not have to validate in order to do these things. Most parsers provide options to read the DTD without validating. Exactly how this is configured varies from parser to parser and API to API. Using SAX you simply have to turn on the `http://xml.org/sax/features/external-general-entities` and `http://xml.org/sax/features/external-parameter-entities` features, as shown here.

```
XMLReader parser = XMLReaderFactory.createXMLReader();
parser.setFeature(
  "http://xml.org/sax/features/external-general-entities", true);
parser.setFeature(
  "http://xml.org/sax/features/external-parameter-entities",
  true);
```

There's no special feature for indicating whether the parser should apply default attribute values or not. However, if the parser does read the DTD, it is required to apply any default attribute values it finds there. Thus turning on these two features has the effect of ensuring that default attribute values are also resolved.

SAX parsers are not required to support these features, although most do. I have seen one or two that did not recognize these features but could validate, so turning on validation instead may be an option. However, if the parser supports neither external general entities nor validation, then it's time to find a better parser.

The primary reason most developers cite for not reading the DTD is performance. Especially if the DTD resides on a remote server, loading and applying it can take a significant amount of time. There are a couple of options to ameliorate this effect, especially if you have advance knowledge of the DTDs the application must process.

If the DTDs are identified by public URIs, catalogs can replace the remote canonical DTDs with local copies. (See Item 47.) If the DTDs are identified via system identifiers and you're using SAX, you can use an `EntityResolver` instead. For example, here's a simple SAX `EntityResolver` that loads all the XHTML 1.0 DTDs once and then serves them out of local memory.

```
import org.xml.sax.*;
import java.io.*;
import java.net.URL;
import java.util.Hashtable;

public class FastXHTML implements EntityResolver {

  private static Hashtable entities = new Hashtable();

  // fill the list of URLs
  static {

    // The XHTML 1.0 DTDs
    addMapping("-//W3C//DTD XHTML 1.0 Strict//EN",
      "http://www.w3.org/TR/xhtml1/DTD/xhtml1-strict.dtd");
    addMapping("-//W3C//DTD XHTML 1.0 Transitional//EN",
      "http://www.w3.org/TR/xhtml1/DTD/xhtml1-transitional.dtd");
    addMapping("-//W3C//DTD XHTML 1.0 Frameset//EN",
      "http://www.w3.org/TR/xhtml1/DTD/xhtml1-frameset.dtd");

    // The XHTML 1.0 entity sets
    addMapping("-//W3C//ENTITIES Latin 1 for XHTML//EN",
```

```
            "http://www.w3.org/TR/xhtml1/DTD/xhtml-lat1.ent");
         addMapping("-//W3C//ENTITIES Symbols for XHTML//EN",
           "http://www.w3.org/TR/xhtml1/DTD/xhtml-symbol.ent");
         addMapping("-//W3C//ENTITIES Special for XHTML//EN",
           "http://www.w3.org/TR/xhtml1/DTD/xhtml-special.ent");
      }

      private static void addMapping(String publicID, String url)  {

        try {
          URL u = new URL(url);
          InputStream in = u.openStream();
          ByteArrayOutputStream out = new ByteArrayOutputStream();
          int c;
          while ((c = in.read()) != -1) out.write(c);
          entities.put(publicID, out.toByteArray());
        }
        catch (Exception ex) {
           // exceptions in static blocks are a real pain
           throw new RuntimeException("Could not initialize " + url);
        }

      }

      public InputSource resolveEntity(String publicID,
       String systemID) throws SAXException {

        if (entities.contains(publicID)) {
          byte[] data = (byte[]) entities.get(publicID);
          InputSource source = new InputSource(systemID);
          source.setPublicId(publicID);
          source.setByteStream(new ByteArrayInputStream(data));
          return source;
        }
        else return null;

      }

    }
```

In the near future, DOM Level 3 Load and Save will add a similar
DOMEntityResolver class for use with DOM.

Some programs that are designed to process only very specific vocabularies may hardwire knowledge of the DTD. The classic example of this is a web browser. The browser handles HTML and only HTML. It knows in advance the replacement text for all the HTML entities such as ` ` and `&Omega;`. It knows which attributes have which default values. It even knows and uses the content models of various elements.

Of course, an application that relies on a presumed copy of the actual DTD (whether by foreknowledge, a local catalog, or an `EntityResolver`) may be tripped up if it encounters a document that points to a modified copy of the DTD. Thus it's still better to read the actual DTD if you reasonably can. However, in cases such as HTML, a document that modifies the DTD but uses the usual public identifier is completely nonconformant, and the author of that document deserves what he or she gets. Modifying a DTD is OK, but you need to assign the modified DTD new system and public IDs.

Another alternative, this one for document producers rather than document consumers, is to set the `standalone` attribute in the XML declaration to yes. (See Item 1.) This is a promise that the external DTD subset makes no contributions to the document's infoset and thus can be safely skipped. That is, it says that no default attribute values are applied that are not also present in the document itself and no entities used in the document are defined. If the document specifies `standalone="yes"`, you may safely forgo reading the external DTD subset. Unfortunately, the `standalone` attribute can be set to yes only when the document contains no white space in element content. (See Item 10.) Since most documents do use such ignorable white space, the `standalone` option is not always available.

None of this should be construed as giving programs any leeway in not reading the internal DTD subset. The XML specification absolutely requires all XML processors to read the internal DTD subset, report any well-formedness errors found therein, apply default attribute values found in attribute declarations in the internal DTD subset, and use entity declarations to resolve external entity references. A parser that does not read or use the internal DTD subset does not adhere to the minimum level of conformance required by XML 1.0.

In the long run, the most reliable results are produced by reading the complete DTD of any document that carries a document type declaration, even if you're not validating. Always insist on reading the complete DTD unless the `standalone` attribute is set to yes. It may take a little longer, but it may also be a lot more correct.

Item 35 Navigate with XPath

Whether you're writing code with DOM, JDOM, dom4j, Sparta, or some other tree-based API, one of the primary tasks is navigating the document to locate particular nodes, whether for query or update. XPath is a very powerful, very robust language for navigating XML documents. It often works better than explicitly specified navigation using methods such as `getChildNode()` or `getNextSibling()`.

Navigation in a tree-based API is a surprisingly complex and error-prone operation. For example, consider a simple contacts file that includes names and phone numbers and claims to follow the DTD shown in Example 35–1.

Example 35–1 | A DTD for a Simple Contacts File

```
<!ELEMENT Contacts (Contact+)>
<!ELEMENT Contact (Name, Phone)>
<!ELEMENT Name (#PCDATA)>
<!ELEMENT Phone (#PCDATA)>
```

A typical document might look like Example 35–2.

Example 35–2 | A Simple Contacts Document

```
<?xml version="1.0"?>
<!DOCTYPE Contacts SYSTEM "contacts.dtd">
<Contacts>
  <Contact>
    <Name>John Doe</Name>
    <Phone>626-555-3456</Phone>
  </Contact>
  <Contact>
    <Name>Joe Smith</Name>
    <Phone>212-555-3456</Phone>
  </Contact>
  <Contact>
```

```
    <Name>Jane and Ben Reilly</Name>
    <Phone>212-555-2341</Phone>
  </Contact>
  <Contact>
    <Name>Mohammed Jones</Name>
    <Phone>718-555-2349</Phone>
  </Contact>
  <Contact>
    <Name>David Smith</Name>
    <Phone>914-555-3145</Phone>
  </Contact>
  <Contact>
    <Name>Xao Li</Name>
    <Phone>212-555-0998</Phone>
  </Contact>
</Contacts>
```

This is very straightforward, very simple record-like data. What can go wrong when processing files like this? Actually, quite a lot, especially when you realize that not all instance documents are likely to be so simple or so valid. In fact, all too often you'll find yourself working with documents like Example 35–3 instead, even if you were promised data that precisely adheres to the DTD in Example 35–1. Invalid data is a fact of life. It's not acceptable to just throw up your hands in disgust because someone sent you a document that's slightly different from what you expected.

Example 35–3 | A Slightly More Realistic Contacts Document

```
<?xml version="1.0"?>
<Contacts>
  <Contact>
    <Name>John Doe</Name>
    <Phone>626-555-3456</Phone>
  </Contact>
  <Contact>
    <Name>Joe
        <!--I need to check whether he prefers Joe or Joseph -->
        Smith
    </Name>
    <Phone>212-555-3456</Phone>
  </Contact>
```

```
<Contact>
  <Name>Jane <![CDATA[& Ben]]> Reilly</Name>
  <Phone>212-555-2341</Phone>
</Contact>
<Contact>
  <Name>Mohammed Jones</Name>
  <Phone>718-555-2349</Phone>
  <Phone>914-555-7698</Phone>
</Contact>
<Contact>
  <Phone>914-555-3145</Phone>
  <Name>David Smith</Name>
</Contact>
<Contact>
  <Name>Jason Smith</Name>
  <Phone></Phone>
</Contact>
<Contact>
  <Name>Xao Li</Name>
  <Name>Jonathan Li</Name>
  <Phone>212-555-0998</Phone>
</Contact>
</Contacts>
```

Potential problems include those listed below.

- Runs of text divided across multiple text nodes in the API although not in the serialized document.
- Runs of text interrupted by comments or processing instructions.

```
<Name>Joe
    <!--I need to check whether he prefers Joe or Joseph -->
    Smith
</Name>
```

- Runs of text interrupted by child elements.

```
<Name>Joseph <Nickname>Bud</Nickname> Smith </Name>
```

- Runs of text interrupted by CDATA sections that result in multiple nodes.

```
<Name>Jane <![CDATA[& Ben]]> Reilly</Name>
```

- Elements that occur two or more times where normally only one would be expected.

```
<Contact>
  <Name>Joe Smith</Name>
  <Phone>718-555-1234</Phone>
  <Phone>914-555-3145</Phone>
</Contact>
<Contact>
  <Name>Xao Li</Name>
  <Name>Jonathan Li</Name>
  <Phone>212-555-0998</Phone>
</Contact>
```

- White-space-only text nodes that change the number of nodes in a sequence. How many child nodes does the above Contact element have? It has three child elements, but most APIs will report at least seven total child nodes because they're counting the white space.
- Elements with an extra, unexpected parent.

```
<Contact>
  <Personal>
    <Name>Joe Smith</Name>
    <Phone>718-555-1234</Phone>
    <Phone>914-555-3145</Phone>
  </Personal>
</Contact>
```

- Nodes that are hiding in an entity reference. For instance, in DOM a node loaded from an external entity reference may be a grandchild of its parent element rather than a child.

```
<Contact>
  &JoeSmith;
</Contact>
```

- Elements that aren't precisely where you expect them. For instance, the Contact element below has the Name child as the second child element rather than the first.

```
<Contact>
    <Phone>914-555-3145</Phone>
    <Name>Joe Smith</Name>
</Contact>
```

- Missing elements. For instance, the following `Contact` element doesn't have a phone number.

```
<Contact>
    <Name>Joe Smith</Name>
</Contact>
```

- Unexpectedly empty elements.

```
<Contact>
  <Name>Jason Smith</Name>
  <Phone></Phone>
</Contact>
```

Some of these problems are mitigated by particular APIs. XOM resolves all entity references. DOM requires parsers to place the maximum possible contiguous run of text in each text node. MSXML throws away white-space-only nodes by default. Nonetheless, all APIs suffer from at least several of these problems.

Validation would catch some of these, though arguably they're not mistakes. For instance, if people do have multiple phone numbers but the schema only allows one, it's the schema that's mistaken, not the document. The instance document more correctly reflects reality than the schema does. The same can be said of a program that assumes every person has exactly one phone number. The software should be changed, not the document.

Is it possible to write a program that behaves correctly even in the face of unexpected changes in document structure? Surprisingly, the answer is yes, it is. Well-written programs can handle a lot of cases their designers did not explicitly plan for. The trick is to write programs that fit document structures loosely rather than tightly. The program should ask only for the information it needs without tying that to information it doesn't really care about. For example, if you want to find Joe Smith's phone numbers, you need to ask for the `Phone` siblings of the `Name` element whose value is Joe Smith. You don't want to ask for the `Phone` sibling of the `Name` element whose first text node is Joe Smith and is a child of a `Contact` element, which is a child of the `Contacts` element, which is the root element of the document. That's too specific. There are too many extra conditions such as "The root element is `Contacts`" that don't have anything to do with what you really want to know.

It is not possible, of course, to write perfectly robust software. For instance, there's no way to find Joe Smith's phone number if it's not in the document somewhere. However, you can write software that behaves reliably on a much broader class of documents and fails gracefully when the information truly isn't there.

XPath is a fourth-generation declarative language that allows you to specify which nodes you want to process without specifying exactly how the processor is supposed to navigate to those nodes. XPath's data model is very well designed to support exactly what almost all developers want from XML. For instance, it merges all adjacent text including that in CDATA sections, skips over comments and processing instructions, includes text from child and descendant elements, and resolves all external entity references. In practice, XPath expressions tend to be much more robust against unexpected but perhaps insignificant changes in the input document.

For example, consider a very simple DOM program fragment that prints all the names in the contacts file.

```
Element contactsElement = doc.getDocumentElement();
NodeList contacts = contactsElement.getChildNodes();

for (int i = 0; i < contacts.getLength(); i++) {
  Node current = contacts.item(i);
  if (current.getNodeType() == Node.ELEMENT_NODE) {
    Element contact = (Element) current;
    NodeList children = contact.getChildNodes();
    for (int j = 0; j < contacts.getLength(); j++) {
      Node candidate = children.item(j);
      if (candidate.getNodeType() == Node.ELEMENT_NODE) {
        // Assuming name is the first child element
        String name = candidate.getFirstChild().getNodeValue();
        System.out.println(name);
        // Assuming there's only one name per contact
         break;
      }
    }
  }
}
```

However, this code is very closely tied to the structure of the document. When actually run on Example 35–3, here's the output:

```
John Doe
Joe

Jane
Mohammed Jones
914-555-3145
Jason Smith
Xao Li
```

You can see that it lost half of Joe Smith's name and missed Ben Reilly completely. It also lost track of Jonathan Li and replaced David Smith with his phone number.

With a little effort, we can improve the DOM code to fix most of the problems. The most important improvement we can make is relying on element names rather than positions. The second most important improvement is using the `getElementsByTagName()` method to search the entire tree rather than just some expected parts of it. The third most important improvement (and the most difficult to implement correctly) is not assuming all text nodes are adjacent. The final fix is removing the assumption that there's only one name per contact. The improved code follows.

```java
NodeList names = doc.getElementsByTagName("Name");

for (int i = 0; i < names.getLength(); i++) {
    Node name = names.item(i);
    String value = getFullText(name);
    System.out.println(value);
}

// ...

public static String getFullText(Node node) {
    StringBuffer result = new StringBuffer(12);
    NodeList children = node.getChildNodes();
    for (int i = 0; i < children.getLength(); i++) {
        Node child = children.item(i);
        int type = child.getNodeType();
        if (type == Node.TEXT_NODE) {
            result.append(child.getNodeValue());
```

```
      }
      else if (type == Node.CDATA_SECTION_NODE) {
        result.append(child.getNodeValue());
      }
      else if (type == Node.ELEMENT_NODE) {
        result.append(getFullText(child));
      }
      else if (type == Node.ENTITY_REFERENCE_NODE) {
        result.append(getFullText(child));
      }
    }
    return result.toString();
  }
```

As you can see, this is somewhat more complex. Note especially the recursion that's necessary to accumulate the complete text of the node. Complexity would increase further in an API that doesn't have an equivalent to `getElementsByTagName()`, a fairly unique feature of DOM.

Is there perhaps an easier way? Yes, there is, and that way is XPath. Consider the following XPath expression.

```
/Contacts/Contact/Name
```

It's about ten times simpler than the DOM version but accomplishes almost as much. This returns the desired content even if the `Name` elements contain CDATA sections and child elements, and no matter how many of them appear in any given `Contact` element. This particular XPath expression would still fail if the hierarchy were not just what was expected, for instance, if the root element were something other than `Contacts` or if a `Name` element were not an immediate child of a `Contact` element. However, an XPath expression that uses the descendant axis would be even more robust. The XPath expression below would still succeed.

```
//Name
```

There are numerous ways to integrate XPath processing into your programs. Most XSLT processors such as Xalan, libxslt, and MSXML include APIs you can use to merge XPath expressions with your own code. Unfortunately, there is as yet no standard API for XPath queries. For example, using Xalan, the above query might look like this:

```
NodeList results = XPathAPI.selectNodeList(doc, "//Name");
for (int i = 0; i < results.getLength(); i++) {
  Node result = results.item(i);
  XObject value = XPathAPI.eval(result, "string()");
  System.out.println(value.str());
}
```

In MSXML, XPath evaluation is built into the DOM implementation classes, which makes for slightly more concise if less portable code. (See Item 31.) For example, here's the same XPath search implemented in JavaScript such as you might use from Internet Explorer.

```
var results = doc.selectNodes("//Name");
for (i=0; i < results.length; i++) {
  var node = results.item(i);
  alert(node.text);
}
```

Many Java APIs are supported by the Jaxen XPath library (http://jaxen. sourceforge.net) including DOM, JDOM, and dom4j. Using Jaxen on top of DOM, the above query would look something like this:

```
XPath expression = new org.jaxen.dom.DOMXPath("//Name");
Navigator navigator = expression.getNavigator();
List results = expression.selectNodes(doc);
Iterator iterator = results.iterator();
while (iterator.hasNext()) {
  Node result = (Node) iterator.next();
  String value = StringFunction.evaluate(result, navigator);
  System.out.println(value);
}
```

There are a few things you need to be wary of when integrating XPath with more traditional code. First of all, XPath queries return node-sets, not single nodes. You should be prepared to iterate through the result, even if you expect only a single node. This handles cases both where the expected node is missing and where there's more than you expected. Avoid methods like `selectSingleNode()` in MSXML and Xalan that hide such results from the library client. They significantly reduce robustness. If you absolutely insist that there can be only one result, then by all means validate the document against a schema that requires this (Item 37) before processing the document, and reject it if it fails the schema. Do not simply assume that all documents passed to the program meet the constraints. Such assumptions fail far more often than most developers initially expect, and over a period of several years almost all such assumptions fail.

Secondly, be aware that you may take a performance hit for choosing XPath, especially if you use the tree-walking descendant and descendant-or-self axes. The following axis also tends to be slow. Some (but not all) XPath engines have major performance problems with the ancestor and ancestor-or-self axes. You can use the child axis and more explicit descent instead. However, as noted above, this does reduce your program's robustness. Like all other performance issues, this should be evaluated within the context of a particular program, system, library, and use case. Some systems have CPU power to spare. Others may be so CPU or memory limited that the cost of even the most basic XPath processing is prohibitive. Sometimes switching to a different XPath engine can produce an order of magnitude improvement in processing particular XPath expressions. I recommend designing the processing for maximum robustness and optimizing the XPath expressions only when and if profiling proves this is a significant bottleneck.

Personally, I'm willing to trade performance for robustness, and I find the opposite opinion (a willingness to trade correctness for performance) completely incomprehensible. XPath-based navigation is both easier to write and easier to write correctly than explicit navigation. It produces much more robust software. If you'd rather process more documents faster, at the cost of processing some of them incorrectly, you can do so; but please at least test the performance of an XPath-based alternative before you rule it out.

Item 36   Serialize XML with XML

XML is itself a fairly efficient serialization format. There's no need or reason to use expensive binary object serialization on XML documents. Even custom-designed binary formats are generally larger, slower, and less robust than XML's plain text formats. (See Item 50.) Generic binary formats like Java's object serialization are much worse. It is much simpler, faster, and more effective to just write the text of the XML document onto a stream or into a string.

For example, I wrote a simple program to load the XML 1.0 specification into a JDOM document object and write it out again as both XML and a serialized object. The binary format was 537,480 bytes long. The original XML document was only 201,918 bytes. Including the full DTD (which is not necessary) adds another 57,135 bytes to the XML document. The total is still less than half the size of the serialized object.

If that's not good enough for you, you can always compress the serialized XML (Item 50), which makes XML even more space efficient. The gzipped binary object in this case is 117,443 bytes long. However, the gzipped XML is only 54,007 bytes long. Any way you slice it, text is more efficient. The best way to store or transmit XML data is as XML, or perhaps as compressed XML if size is very important. Object serialization buys you nothing.

The reverse is not necessarily true. In some circumstances, it may indeed make sense to transmit binary data using text-based XML formats instead of the native format. A number of developers who have written replacements for Java's object serialization using XML report significant savings of both time and space. These include the following:

- Mark Wutka's JOX (http://www.wutka.com/jox.html)
- Bill LaForge's Quick (http://qare.sourceforge.net/web/2001-12/products/quick/index.html)
- Brendan Macmillan's JSX (http://www.csse.monash.edu.au/~bren/JSX/)
- KOML, The Koala Object Markup Language (http://koala.ilog.fr/XML/serialization/)
- CastorXML (http://castor.exolab.org/)
- Sun's long-term persistence for JavaBeans (`java.beans.XMLEncoder` and `java.beans.XMLDecoder`)

And this is just Java! I won't even attempt to list the similar tools you'll find for Python, Perl, C#, C++, and other languages. .NET has an XML-based object serialization in its core class library.

Of course, binary object serialization is more than just a storage format. It's also a critical component of network computing systems like CORBA and Java's Remote Method Invocation (RMI). These systems depend on complex, serialized binary objects. However, it's no coincidence that in the real world, both of them are getting creamed by the success of much simpler XML-based protocols such as XML-RPC and SOAP, as well as more RESTful systems like RSS. This may well be an example of the triumph of worse is better. Both XML-RPC and SOAP are missing numerous features of the more complex protocols:

- Transactions
- Remote garbage collection
- Callbacks
- Stubs and skeletons
- Remote class loading

However, I have to say I'm not at all convinced these are required for most useful work. What most developers need is a straightforward way to move bundles of data from point A to point B on the network, with some confirmation that the data got there. This much both XML-RPC and SOAP provide. RESTful systems like RSS do an even better job. More than this may not be necessary most of the time.

Bottom line: If you need to transmit or store XML, transmit or store XML. Do not transmit or store some other variation of the XML document. XML is syntax, and only Unicode in angle brackets is real XML. All other formats are just poor copies that often don't perform as well as XML itself.

Item 37   Validate Inside Your Program with Schemas

Rigorously testing preconditions is an important characteristic of robust, reliable software. Schemas make it very easy to define the preconditions for XML documents you parse and the postconditions for XML documents you write. Even if the document itself does not have a schema, you can write one and use it to test the documents before you operate on them. It is quite hard to attach a DTD to a document inside a program. Fortunately, however, most other schema languages are much more flexible about this.

For example, let's suppose you're in charge of a system at *TV Guide* that accepts schedule information from individual stations over the Web. Information about each show arrives as an XML document formatted as shown in Example 37–1.

Example 37–1 | An XML Instance Document Containing a Television Program Listing

```
<Program xmlns="http://namespaces.example.com/tvschedule"
  <Title>Reality Bites</Title>
  <Description>
  Elimination tournament in which contestants eat a
  succession of gross items until only one is left standing.
  Tonight's episode features rancid apples, insects, and
  McDonald's Happy Meals.
  </Description>
  <Date>2003-11-21</Date>
  <Start>08:00:00-05:00</Start>
  <Duration>PT30M</Duration>
  <Station>KFOX</Station>
</Program>
```

Every day, around the clock, stations from all over the country send schedule updates like this one that you need to store in a local database. Some of these stations use software you sold them. Some of them hire interns to type the data into a password-protected form on your web site. Others use custom software they wrote themselves. There may even be a few hackers typing the information into text files using emacs and then telnetting to your web server on port 80, where they paste in the data. There are about a dozen different places where mistakes can creep in. Therefore, before you even begin to think about processing a submission, you want to verify that it's correct. In particular, you want to verify the following.

- The root element of the document is `Program`.
- All required elements are present.
- No more than one of each element is present.
- The `Title` element is not empty.
- The date is a legal date in the future.
- The `Start` element contains a sensible time.
- The duration looks like a period of time.
- The station identifier is a four-letter code beginning with either K or W.
- The station identifier maps to a known station somewhere in the country, which can be determined by looking it up in a database running on a different machine in your intranet.

You could write program code to verify all of these statements after the document was parsed. However, it's much easier to write a schema that describes them declaratively and let the parser check them. The W3C XML Schema Language, RELAX NG, and Schematron can all handle about 85% of these requirements. They all have problems with the requirement that the date be in the future and that the station be listed in a remote database. These will have to be checked using real programming code written in Java, C++, or some other language after the document has been parsed. However, we can make the other checks with a schema. Example 37–2 shows one possible W3C XML Schema Language schema that tests most of the above constraints.

Example 37–2 | A W3C XML Schema for Television Program Listings

```
<?xml version="1.0"?>
<xsd:schema xmlns:xsd="http://www.w3.org/2001/XMLSchema">

  <xsd:element name="Program">
    <xsd:complexType>
      <xsd:all>
        <xsd:element name="Title">
          <xsd:simpleType>
            <xsd:restriction base="xsd:string">
              <xsd:minLength value="1"/>
            </xsd:restriction>
          </xsd:simpleType>
        </xsd:element>
        <xsd:element name="Description" type="xsd:string"/>
        <xsd:element name="Date"        type="xsd:date"/>
        <xsd:element name="Start"       type="xsd:time"/>
        <xsd:element name="Duration"    type="xsd:duration"/>
        <xsd:element name="Station">
          <xsd:simpleType>
            <xsd:restriction base="xsd:token">
              <xsd:pattern value="(W|K)[A-Z][A-Z][A-Z]"/>
            </xsd:restriction>
          </xsd:simpleType>
        </xsd:element>
      </xsd:all>
    </xsd:complexType>
  </xsd:element>

</xsd:schema>
```

For simplicity, I'll assume this schema resides at the URL `http://www.example.com/tvprogram.xsd` in the examples that follow, but you can store it anywhere convenient.

There are several different ways to programmatically validate a document, depending on the schema language, the parser, and the API. Here I'll demonstrate two: Xerces-J using SAX properties and DOM Level 3 validation.

Xerces-J

The Xerces-J SAX parser supports validation with the W3C XML Schema Language. By default, it reads the schema with which to validate documents from the `xsi:schemaLocation` and `xsi:noNamespaceSchemaLocation` attributes in the instance document. However, you can override these with the `http://apache.org/xml/properties/schema/external-schemaLocation` and `http://apache.org/xml/properties/schema/external-noNamespaceSchemaLocation` SAX properties. In this example, the documents being validated have namespaces, so we'll set `http://apache.org/xml/properties/schema/external-schemaLocation` to `http://www.example.com/tvprogram.xsd`. Then, we'll turn on schema validation by setting the `http://apache.org/xml/features/validation/schema` feature to true.

```
XMLReader parser = XMLReaderFactor.createXMLReader(
  "org.apache.xerces.parsers.SAXParser");
parser.setProperty(
"http://apache.org/xml/properties/schema/external-
schemaLocation",
  "http://namespaces.example.com/tvschedule"
  + " http://www.example.com/tvprogram.xsd");
parser.setFeature(
  "http://apache.org/xml/features/validation/schema",
  true);
```

We'll also have to register an `ErrorHandler` to receive any validation errors that are detected. Because validity errors aren't necessarily fatal unless we make them so, we'll rethrow the `SAXParseException` passed to the `error()` method. Example 37–3 shows an appropriate `Error Handler` class.

Example 37–3 | A SAX `ErrorHandler` That Makes Validity Errors Fatal

```
import org.xml.sax.*;

public class ErrorsAreFatal implements ErrorHandler {

  public void warning(SAXParseException exception) {
    // Ignore warnings
  }

  public void error(SAXParseException exception)
   throws SAXException {

    // A validity error; rethrow the exception.
    throw exception;

  }

  public void fatalError(SAXParseException exception)
   throws SAXException {

    // A well-formedness error
    throw exception;

  }

}
```

This `ErrorHandler` also needs to be installed with the parser.

```
parser.setErrorHandler(new ErrorsAreFatal());
```

Finally, the document can be parsed. The parser checks it against the schema as it parses. At the same time, the `ContentHandler` methods accumulate the data into the fields. Since SAX parsing interleaves parser operation with client code, all the data collected should be stored until the complete document has been validated. Only then can you be sure the document is valid and the information should be committed. Example 37–4 demonstrates one way to build a `TVProgram` object that stores this data. The constructor is private, so the only way to build such an object is by passing an `InputStream` containing a `TVProgram` document to the `readTVProgram()` method. The `TVProgram` object is actually created before the parsing starts. However, it's not returned to anything outside this class until the input document has been parsed and any constraints verified. If a constraint is violated, then an exception is thrown.

Example 37–4 | A Program That Validates against a Schema

```java
import java.util.*;
import java.io.*;
import org.xml.sax.*;
import org.xml.sax.helpers.*;

public class TVProgram extends DefaultHandler {

  private String title;
  private String description;
  private Date   startTime; // includes both date and time
  private int    duration;  // rounded to nearest second
  private String station;   // rounded to nearest second

  private TVProgram() {
    // Data will be initialized in the readTVProgram() method
  }

  private static XMLReader parser;

  // Initialization block. No need to load a new parser for
  // each document.
  static {
    try {
      parser = XMLReaderFactory.createXMLReader(
        "org.apache.xerces.parsers.SAXParser");
      parser.setProperty(
"http://apache.org/xml/properties/schema/external-schemaLocation",
        "http://namespaces.example.com/tvschedule"
        + " http://www.example.com/tvprogram.xsd");
      parser.setFeature(
        "http://apache.org/xml/features/validation/schema",
        true);
      parser.setErrorHandler(new ErrorsAreFatal());
    }
    catch (SAXException e) {
     throw new RuntimeException(
        "Handling exceptions in static initializers is tricky");
    }
  }
```

```
public static TVProgram readTVProgram(String systemID)
 throws SAXException, IOException {

  TVProgram program = new TVProgram();
  parser.setContentHandler(program);
  parser.parse(systemID);

  // If no exception has been thrown yet, then the document
  // must be valid. However, we still have to check the
  // constraints the schema couldn't:
  checkDateInFuture(program.startTime);
  checkStationExists(program.station);

  // If we get here, everything's fine.
  return program;

}

private static void checkDateInFuture(Date date)
 throws SAXException {

  // Java code to compare the date to the current time

}

private static void checkStationExists(String station)
 throws SAXException {

  // JDBC code to look up the station call letters in our
  // database

}

// Various ContentHandler methods that will fill in the fields
// of this object. This could be a separate class instead...

// Various setter and getter and other methods...

}
```

Presumably, after such an object has been read, other code will store it in a database or otherwise work with it. And, of course, building an object that exactly matches the data in the document is far from the only way to model the data. All these details will depend on the business logic in the rest of the program. However, the input checking through validation will normally be similar to what's shown here.

DOM Level 3 Validation

DOM Level 3 provides a detailed API for validation. This API can be used to validate against any schema language the parser supports, although DTDs and W3C XML Schema Language schemas are certainly the most common options.

Caution *This section is based on working drafts of the relevant specifications and experimental software. The broad picture presented here is correct, but a lot of details are likely to change before DOM Level 3 is finalized.*

Unlike SAX, DOM objects can be validated when the document is first parsed or at any later point. You can also validate individual nodes rather than validating the entire document. To validate while parsing, you set the following features on the document or document builder's `DOMConfiguration` object.

- `schema-type`: A URI identifying the schema language used to validate. Values include `http://www.w3.org/2001/XMLSchema` for the W3C XML Schema Language and `http://www.w3.org/TR/REC-xml` for DTDs.
- `schema-location`: A white-space-separated list of URLs for particular schema documents used to validate.
- `validate`: If true, all documents should be validated. If false, no documents should be validated unless `validate-if-schema` is true.
- `validate-if-schema`: Validate only if a schema (in whatever language) is available, either one set by the `schema-location` and `schema-type` parameters or one specified in the instance document using a mechanism such as a `DOCTYPE` declaration or an `xsi:schemaLocation` attribute.

For example, here's the DOM Level 3 code to parse the document at `http://www.example.net/kfox.xml` while validating it against the schema at `http://www.example.com/tvprogram.xsd`.

```
DOMImplementation impl = DOMImplementationRegistry
   .getDOMImplementation("XML 1.0 LS-Load 3.0");
if (impl == null || !impl.hasFeature("Core", "3.0") {
  throw new Exception("DOM Level 3 not supported");
}
```

```
DOMImplementationLS implLS = impl.getInterface("LS-Load", "3.0");
DOMBuilder builder = implLS.createDOMBuilder(
  DOMBuilder.MODE_SYNCHRONOUS,
  "http://www.w3.org/2001/XMLSchema");
DOMConfiguration config = builder.getConfig();
config.setParameter("validate", Boolean.TRUE);
config.setParameter("schema-location",
  "http://www.example.com/tvprogram.xsd");
config.setParameter("schema-type",
  "http://www.w3.org/2001/XMLSchema");
builder.setErrorHandler(new DOMErrorHandler() {
  public boolean handleError(in DOMError error) {
    System.err.println(error.getMessage());
  }
});
Document doc = builder.parseURI(
  "http://www.example.net/kfox.xml");
```

Currently, this API is only experimentally supported by Xerces and the Xerces-derived XML for Java, but more parsers should support it in the future.

If you make modifications to a document, DOM3 allows you to revalidate it to make sure it's still valid. This is an optional feature, and not all DOM Level 3 implementations support it. If one does, each `Document` object will be an instance of the `DocumentEditVal` interface as well. Just cast the object to this type and invoke the `validateDocument()` method as shown below.

```
if (doc instanceof DocumentEditVal) {
  DocumentEditVal docVal = (DocumentEditVal) doc;
  try {
    boolean valid = docVal.validateDocument();
  }
  catch (ExceptionVAL ex) {
    // This document doesn't have a schema
  }
}
```

You can even continuously validate a document as it is modified. If any change makes the document invalid, the problem will be reported to the registered `DOMErrorHandler`. Just set the `continuousValidity Checking` attribute to true.

```
docVal.setContinuousValidityChecking(true);
```

This is particularly useful if the modifications are not driven by the program but by a human using an editor. In this case, you can even check the data input for validity before allowing the changes to be made.

If you need to change the schema associated with a document, set the `schema-location` and `schema-type` parameters on the document's `DOMConfiguration` object.

```
DOMConfiguration config = doc.getConfig();
config.setParameter("schema-type",
                    "http://www.w3.org/2001/XMLSchema");
config.setParameter("schema-location",
                    "http://www.example.com/schema.xsd");
```

To validate this document, you would then call `validateDocument()` as described above.

Validation with DOM differs from validation with SAX in that you don't actually begin working with the document until after it has been validated. Thus there's no need to worry about committing the data in pieces. This is a common difference between SAX and DOM programs. A second advantage is that DOM validation can be reversed so that you build the document in memory and then check for validity before outputting it. You can even check every node you add to the `Document` object for adherence to a schema immediately and automatically.

Whether you validate with SAX or DOM, whether you do so continuously or just once when the document is first parsed, and whether the schema is a DTD, a W3C XML Schema Language schema, or something else, validation is an extremely useful tool. Even if you don't reject invalid documents, you can still use the result of validity checking to determine what to do with any given document. For instance, you might validate documents against several known schemas to identify the document's type and dispatch the document to the method that processes that type. Validation is an essential component of robust, reliable systems.

4 | Implementation

XML documents don't live in a vacuum. They are parts of larger systems. They are written in and read by a variety of software tools, transmitted across networks in a variety of formats using various protocols, and stored in file systems and databases. They interact with other processes. A single document may be read and written by many different people and programs during its existence, each of whom may interpret it in a different way.

This final part explores issues that arise when looking at XML documents as parts of larger systems. These include verification, data integrity, compression, authentication, caching, content management, and the like. Sometimes these services can be performed in the external processes that manage, manipulate, and transmit the XML documents. Other times the need for these services requires changes in the design and structure of the XML documents and applications themselves.

Item 38 Write in Unicode

You may work in English, but these days it's no great surprise if some of your coworkers or customers are more comfortable in French, Chinese, or Amharic. One of the most underrated advantages of XML is its internationalization support. Much of this is a direct result of its dependence on Unicode. In effect, every XML document is read in Unicode. Even if the document is written in a different character set such as ISO-8859-1 or SJIS, the parser converts it to Unicode on input. Thus it behooves you to know how to properly process Unicode data.

How difficult this is varies greatly from one language or environment to the next. In Python 2.2 it's relatively easy. In Java it's not too hard, but there are some pitfalls laid out to trap the unwary. In Perl 5.0 it's nearly impossible, but more recent versions of Perl are much better, especially Perl 5.8 and later. In C and C++ Unicode normally requires types other than string and char. In many cases (including C, C++, Python, Perl, and Java) a lot depends on exactly which version of the language you're using. In general, you should strive to use the most recent version of the language if at all possible. In all cases I'm aware of, the more recent version always has Unicode support that's as good as or better than the earlier versions.

Note *This is not in conflict with Item 2, Mark Up with ASCII if Possible. ASCII is still the best choice for markup (that is, element names, attribute names, and so on), especially markup that needs to be shared among many different developers with many cultures and languages. The simple fact is that English and ASCII are the lowest common denominator for technical communication around the world.*

However, the situation is very different for content; that is, for PCDATA and attribute values. Here, the text must be highly localized. For example, consider the MegaBank Statement Markup Language one more time. If the bank operates internationally, it may need to transmit information back and forth between branches in France, the United States, Japan, China, Brazil, and many other countries. Programs that process this data work more effectively if the structure and markup of the documents don't vary from country to country. The markup should be the same across national boundaries.

On the other hand, each individual document is probably local to a particular country. The information changes from one customer to the next. M. Béla Delanoë of Lyons should receive a statement that shows his name with all the accents in place. Iwahashi-san of Tokyo should receive a message written in Kanji, not Romaji. The content needs to be localized. By far the easiest way to do that for a worldwide audience is to use Unicode.

Choosing an Encoding

Given that you've wisely chosen to use Unicode for your documents, the next question is which encoding of Unicode to pick. Unicode is a character set that assigns almost 100,000 characters to different numeric code points. The characters assigned code points from 0 to 65,535 are sometimes referred to as Plane 0 or the Basic Multilingual Plane (BMP for short). The BMP includes most common characters from most of the world's living languages including the Roman alphabet, Cyrillic, Arabic,

Greek, Hebrew, Hangul, the most common Han ideographs, and many more. Plane 1, spanning code points 65,536 to 131,071, includes musical notation, many mathematical symbols, and several dead languages such as Old Italic. Plane 2 (code points 131,072 to 196,607) adds many less common Han ideographs. Plane 14 includes language tags XML developers can safely ignore. (They should use the `xml:lang` attribute instead.) The other planes are as yet unpopulated.

Unicode does not specify a single unique binary representation for any of the code points in any of the planes, however. They can be encoded as four-byte big-endian integers, four-byte little-endian integers, or in some more complex but efficient way. Indeed, there are several common encodings of the Unicode character set in practical use today. However, only two are worthy of serious consideration, UTF-8 and UTF-16. UTF-8 should be the default choice for most documents that don't contain large amounts of Chinese, Japanese, or Korean text. Documents that do contain significant amounts of Chinese, Japanese, or Korean should be encoded in UTF-16.

UTF-8

UTF-8 (Unicode Transformation Format, 8-bit encoding form) is a very clever encoding that uses different numbers of bytes for different characters. Characters in the ASCII range (0–127) occupy one byte each. Characters from 128 to 4095 occupy two bytes each. The rest of the characters in Plane 0 occupy three bytes each. Finally, all the other characters in Planes 1 through 15 occupy four bytes each.

This scheme has a number of useful characteristics. First among them is that UTF-8 is a strict superset of ASCII. Every ASCII text file is also a legal UTF-8 document. This makes UTF-8 much more compatible with the installed software base, especially when working primarily in English. Also important is that none of the ASCII characters ever appear as parts of another character. That is, when you encounter a byte with a value between 0 and 127, it is always an ASCII character.

Second, UTF-8 is byte order independent. A UTF-8 document on a big-endian UNIX system is byte-for-byte identical to the same document on a little-endian Windows system. Byte order marks are not necessary, though they are allowed.

Third, the particular encoding scheme used is such that by looking at any one byte, a program can determine, based on that byte alone, whether or not it's the only byte of a single-byte character, the first or second byte of a two-byte character, or the first, second, or third byte of a three-byte character. The character boundaries can be inferred from the bytes alone. You do not need to start at the beginning of a stream or a file to read text from the middle. By reading at most three bytes starting at any position in the file, a program can align itself on the character boundaries.

Finally, for documents that use the Roman alphabet primarily, UTF-8 documents tend to be smaller than other Unicode encodings because each ASCII character takes up only one byte. The additional characters in other Roman alphabet languages (e.g., French, Turkish) don't make a huge difference. Non-Roman alphabets like Arabic and Greek use two bytes per character, which is no bigger than they are in other Unicode encodings. However, in languages with ideographic characters, such as Chinese, Japanese, and Korean, each character occupies three bytes or more, which makes text significantly larger than it would be in UTF-16.

UTF-16

UTF-16 (Unicode Transformation Format, 16-bit encoding form) is a more obvious encoding that uses two bytes for most characters, including the most common Chinese, Japanese, and Korean ideographs. Some less common ideographs are encoded in Plane 1 and represented with surrogate pairs of four bytes each. However, though you might use one or two of these, they're unlikely to make up the bulk of any document. Thus a document containing large amounts of Chinese, Japanese, or Korean text can be a third smaller in UTF-16 than it would be in UTF-8.

Note *On the other hand, ideographic languages stuff a lot of information into a single character. For example, the Japanese word for tree is 木. That single character is three bytes in UTF-8 and two bytes in UTF-16. By contrast the English word for* tree *needs four bytes in UTF-8 and eight bytes in UTF-16. The English word* grove *takes five bytes in UTF-8. The Japanese equivalent, 林, takes only three bytes. The word* forest, 森, *takes six bytes in English but still only three bytes in Japanese. Ideographic languages are quite space efficient to start with, regardless of encoding. Chinese is probably the most efficient, Korean the least, with Japanese somewhere in between.*

However, UTF-16 does not have all the other nice qualities of UTF-8, so it should not be used as your default Unicode encoding unless you're working with ideographic languages, even when space is not an issue. UTF-16 is not byte order independent, it does not allow character boundaries to be easily detected, and it tends to contain many embedded nulls.

The normal solution to the byte order problem is to place a byte order mark (#xFEFF) at the beginning of the document. If the first two bytes the program reads are FE and FF, the document is written in big-endian UTF-16. However, if the first two bytes the program reads are FF and FE, the document is written in little-endian UTF-16. (FFFE is not a legal Unicode character, so there's no chance of misidentifying a legal character as the byte order mark in the opposite encoding.) XML explicitly allows a byte order mark to appear in the first two bytes of a document. This is the only thing that may appear before the XML declaration.

UTF-16 does not provide any foolproof mechanism to detect character boundaries. However, this shouldn't be an issue for streaming applications, which can simply start at the beginning and read two bytes at a time from that point forward. Some random access programs can simply assert that character boundaries occur only at even indexes (byte 0, byte 2, byte 4, and so on). If this is not an option, one useful heuristic is that zero bytes are much more likely to occur as the first byte of a character than the second, especially in markup and code where most characters are taken from the ASCII character set anyway.

Non-Unicode Character Sets

Having said all this, please keep in mind that this only applies to generating XML and processing XML with non-XML-aware tools such as text editors and grep. When an XML parser reads a document, it will translate the document's declared encoding to Unicode before presenting it to the client application. No properly designed XML system should ever depend on the document's original encoding.

Thus you can write XML documents in other encodings such as ISO-8859-1 (Latin-1) if this works better with your existing tools. Different branch offices in different countries can and do use different encodings, all of which are resolved by the parser when the document is processed. However, other than UTF-8 and UTF-16, XML processors are not required to recognize and understand other character sets. In practice,

ISO-8859-1 does seem ubiquitous. However, the other standard character sets such as ISO-8859-2 through ISO-8859-16, ISO-2022-JP, and Big5 are often unsupported. Even ASCII is not recognized by all parsers, so it tends to get labeled as UTF-8, which is recognized. (Remember, any ASCII document is also a legal UTF-8 document.) UTF-8 and UTF-16 are much more interoperable across processes. Use UTF-8 if you plausibly can.

A char Is Not a Character

The prime problem with Unicode in most programming languages is that a Unicode character is not equivalent to the native char type. For instance, on many systems, a C char is one signed byte. This allows 128 characters that cover the ASCII range (barely) but fails as soon as you need an *ü* or an *é*. On other systems, the C char type is an unsigned byte that provides 256 characters. This works adequately for most Latin-alphabet languages, though different languages have to use different character sets and not all languages can be processed simultaneously. It fails completely when faced with a language such as Japanese that has more than 256 characters. This has led to the development of wide character types such as wchar. However, the effective size of wchar varies from seven bits to four bytes, depending on platform and compiler, and may use the platform default character set rather than Unicode.

In Java a char is two unsigned bytes and is based on Unicode. That's room for 65,536 different characters, which should be enough except that some languages (notably Chinese) have more than 70,000 characters. (The exact number is debated, but everyone agrees it's a lot.) Thus even two-byte chars like those found in Java don't adequately handle Unicode, which covers Chinese and a lot more. To some extent, this was hidden up through Unicode 3.0 because Unicode hadn't actually defined any characters with code points beyond 65,535; but that began to change in Unicode 3.1, and the process seems likely to accelerate in the future.

One common misconception about Unicode is that each Unicode character occupies exactly two bytes. In fact, Unicode has space for over one million characters, which clearly can't be represented in two bytes. This misconception arose because until Unicode 3.1 all Unicode characters were assigned to code points below 65,536. However, in Unicode 3.1 several scripts, including musical and mathematical symbols, were assigned to Plane 1 with code points above 65,536. More will be assigned there in the future. This means that more than two bytes and more than one Java char are necessary to hold a single Unicode character. In fact, a Java char does not encode a Unicode character. Rather, it represents a UTF-16 code point. Characters with code points less than or equal to 65,535 are represented with one Java char. Characters with code points greater than 65,535 are represented with two Java chars using surrogate pairs. However, the two chars that make up the surrogate pair account for just one Unicode character.

Normally, this distinction is not a big deal when processing XML. The parser passes strings or char arrays to the application that contain all necessary chars. On rare occasions it's possible for a parser that splits XML text across multiple method calls to pass in half of one character at the end of one string and the other half at the beginning of the next, but this is unlikely to occur and generally doesn't cause any major problems even when it does.

The proper handling of Unicode is slightly (but only slightly) more troublesome when writing XML. Here, you cannot simply assume that the characters and the strings are as you need them to be. You need to use classes that convert the native char type, whatever it is, into proper UTF-8 or UTF-16. Alternately, you can use other encodings as long as the XML document carries an encoding declaration identifying which encoding you are using. In Java, the `OutputStreamWriter` class is up to this task. Python makes this fairly easy, and Perl 5.6 and later generate UTF-8 by default. Standard C and C++ don't have anything like this, but most platform-dependent APIs, such as the Unicode stream I/O functions in the Microsoft runtime library on Windows (fwprintf, fputwc, fputws, and so on) or glibc 2.2 and later in Linux, support Unicode output, typically in UTF-8 and/or UTF-16.

Normalization Forms

For reasons of compatibility with legacy character sets, as well as out-and-out mistakes, a number of characters have more than one representation in Unicode. For example, the umlaut character can be represented as either the single character *ü* or as a *u* followed by a combining diaresis. XML 1.0[1] treats these two forms as distinct. For example,

---

1. This is one of the few changes that may be made in XML 1.1. However, exactly how or when characters will be normalized has not yet been finalized.

Münchn (München) is not the same as Münchn (München). You can see that this might be a bit of a problem.

While such differences are not significant to XML parsing, they may very well be significant to applications that build on top of XML. You should normalize all text that comes into your program before acting on it. Unicode defines four separate normalization algorithms, suitable for different needs. Probably the most generally useful is Normalization Form C (NFC). This tends to produce text that is best displayed by existing software. However, for sorting, searching, indexing, and so forth, Normalization Form KC (NFKC) is usually more appropriate. It's similar to NFC except that it's a little more aggressive in unifying characters. In particular, stylistic variants such as the fi ligature would be replaced by the two letters f and i, whereas NFC would not unify them. Both NFC and NFKC unify stylistically equivalent sequences and characters such as *ü* and a *u* followed by a combining diaresis.

Actually implementing the various normalization algorithms is relatively tricky, although it mostly involves table lookups. It is a task best left to the experts. Fortunately, high-quality open source and public domain code is available that can do the job for you.

- The Unicode Consortium has published sample algorithms in Java at http://www.unicode.org/unicode/reports/tr15/Normalizer.html.
- IBM's International Components for Unicode (ICU, http://oss. software.ibm.com/icu/) are a high-quality class library for performing normalization and many other tasks. The complete library is a little large for some tastes, but many developers rebuild it with only the parts their own programs need.
- Perl has the Unicode::Normalize module, which you can download from CPAN.

A Google search will turn up numerous other options. Normalization is still something of an esoteric subject. Few developers realize how much they need this, so it hasn't made its way into the standard libraries in major programming languages just yet. Indeed it may not be necessary in pure ASCII environments. However, as soon as you move beyond the ASCII character set and the English language, normalization of strings becomes very important.

Sorting

Many CS101 textbooks demonstrate sorting on strings by using code point order. Unfortunately this does not work in the real world, even in ASCII, much less in Unicode. Most obviously, real sorts (such as that found in the index in the back of this book) sort capital letters identically to their lowercase equivalents. *Lichenstein* should appear after *language,* not before it as it does when ordered by code points. Less obviously, the punctuation marks generally appear before all letters whether they're # (ASCII code point 35), [(ASCII code point 91), or ~ (ASCII code point 126). And of course sorting is language dependent. While converting all characters to upper case and lexically ordering the resulting strings may give passable results in English, it fails completely in languages like French where *è* and *é* are intermixed with *e* even though in almost all character sets the code points for *è* and *é* come well after *z.*

Text comparison and sorting has to be done in a locale-sensitive manner. You need to know which language you're sorting, and you need to use an appropriate collation table, as well as normalizing the data before you sort. In Java, the `java.text.Collator` class performs locale-sensitive string comparison. IBM's aforementioned International Components for Unicode provide more powerful and configurable options. How fancy you want to get depends on your needs and the language or languages of the documents you're processing. The main thing to remember is that any time you're using code point order, you're doing it wrong. Code point order is never adequate for sorting something that will be shown to a person.

Item 39   Parameterize XSLT Stylesheets

There's an old programmer's adage that the only numbers in programs should be 0, 1, and infinity. Everything else should be a named constant. The same can be said for styles in XSLT stylesheets. Sooner or later somebody is going to want to customize anything they can customize. To enable this, use named variables (an XSLT variable is much like a C++ const) instead of hard-coding styles like 12pt or bold.

The key to this is top-level `xsl:variable` and `xsl:param` elements. These are direct children of the root `xsl:stylesheet` element. Each such element has a `name` attribute that sets the name of the variable (or parameter) and a `select` attribute that sets the value of the variable (or parameter) using an XPath expression. For example, the following `xsl:variable` and `xsl:param` elements set various font properties.

```
<xsl:variable name="body-font-name" select="'Times New Roman'"/>
<xsl:variable name="body-font-size" select="'10pt'"/>
<xsl:param name="code-font-name" select="'Courier'"/>
<xsl:param name="code-font-size" select="'12pt'"/>
```

The value of each of these variables/parameters is a literal string. A value can also be a number.

```
<xsl:variable name="start-page" select="25"/>
<xsl:variable name="columns" select="2"/>
```

A variable can even be set to a node-set. For example, the code below would set the variable headings to all the level 1 and level 2 headings in a typical DocBook document.

```
<xsl:variable name="headings" select="//sect1/title |
//sect2/title"/>
<xsl:variable name="columns" select="2"/>
```

However, for variables and parameters that define constants, it's normally more plausible to use simple string, numeric, and perhaps boolean values.

Variables and parameters can also be set to result tree fragments by omitting the `select` attribute and using a template inside the `xsl:variable` or `xsl:param` element instead, as demonstrated below.

```
<xsl:variable name="body-font-name">Times</xsl:variable>
<xsl:variable name="body-font-size">10pt</xsl:variable>
<xsl:param name="code-font-name">Courier</xsl:variable>
<xsl:param name="code-font-size">12pt</xsl:variable>
<xsl:variable name="columns">2<xsl:variable/>
```

The result tree fragments are normally converted to the necessary type automatically. Using these result tree fragments like node-sets is more useful for purposes other than stylesheet parameterization. Here, they're mostly being used as an alternate, slightly more convenient syntax for strings.

Variables and parameters are dereferenced within other XPath expressions in the XSLT stylesheet by placing a dollar sign in front of the variable name, for example, `$body-font-name` and `$body-font-size`. These two templates transform DocBook paragraphs and program listings into XSL-FO `fo:block` elements. The styles for the paragraph are determined by the `body-font-family` and `body-font-size` variables. The styles for the program listing are given by the `code-font-family` and `code-font-size` parameters.

```
<xsl:template match="para">
  <fo:block font-family="{$body-font-family}"
            font-size="{$body-font-size}">
    <xsl:apply-templates/>
  </fo:block>
</xsl:template>

<xsl:template match="programlisting">
  <fo:block font-family="{$code-font-family}"
            font-size="{$code-font-size}"
            white-space-collapse="false">
    <xsl:apply-templates/>
  </fo:block>
</xsl:template>
```

In this example, since the `font-family` and `font-size` attributes are part of the output vocabulary, rather than XSLT-defined attributes, it's necessary to put the variable reference inside curly braces to indicate that the value is an XPath expression that should be evaluated. In an XSLT attribute that expects an XPath expression, such as the `test` attribute of `xsl:if` or the `select` attribute of `xsl:copy-of`, this isn't necessary.

Variables and parameters can also be used to direct the flow of control in the stylesheet, as well as to select particular characteristics in the output. For example, a boolean parameter could be used to specify whether to include a table of contents, a list of figures, a list of tables, an index, and so forth. These could all be set as shown below.

```
<xsl:param name="include-table-of-contents" select="true()"/>
<xsl:param name="include-list-of-figures" select="false()"/>
<xsl:param name="include-list-of-tables" select="false()"/>
<xsl:param name="include-index" select="true()"/>
```

When processing the book the stylesheet would use the values of these variables to determine whether or not to call particular templates.

```
<xsl:template match="book">
  <xsl:if test="$include-table-of-contents">
    <xsl:call-template name="make-table-of-contents"/>
  </xsl:if>
  <xsl:if test="$include-list-of-figures">
    <xsl:call-template name="make-list-of-figures"/>
  </xsl:if>
  <xsl:if test="$include-list-of-tables">
    <xsl:call-template name="make-list-of-tables"/>
  </xsl:if>
  <xsl:if test="$include-index">
    <xsl:call-template name="generate-index"/>
  </xsl:if>
</xsl:template>
```

Variables and parameters enable customizers to make small changes to the final output without modifying or overriding the templates, a much more difficult operation. XSLT stylesheets are programs, and they require the skills of a programmer to write. If you give typical print designers an XSLT stylesheet and ask them to change it to suit their needs, you're lucky if the results are well-formed, much less correct. However, such designers are normally capable of selecting the names and sizes of fonts, the number of columns, the widths of pages, and so on. In fact, they can probably do a much more attractive job of that than the typical programmer can. Each field has its own strengths. The XSLT programmer's task is to enable the designer to do his or her job without requiring XSLT expertise.

There are several ways the values of a top-level variable or a parameter can be adjusted.

- The user can edit the stylesheet directly to type in a new value of the `select` attribute that sets the variable or parameter.
- An `xsl:variable` or `xsl:param` element inside a template can override the value of the global variable or parameter with the same name.
- When stylesheet A imports stylesheet B, the definitions in the importing stylesheet A take precedence over the definitions in the imported stylesheet B.

- Parameters (but not variables) can be modified from the environment that invokes the stylesheet, for instance, by a command line flag or an API call.

Which of these is used to customize a stylesheet depends on who is doing the customizing and why. For instance, developers who are importing the stylesheet into their own stylesheets would be likely to simply override a value with their own `xsl:param` element. However, people who are applying your stylesheet to their own documents might just set command line flags.

Note *A variable or a parameter can be shadowed by a different binding, but it cannot be changed. That is, its value is fixed. This sounds a little strange. After all, a variable that can't change is more like a constant. The terminology here is taken more from the mathematical notion of a variable than the common programming notion of a variable.*

Large stylesheets can and should collect related variable definitions into their own files, which can be imported or included from the master stylesheets. This centralizes them in one place where any customizer can look to adjust the output. This is similar to using a .h header file in C.

A parameter (but not a variable) can be adjusted when the stylesheet is invoked from the environment. Exactly how this is done varies from processor to processor. However, it's generally accomplished via a system property or command line argument passed to the processor when invoking it. For example, in xsltproc the `--stringparam` flag is followed by the name and the value of the parameter to set. I use xsltproc to generate the RSS feeds for my Cafe au Lait and Cafe con Leche web sites. The default parameter values are set up for Cafe con Leche as follows.

```
<xsl:param name="url">http://www.cafeconleche.org/
</xsl:param>
<xsl:param name="sitename">Cafe con Leche</xsl:param>
```

However, I can use the same stylesheet for Cafe au Lait by passing the appropriate command line options from the cron job that drives the transform.

```
xsltproc cafe.xsl http://www.cafeconleche.org/
xsltproc --stringparam url http://www.cafeaulait.org/
```

```
--stringparam sitename "Cafe au Lait"
cafe.xsl http://www.cafeaulait.org/
```

In this case, the parameter is used to feed in external information (the name and base URL of the site) that is not available in the documents themselves.

In an XSLT API, there will normally be a method call for setting the values of the parameters before using the stylesheet. For instance, in TrAX the `javax.xml.transform.Transformer` class has `setParameter()` and `getParameter()` methods.

```
transformer.setParameter("url", "http://www.cafeaulait.org/");
transformer.setParameter("sitename", "Cafe au Lait");
```

The exact API calls or command line options will vary from one processor to the next. However they're set, though, external values take precedence over the local definitions in the stylesheet. Whether set internally or externally, using parameters instead of hard-coded values makes stylesheets much more maintainable and extensible.

Item 40   Avoid Vendor Lock-In

Although XML is a nonproprietary, vendor-independent technology, it doesn't have to stay that way. Be extremely cautious of any tool that would tie you to one vendor's systems. In some cases the lock-in is obvious. For instance, one vendor went so far as to patent its DTDs. That's easy to avoid. But sometimes the lock-in is less obvious. The real danger is complexity. If the system is so complex that you cannot imagine writing your own tools to process the documents it uses, avoid it. It's one thing to buy a useful tool from a vendor that will save a you a couple of weeks of programmer time. It's a completely different thing to depend on a system that you couldn't reimplement given a couple of years of expert developer time.

Things to watch out for include the following.

- Opaque, binary data used in place of marked-up text. Base64 encoding a proprietary, undocumented binary format and then stuffing it between two tags does not make it XML. Structure should be indicated by tag names.

- Overabbreviated, unclear element and attribute names like `F17354` and `grgyt`. Tag names should be obviously related to what they contain.

- Binary encodings of XML that can't be processed with open tools, most especially those that rely on patented algorithms.

- APIs that try to shield developers from the raw XML, especially when the API becomes the spec. The web services space is rife with these. Specifications for web services need to be defined in terms of the XML transmitted, not the methods called.

- Products that focus on the Infoset to the exclusion of real XML. The Infoset is a useful vocabulary for talking about XML, but it is not XML. The only interoperable form of XML is Unicode in angle brackets. All transmissions between different systems should take place as real XML text.

- Alternate serializations of XML. Once again, there is no XML other than Unicode in angle brackets. The Unicode in angle brackets can be hidden in different forms such as raw ASCII text files, gzipped data, or database fields. However, it always comes back to Unicode characters in a row. Beware of formats that attempt to replace rather than encode Unicode characters in a row.

Make sure the XML that your tools emit is standards-compliant, well-formed XML 1.0. At one time or another various vendors have published formats and tools that attempt to "fix" things they feel are broken in XML. For instance, some early Microsoft formats such as CDF were case-insensitive and used XML declarations like this:

```
<?XML version="1.0"?>
```

Needless to say, this could only be parsed by Microsoft's parser, not by everybody else's. For the most part the market has resoundingly rejected such fundamental nonconformance, so you don't have to worry a lot about it today. Nonetheless, in the last month alone I've seen two different companies pushing their own nonstandard and noninteroperable (with each other or anybody else) variants of XML. Worse yet, they're labeling their tools as XML tools and obscuring the difference between what they're doing and real XML. Casual XML users could easily be fooled into thinking that what they're buying from these companies makes them XML-compliant, even though it won't work with any of the other products on the market. Always remember that well-formed Unicode in angle brackets is the absolute minimum for XML. Don't accept any tool that tries to get away with less.

Variations of this approach take a different, less obvious path. Schema languages can be changed from standard, vendor-independent languages such as DTDs, the W3C XML Schema Language, or RELAX NG to proprietary systems like Microsoft's XML Data Reduced (XDR) or the patented XLinkIt. Don't accept languages based on such owned foundations. Insist on nonproprietary schema languages as the normative definitions of any XML application you use.

Stylesheet languages have also been subject to vendor efforts to embrace and extend them in ways that are incompatible with the pure language. The worst offender here is Microsoft's XSLT implementation. Internet Explorer 5 shipped with an XSLT engine that partially implemented an early working draft of XSL. At the time this was understandable because there wasn't anything better, although if nothing else it was a serious error in judgment to ship software based on such an early, rapidly changing draft specification. However, Microsoft continued to ship this nonconformant engine in later versions of Internet Explorer even after the final version of XSLT was available. The company eventually wrote a parser and transformer that did implement the specification. However, Microsoft then configured the installer so that it did not actually replace the original, broken transformer. Worst of all, even after shipping a conformant engine, the company's web sites and trainers continued to evangelize and teach the old, experimental version of XSLT that was never implemented by anyone other than Microsoft.

Microsoft finally shipped a mostly conformant version of Internet Explorer in version 6, but even the allegedly conformant IE6 still has numerous standards compliance issues, among them those listed below.

- Internet Explorer only recognizes the phantom MIME type text/xsl, not standard types like text/xml and application/xml+xslt. No text/xsl MIME type has been or is likely to be registered with the IANA. The XSLT specifications are clear that you should use text/xml or application/xml to identify XSLT stylesheets in xml-stylesheet processing instructions until the more specific MIME type application/xml+xslt has completed the registration process.
- By default, the MSXML parser IE uses throws away all white-space-only nodes before transforming. Microsoft has made the jesuitical argument that this takes place during parsing and tree construction

rather than during transformation, so it's allowed by the specification. The same argument applies equally to the claim that it's OK to turn all text nodes in the document to "All work and no play makes Jack a dull boy." I don't buy it.

Worst of all, the latest versions of IE6 and MSXML still accept the old, broken half XSLT beta/half meat byproduct syntax from IE5, thus continuing to foist this monstrosity on the world.

Perhaps the least offensive effort to "embrace and extend" the independent standards is in the area of APIs. XML deliberately does not define a standard data model or API. Interoperability comes through shared document syntax, not through a common API or binary representation. Of course, we do need APIs to process XML; but each developer is free to choose the one that works best for him or her. I may use JDOM and you may use SAX, but we can still understand each other as long as we pass XML back and forth. However, as Item 31 indicates, using a standard API like SAX or DOM that's implemented by many parsers does make your code more portable and allow you to switch vendors as necessary or convenient.

Another common way to attempt to lock you in to particular tool sets is to hide the XML behind an apparently simple API. This is particularly common in the web services world. As long as the API works, and as long as you stick with the same vendor, you may not notice a problem. However, if you try to migrate off that vendor's tools or introduce a new platform that the vendor doesn't support, you may find that it's not so easy to get your data out of the proprietary system. Here a lot depends on just how well the vendor has documented all its different XML formats. If it has, that's not such a big deal. If it hasn't, the migration process will be considerably more challenging. You might even discover that the vendor has chosen to encode key information in binary data, all wrapped up in a nice Base64 package, and hasn't told you anything about the format of that binary data. Before committing to an API, always inspect the formats it generates and the documentation for those formats. Make sure you're not limited to that one library for producing and consuming the data.

XML is designed for openness. It is a text-based format because text is less opaque and more interoperable than binary formats. In practice XML data is far easier to reverse engineer, exchange, and export than almost any traditional data format. Needless to say, this is good news for users but bad news for companies that have built business models around locking data up into their proprietary formats. Some of these companies are trying to stuff the XML genie back into proprietary bottles. Fortunately, there are many more genuinely open tools for working with XML than closed ones. Be a little skeptical when evaluating vendor hype, especially if the vendor is promising to save you from all the evils of XML, and you should be fine.

Item 41   Hang On to Your Relational Database

Over the years I've been teaching XML, I've noticed that one perennial question is whether XML somehow replaces relational databases. Typically, this question is asked by IT managers who've had one too many Oracle salespersons visit the company and hoist them up by the toenails to see how much money they can shake out of their pockets. Often, the question is posed with an almost pleading tone, "Please tell me I can finally throw away my relational database. Please."

Sadly, for these managers the answer is no, they cannot throw away their relational database. (They may well be able to replace the ridiculously expensive Oracle with the ridiculously cheap MySQL or PostgreSQL, but that's a subject for another book.) XML is not a database. It was never meant to be a database. It is never going to be a database. Relational databases are proven technology with more than 20 years of implementation experience. They are solid, stable, useful products. They are not going away. XML is a very useful technology for moving data between different databases or between databases and other programs. However, it is not itself a database. Don't use it like one.

First of all, relational databases are based on very clear, well-understood mathematical principles. Storing all data in normalized tables makes for very robust (if sometimes slow) systems. Of course, not all the world's data fits neatly into rows and columns. A list of transactions made against a bank account with dates and amounts fits very easily into a table. The bank's privacy policy for that account does not. Narrative documents such as privacy policies, mortgage contracts, annual reports, deposit instructions, and more really don't look anything like tables. This is where XML enters the picture and where a native XML database that does understand the structure of XML documents might come in handy.

Secondly, while the interface to a relational database is based on a mathematical abstraction of fields and tables, the underlying physical storage almost certainly is not. Relational databases keep indexes on the data, store the same data in multiple places, cache particular results, and perform a host of other tricks to attempt to optimize performance. Big iron databases like Oracle even go so far as to manage their own disk partitions to try to eke out every last nanosecond of performance. XML documents do none of this. The physical storage model of an XML document is very close to the mental model most developers have of it, whether event-based like SAX or tree-based like DOM. No effort is spent on optimization. Thus storing all your data inside XML documents instead of in a relational database is almost certainly going to kill performance on an application of any reasonable size.

All of that having been said, however, there are still many uses for which XML makes a lot of sense in the database world. XML is not a database, but it is a wonderful format for exchanging data between different databases, or between databases and nondatabase systems. By 2003 most major database software ranging from MySQL to FileMaker Pro to Microsoft SQL Server to Oracle have functionality for importing and exporting XML documents. There are no standards in this arena, so how you do it depends heavily on which database you've chosen. For example, FileMaker Pro developers write XSLT stylesheets that transform to and from a native FileMaker syntax to whatever format the developer is receiving (on input) or wants to produce (on output). Other systems rely on schemas or custom mapping files to match XML data to relational fields and records.

This all works very well as long as the XML documents being stored contain the same sort of data that has traditionally gone into relational databases: accounts receivable, passenger manifests, invoices, student records, sales statistics, and so on. It begins to break down as soon as you start trying to store ad copy, privacy policies, legal briefs, street maps, assembly diagrams, document schemas, sixteenth-century Italian love poetry, and other kinds of things that are written in XML but that have not traditionally been stored in relational databases.

If you have large collections of narrative or other semistructured data in XML (or in a format that can easily be moved to XML), it may be time to consider putting that data in a native XML database. This is a database management system in which the fundamental structure is an XML document rather than a table. The mathematics of XML database systems aren't as formal or as well understood as the mathematics of relational databases, and the standards are just beginning to be developed. (The query language is a working draft and does not include any update, insert, or delete functionality, all of which vendors have to invent their own extensions for.) Still, native XML databases do fit some problems that relational databases don't.

Since native XML databases are very bleeding edge technology, there's a lot of research, experimentation, and hype in the field. No two products in this space work as similarly as do any two SQL databases. Nonetheless, some order is beginning to congeal from the primordial chaos, and I can thus make a few assertions about the characteristics of most native XML databases, which I will do by analogy with the more familiar relational systems.

- A relational database contains tables of records. An XML database contains collections of documents.
- All the records in a table have the same schema. All the XML documents in a collection have the same DTD (maybe). This is perhaps the area in which different systems differ the most. Some databases use DTDs. Some use the W3C XML Schema Language. Some allow merely well-formed documents with no schema of any type. Others do not. Some require that all documents in a collection have the same structure, valid or not. Others do not.
- A relational record is an unordered list of named values. An XML document is an ordered tree of named elements.
- A SQL query returns an unordered set of records. An XQuery returns an ordered sequence of nodes.

If you dig deeper into how these databases implement storage and optimize queries, you will find even more differences both with each other and with traditional relational databases. However, one very good characteristic that the native XML databases have adopted wholeheartedly from the relational world is the separation of the data model from the physical model. Although the data model and query language is not standardized across XML databases as it is with SQL databases, every XML database does separate its data model and query language from its physical model. You do not need to directly concern yourself with the physical model the XML database uses, only indirectly as it impacts performance.

I do not suggest using a native XML database for data that does fit well into tabular structures. In practice, relational databases like Oracle, FileMaker Pro, and MySQL are far more reliable, much better supported, and easier to use and administer; and they perform far better than a typical native XML database. More than anything else this reflects the relative maturity of relational databases (more than 20 years) and native XML databases (less than 5 years). One day native XML databases may be as robust, reliable, and fast as relational databases, but that day is not today. In the meantime, however, there are some problems that don't fit the relational model very well, and for these applications a native XML database may be appropriate. These situations include the following:

- Content management systems for newspapers and magazines
- Page-based, written web sites with lots of static, narrative content
- A contracts and briefs database for a law firm
- Patient records in a doctor's office
- The dissertations submitted by Ph.D. candidates at a university
- Software documentation and specifications, including UML diagrams

Anywhere you see people storing data as folders full of Word documents, static HTML pages, or some equivalent, you're looking at an opportunity for a native XML database.

I know there are a few relational database aficionados among my readers who are right now jumping up and shouting, "But an RDBMS can do all those things!"—and they're right. An RDBMS can do these things too. But a hammer can pound a screw into wood. That doesn't make it a good idea, nor does it work nearly as effectively as a screwdriver. Not all of the world's data is a table (or an object, or a tree). Spending too much time with one very powerful tool like an RDBMS tends to cause a kind of developer myopia that makes the relational database seem like the right tool for all tasks. But there is no universal tool. Use relational databases for what they're good for, and use XML for what it's good for. It's easy to connect them to each other as necessary. Don't try to make either one do everything.

Item 42   Document Namespaces with RDDL

All the warnings in the namespace specification that there is not necessarily anything at the end of a namespace URL have not stopped people from typing namespace URLs into their browser location bars and clicking the Go button. If you don't want your error logs filling up with requests for nonexistent documents, you need to put something there. The right thing to put there is a Resource Directory Description Language (RDDL) document. This provides human-readable XHTML documentation for people and machine-readable XLinks for software.

For example, consider the MegaBank Statement Markup Language (MBSML) introduced in Item 5. This was specified as being in the namespace http://namespaces.megabank.com/statement. Assuming you or the company you work for already owns megabank.com (if you don't, what are you doing defining namespaces in that domain?), the first step is to set up a web server at namespaces.megabank.com if one doesn't already exist. This is normally not a high-volume site (at least compared to the server that lets customers check credit card balances, for example), so a cheap Linux box or a virtual host on an existing server will likely be more than sufficient.

The next step is to put a page at the URL http://namespaces.megabank. com/statement. Initially, almost anything that stops your error logs from filling up is sufficient. For example, here's an incredibly simple page I adapted from the one the W3C puts at the XSLT namespace URI.

```
<html>
<head>
  <title> MegaBank Statement Markup Language </title>
</head>
<body>
<p>
This is the XML namespace for the <a
href="http://developer.megabank.com/xml/">MegaBank Statement
Markup Language</a>.
</p>
<hr />
<address>
  <a href="mailto:webmaster@megabank.com">Webmaster</a>
</address>
</body>
</html>
```

That's good enough to start, but longer term you'd like something that provides a little more information. There are many things you might reasonably expect to find at the end of a namespace URL:

- Schemas
- DTDs
- Stylesheets
- Processing software
- Documentation

Indeed, any given application might have several of each of these. It is precisely this plethora of possibilities for the end of a namespace URL that led the W3C XML Working Group to punt on the issue of exactly what to put there. Unfortunately, their nondecision just increased the confusion as novice XML developers peppered xml-dev and other mailing lists with questions about how to use XSLT on a computer that wasn't connected to the Internet and thus couldn't load http://www.w3.org/1999/XSL/Transform. After a couple of years of this, Tim Bray and Jonathan Borden decided that it might actually make sense to put a document at the end of a namespace URL, and they invented RDDL as the format for such documents.

RDDL solves the question of what to put at the end of a namespace URL by introducing an additional layer of indirection. A RDDL document is not a specification for the namespace. It is not a schema for the namespace. It is not a stylesheet for documents in the namespace. It is not software for processing content from that namespace. Instead, it is a directory pointing to any, some, or all of these things, neatly wrapped up inside well-formed and valid strict modular XHTML that browsers can display to end users.

The minimal RDDL document is just an XHTML document whose document type declaration points to the RDDL DTD instead of the normal XHTML DTD and whose root element also declares the RDDL and XLink namespaces. (In fact, you can even leave out the document type declaration if you want to.)

```
<!DOCTYPE html PUBLIC "-//XML-DEV//DTD XHTML RDDL 1.0//EN"
                  "http://www.rddl.org/rddl-xhtml.dtd">
<html xmlns="http://www.w3.org/1999/xhtml"
      xmlns:xlink="http://www.w3.org/1999/xlink"
      xmlns:rddl="http://www.rddl.org/">
<head>
  <title> MegaBank Statement Markup Language (MBSML) </title>
</head>
<p>
This is the XML namespace for the <a
href="http://developer.megabank.com/xml/">MegaBank Statement
```

```
Markup Language</a>.
</p>
<hr />
<address>
  <a href="mailto:webmaster@megabank.com">Webmaster</a>
</address>
</body>
</html>
```

You can put absolutely any valid strict XHTML markup you care to use in the RDDL document: unordered lists, tables, images, objects, headings, hypertext links, and so on. All of this is normally designed so that the page will look good in a browser to a human reader. Generally, you want to give people reading the document a brief summary of the application that uses the namespace or tell them where they can go to learn everything they need to know.

So far this is nothing you couldn't do with HTML. What RDDL brings to the table is one additional element, which is not shown to human readers but which does provide helpful hints to automated software. This element has the local name resource and lives in the RDDL namespace (http://www.rddl.org/). Each `rddl:resource` element is a simple XLink that points to some related resource: a schema, a stylesheet, a specification, and so on. For example, here's a `rddl:resource` element that locates the main DTD for MBSML.

```
<rddl:resource xlink:type="simple"
   xlink:href="http://developer.megabank.com/xml/mbsml.dtd" />
```

This `rddl:resource` element can be placed in the RDDL document anywhere a `div` or other block-level element may appear. Browsers ignore any tags they don't recognize. Consequently, this has no effect on the content displayed to a person. However, RDDL-aware software looking for these related resources can extract just the `rddl:resource` elements and ignore everything else.

Sometimes it is convenient to include some content inside the `rddl:resource` element. As long as this is normal well-formed XHTML that's not a problem. For example, the following `rddl:resource` element contains both XLinks for the automated processors and a plain-vanilla HTML link with descriptive text for humans.

```
<rddl:resource xlink:type="simple"
  xlink:href="http://developer.megabank.com/xml/mbsml.dtd">
  <p>
  The MegaBank Statement Markup Language has a non-normative
  <a href="http://developer.megabank.com/dtds/mbsml.dtd">DTD</a>
  for use with parsers that don't support schemas. However,
  in the event of a conflict between the DTD and the schema,
  the schema is authoritative.
  </p>
</rddl:resource>
```

A `rddl:resource` element can even contain another `rddl:resource` element. Such nested `rddl:resource` elements have no special relationship to each other. Each is treated on its own. In essence, all the information needed to process any one `rddl:resource` element is contained completely within the start-tag.

Natures

While a human may be able to read the explanatory text in order to figure out which links point to schemas and which links point to stylesheets, software needs somewhat more formal hints to ensure that a validator doesn't try to validate a document against a stylesheet or that a browser doesn't try to format a document as described by a DTD. To this end, the `xlink:role` attribute may contain a URL that indicates the nature of the resource likely to be found at the other end of the simple link. For example, this `rddl:resource` element locates a W3C XML Schema Language schema:

```
<rddl:resource xlink:type="simple"
    xlink:href="http://developer.megabank.com/xml/mbsml.xsd"
    xlink:role="http://www.w3.org/2001/XMLSchema" />
```

This `rddl:resource` element locates a DTD:

```
<rddl:resource xlink:type="simple"
    xlink:href="http://developer.megabank.com/xml/mbsml.dtd"
    xlink:role="http://www.isi.edu/in-
notes/iana/assignments/media-types/application/xml-dtd"
  />
```

This `rddl:resource` element locates a CSS stylesheet:

```
<rddl:resource xlink:type="simple"
    xlink:href="http://developer.megabank.com/xml/mbsml.xsd"
    xlink:role="http://www.isi.edu/in
-notes/iana/assignments/media-types/text/css" />
```

As in these examples, most nature URIs are derived from either XML namespace URLs or MIME media type URLs. The RDDL specification

Table 42–1 | RDDL Natures

URI	Nature
http://www.isi.edu/in-notes/iana/assignments/media-types/text/css	CSS stylesheet
http://www.isi.edu/in-notes/iana/assignments/media-types/application/xml-dtd	DTD
http://www.rddl.org/natures#mailbox	Mailbox
http://www.w3.org/TR/html4/	HTML 4 document
http://www.w3.org/TR/html4/strict	Strict HTML 4 document
http://www.w3.org/TR/html4/transitional	HTML 4 transitional document
http://www.w3.org/TR/html4/frameset	HTML 4 Frameset document
http://www.w3.org/1999/xhtml	XHTML document
http://www.w3.org/TR/xhtml1/DTD/xhtml1-strict	XHTML 1.0 strict document
http://www.w3.org/TR/xhtml1/DTD/xhtml1-transitional	XHTML 1.0 transitional document
http://www.w3.org/2000/01/rdf-schema#	Resource Description Framework Schema[a]
http://www.w3.org/2000/10/XMLSchema	XML Schema module
http://www.xml.gr.jp/relax	RELAX schema[b]
http://www.xml.gr.jp/xmlns/relaxCore	RELAX core grammar
http://www.xml.gr.jp/xmlns/relaxNamespace	RELAX namespace grammar
http://www.ascc.net/xml/schematron	Schematron schema
http://www.rddl.org/natures#SOCAT	An OASIS Open Catalog[c]
http://www.w3.org/TR/REC-xml.html#dt-chardata	XML character data
http://www.w3.org/TR/REC-xml.html#dt-escape	Escaped XML text
http://www.w3.org/TR/REC-xml.html#dt-unparsed	Unparsed binary data
http://www.ietf.org/rfc/rfc2026.txt	An IETF RFC
http://www.iso.ch/	An ISO standard

[a] Not the same thing as a W3C XML Schema Language schema.
[b] RELAX is a precursor to RELAX NG. A RELAX NG nature is a likely candidate for the future.
[c] See Item 47.

currently defines the 22 roles listed in Table 42–1. However, new ones are added regularly; you are free to invent and use your own. Most software will silently ignore any `rddl:resource` elements with unfamiliar natures.

Purposes

Natures are not unique. An XML application in a single namespace may have several schemas, even in one schema language. It may have more than one DTD. (XHTML 1.0 has three.) The schema or DTD may be broken up into many modules. Stylesheets, software, documentation, and other related resources may be even more diverse. The specific kinds of resources that are related to a namespace can be further subdivided by purpose. A URI identifying the purpose is included in the `rddl:resource` element's `xlink:arcrole` attribute. For example, here are three different `rddl:resource` elements describing different resources related to MBSML.

```
<rddl:resource xlink:type="simple"
    xlink:href="http://developer.megabank.com/xml/spec.html"
    xlink:role="http://www.w3.org/TR/html4/"
    xlink:arcrole
      ="http://www.rddl.org/purposes#normative-reference"
>
  <p>
  The
  <a href="http://developer.megabank.com/xml/spec.html">MegaBank
  Statement Markup Language Specification 1.0</a>
  </p>
</rddl:resource>
<rddl:resource xlink:type="simple"
    xlink:href="http://developer.megabank.com/xml/tutorial.html"
    xlink:role="http://www.w3.org/TR/html4/"
    xlink:arcrole
      ="http://www.rddl.org/purposes#non-normative-reference"
>
  <p>
    Alan Williams has written a nice
    <a href="http://developer.megabank.com/xml/tutorial.html">
    tutorial</a> describing the MegaBank Statement Markup
    Language.
  </p>
```

```
</rddl:resource>
<rddl:resource xlink:type="simple"
    xlink:href
      ="http://developer.megabank.com/xml/canonicalization.html"
    xlink:role="http://www.w3.org/TR/html4/"
    xlink:arcrole="http://www.rddl.org/purposes#canonicalization"
>
  <p>
    Before comparing documents, it is necessary to
    <a href=
    "http://developer.megabank.com/xml/canonicalization.html">
    canonicalize</a> them.
  </p>
</rddl:resource>
```

All three resources have the same nature (HTML 4.0 document). However, they have different purposes. The first refers to the normative specification of MBSML. The second refers to a non-normative tutorial. The third points to a description of a canonicalization algorithm for MBSML documents.

Purposes tend to be application specific. Table 42–2 lists those purposes that have been identified.

Table 42–2 | RDDL Purposes

URI	Purpose
http://www.rddl.org/purposes#validation	DTD validation
http://www.rddl.org/purposes#schema-validation	Schema validation
http://www.rddl.org/purposes#module	DTD module
http://www.rddl.org/purposes#schema-module	Schema module
http://www.rddl.org/purposes#entities	Entity definition
http://www.rddl.org/purposes#notations	Notation definition
http://www.rddl.org/purposes#software-module	Software module
http://www.rddl.org/purposes#software-package	Software package
http://www.rddl.org/purposes#software-project	Software project
http://www.rddl.org/purposes#JAR	Java .jar file
http://www.rddl.org/purposes#software-directory	Software directory
http://www.rddl.org/purposes#reference	Documentation

Table 42–2 | *continued*

URI	Purpose
http://www.rddl.org/purposes#normative-reference	Authoritative documentation
http://www.rddl.org/purposes#non-normative-reference	Nonauthoritative documentation
http://www.rddl.org/purposes#prior-version	A prior version
http://www.rddl.org/purposes#definition	Definition
http://www.rddl.org/purposes#icon	Icon
http://www.rddl.org/purposes#alternate	An alternate form
http://www.rddl.org/purposes#canonicalization	A canonicalization algorithm
http://www.rddl.org/purposes#directory	Another RDDL document
http://www.rddl.org/purposes#target	The namespace URL this document describes

Natures, purposes, and links together provide enough information for many processes to do something useful with a namespace URL, instead of merely using it as an opaque identifier. Even more importantly, putting HTML at the end of namespace URLs gives us curious humans something plausible to look at when we inevitably type the namespace URLs into web browsers.

Item 43   Preprocess XSLT on the Server Side

One of the original goals of XML was to create "SGML for the Web" to allow markup with arbitrary vocabularies to be served to web browsers. To a large extent, this goal has not been met. While some of the latest versions of web browsers support full XML display, many do not; and I am not one who believes that it's acceptable to throw away even 1% of your potential readers just because the web designers think they need some cool new feature that's only available in Internet Exploder 8.0. In 2003, I know people still using Netscape 1 and Netscape 2. Recently I even spent a few minutes surfing with MacWeb. (Remember that one, old-timers?) With proper attention to design, it's still possible to serve these readers well, as long as you focus on serving readers instead of on making the web site look cool. Surprisingly, it is possible to serve old browsers XML, as long as you don't let them know that's what you're doing.

XML served over the Web requires a stylesheet to teach the browser how to format the content it has received. CSS works on the client side, at least as well as anything does. However, it really requires a very modern web browser: Internet Explorer 6, Netscape 6, Mozilla 1.0, Safari 1.0, or Opera 4 or later. This may be plausible in an intranet environment, but it just doesn't fly on the public Internet.

Browser support for XSLT is even more limited (and that's being polite). Internet Explorer 5.0 and 5.5 do not support XSLT, Microsoft's claims to the contrary notwithstanding. Instead they support something I like to call (with apologies to Douglas Adams) a language almost, but not quite, entirely unlike XSLT. Internet Explorer 6.0 does support real XSLT but it still has some nasty bugs. Netscape 4.x and earlier have no support for XSLT. Netscape 6.0 and later and Mozilla do support XSLT, but for various technical reasons it's extremely hard to convince Netscape/Mozilla to actually use an XSLT stylesheet. (It's roughly on a par with convincing a Vogon not to knock your planet down for an interstellar byway.) Opera, Konqueror, Safari, Lynx, and most other browsers don't even attempt to support XSLT.

Fortunately, therefore, it's not very hard to convince the web server to do the transformation work for you. Most XSLT engines including Saxon and Xalan provide servlets that automatically transform XML documents to HTML documents according to an XSLT stylesheet. By using these, you can send clients plain-vanilla HTML that can be read by web browsers going back to Mosaic 1.0. Many application servers such as Apache Cocoon also have built-in support for this process. You can post XML documents on the web server, but the clients only see HTML. With reasonable caching, it's not even that big of a performance hit. (Without caching, this can be a nasty performance hit. Worst case scenario: Some naïve, custom solutions I've seen load an entire Java virtual machine from scratch every time a page is requested. However, the major implementations of server-side transformation aren't nearly this stupid.)

Servlet-Based Solutions

If a servlet engine such as Tomcat or Jetty is already running on the web server, the simplest way to add XSLT support is by using one of the prewritten servlets. The downside to this is that you can't always easily map existing URLs and documents into such a system, but this approach does let you put up new content in new directories very quickly.

Saxon

Michael Kay's Saxon includes a simple servlet in its samples directory that performs basic transformations. This isn't really intended as a full-blown, server-side transformation engine—just a little code to show you how to roll your own. Still it's impressively small and should work well with any servlet container such as Tomcat or JRun. Once you've installed this servlet (or a customized version of it) on your server, you'll be able to load XML documents through URLs that look like this:

> http://www.example.com/servlets/SaxonServlet?source=doc.xml&
> style=sheet.xsl

The `source` parameter is a URL pointing to the XML document. The `style` parameter is a URL pointing to the stylesheet to use for the transformation. Both are relative to the location of the servlet context. However, with a little custom coding, it's easy to select a different base directory for either or both.

Note *Internet Explorer has a nasty habit of relying on the last few letters of the URL to determine the MIME type. When IE sees a URL ending in .xml or .xsl, even in the query string, it treats the result as XML, regardless of what the MIME type actually is. You can add an unused parameter to the query string to avoid this, as demonstrated below.*

http://www.example.com/servlets/SaxonServlet?source=doc.xml&
style=sheet.xsl&IE=braindamage

When the user requests such a URL, the servlet calls TrAX to transform the input document according to the instructions in the stylesheet and then sends the result to the client browser. The output document is streamed to the client as quickly as possible. The entire transformation does not need to be complete before the first byte of data is sent (though XSLT is really not designed for streaming, and generally quite a bit of work will need to be done before the first byte is sent, just not all of the work).

This servlet is half caching: It holds onto the compiled stylesheet so it doesn't have to reparse it every time it's used. Furthermore, it's thread safe so the same servlet and stylesheet can be used for multiple requests simultaneously. However, it does not store the transformed document. Thus a file must be read from disk and the transformation applied every time the document is requested. Since most web servers do not cache documents loaded with query strings, this can be a performance issue on a high-volume server. If you use this servlet for important work, one of the first things you should probably add is an output cache that holds the transformed document. If the server has a lot of RAM and serves fairly small documents, you may want to store them in memory. Otherwise, you can save them in a temporary directory somewhere on the disk, perhaps saving only the most frequently requested files.

Xalan

Xalan-J includes several sample servlets that can process XSLT on the server side. These include a servlet that reads an `xml-stylesheet` processing instruction in the XML document to figure out which stylesheet to apply and a servlet that uses the CGI query string to set XSLT parameters. (See Item 39.) Xalan also provides a Java Server Page implementation. However, the Xalan samples don't do any caching, so they're even less suited to production use than the Saxon servlet.

In fact, since all these servlets are based on the generic TrAX API rather than on the specifics of Xalan or Saxon, you can use them with either processor or others. Since you'll normally want to customize the servlets anyway, you'll probably want to borrow code from all of them when it seems useful to you.

Apache

If, like over half of web masters, you're using the Apache HTTP server, you have numerous options for serving XML documents by transforming them through XSLT. These range from simple third-party modules like mod-xslt to full-blown application servers such as Cocoon and AxKit.

Cocoon started its life as a "simple servlet for XSL styling of XML content"[1] like the Saxon and Xalan servlets discussed previously. However, in the last few years it has become much more. Unlike the sample servlets discussed so far, the Cocoon application server is designed for production use. Cocoon can process every XML document a server serves, not just transforming it with XSLT but also merging in XIncludes, integrating the results of SQL queries, producing PDF output for printing, and more. It does quite a bit more than simple transformation, and it does it well.

---

1. "Understanding Apache Cocoon." Accessed online in June 2003 at http://xml.apache.org/cocoon/userdocs/concepts/index.html.

Cocoon is a bit on the heavyweight side. It requires a solid servlet engine like Apache Tomcat. However, if you want a very flexible system based on XML that integrates content from many different data sources to produce output in many different formats, Cocoon is going to make your day.

Perl programmers may prefer the Apache ASP module (http://www.apache-asp.org). Like Cocoon, this provides automatic XSLT transformation capabilities and a lot more. However, it's based on Perl and Microsoft's Active Server Pages syntax rather than Java and XML. Like Cocoon, it's probably overkill if all you want to do is automatically transform a few XML documents. mod_perl is required.

Another alternative for Perl programmers is Matt Sergeant's AxKit (http://axkit.org/), another application server based on Perl that provides on-the-fly XSLT conversion of XML documents. AxKit also uses a built-in Perl interpreter so Perl code can be embedded in XML documents and executed when the page is requested. (This is like Java Server Pages or Active Server Pages except Perl replaces Java and Visual Basic.) Like Cocoon, AxKit uses pipelines to feed the output of one process into the input of the next, ultimately producing output in a variety of formats that can be customized to particular clients. Thus you could send XML and XSLT to Internet Explorer 6, XML and CSS to Opera, and plain HTML to Netscape 4. Transformations and their outputs can be optionally cached to improve performance.

IIS

Microsoft's Internet Information Services (IIS) is the second most popular web server on the Net today. However, it's a distant second, and thus there aren't nearly as many high-quality options for adding XSLT support as there are for Apache.

Microsoft publishes an unsupported XSL ISAPI Filter. Like other ISAPI filters, it sits between the requests and the file system, making changes as documents are requested. In particular, it transforms documents according to an XSLT stylesheet before forwarding them to the client that made the request. It can cache stylesheets and apply different stylesheets to match the browser or XML document type. This filter also supports pipelining of stylesheets so that the output of one transformation can be become input to the next. It can also transform ASP-generated content, as well as static XML files. It's based on the MSXML parser/XSLT engine and thus shares that engine's bugs.

Michael Rothwell's published XSLTFilter (http://www.xsltfilter.com/), a shareware ISAPI filter that works with ASP on IIS, and is much more suitable for practical use than the XSL ISAPI Filter. It uses the Gnome project's libxslt processor, which is significantly more conformant to the XSLT specification than MSXML. XSLTFilter also has the useful ability to tidy up traditional malformed HTML and then transform it as well.

Whichever server you use, and whatever your favorite language is, chances are good there's a server-side XSLT plug-in for you. It is far more reliable to use this plug-in to transform the documents on the server where you control the environment than to send the XML document and stylesheet to the client and hope it has the necessary software to transform the document itself. Since XSLT is a fairly processor- and memory-intensive process, this can place a significant load on the server. However, since web pages are normally not too large you can support this with a beefy enough server. Do not let the disappointing lack of client-side XSLT support prevent you from using XML and separating content from presentation or taking advantage of the full power of XSLT.

Item 44   Serve XML+CSS to the Client

Given the limitations of the installed base of browsers, I'm not sure I would ever recommend serving XML directly rather than transforming on the server side. However, most current desktop web browsers do have reasonable support for direct display of XML documents with attached CSS stylesheets. The exact part of CSS any browser supports varies from one to the next, but browsers that include some reasonable level of CSS support include Internet Explorer 5.0 and later, Opera 4.0 and later, Netscape 6.0 and later, Mozilla, Safari, and Konqueror. Support for CSS is much better on the client side than support for XSLT. If you really want to serve XML documents directly to clients, CSS is the way to go.

Unlike HTML, XML does not normally include the CSS directly inside the document. Instead, a separate stylesheet is referenced by an `xml-stylesheet` processing instruction in the document prolog. This stylesheet has an `href` pseudo-attribute containing a relative or absolute URL pointing to the stylesheet and a `type` pseudo-attribute containing the MIME media type text/css. For example, an RSS document might begin like this:

```
<?xml version="1.0"?>
<?xml-stylesheet type="text/css" href="styles/rss.css"?>
<rss>

...
```

A recent web browser that loaded this document would know that the processing instruction means it should load and apply the CSS stylesheet found at the relative URL styles/rss.css. Most other applications would ignore the processing instruction.

You can even provide multiple stylesheets for different media by setting the optional `media` pseudo-attribute to one of these values:

- `screen`: typical computer monitors
- `tty`: monospaced text terminals such as xterm windows, DEC VT-100s, and IBM 3270s
- `tv`: televisions
- `projection`: wall and movie screen display
- `handheld`: PDAs, cell phones, and similar small devices
- `print`: paper that comes out of a laser, inkjet, or other printer
- `braille`: braille tactile feedback devices used by blind persons
- `aural`: speech synthesizers
- `all`: stylesheet appropriate for all devices

The browser should then pick the stylesheet that most closely matches its environment. For example, these instructions specify different stylesheets for printers, monitors, and speech synthesizers.

```
<?xml-stylesheet type="text/css" media="print"
                 href="styles/rss_print.css"?>
<?xml-stylesheet type="text/css" media="screen"
                 href="styles/rss_screen.css"?>
<?xml-stylesheet type="text/css" media="aural"
                 href="styles/rss_aural.css"?>
```

The `media` pseudo-attribute can also contain a comma-separated list of media types, in which case it applies to all listed media. For example, the `xml-stylesheet` processing instruction that follows applies to print, screen, and projection media.

```
<?xml-stylesheet type="text/css"
                 media="print, screen, projection"
                 href="styles/rss_main.css"?>
```

If more than one stylesheet is available for a given medium, all are applied, using the normal cascading rules of CSS to resolve conflicts. For example, faced with the following batch of stylesheet processing instructions, a web browser that was printing the XML document would use both `rss_main.css` and `rss_print.css` but not `rss_screen.css` or `rss_aural.css`.

```
<?xml-stylesheet type="text/css"
                 media="print, screen, projection"
                 href="styles/rss_main.css"?>
<?xml-stylesheet type="text/css" media="print"
                 href="styles/rss_print.css"?>
<?xml-stylesheet type="text/css" media="screen"
                 href="styles/rss_screen.css"?>
<?xml-stylesheet type="text/css" media="aural"
                 href="styles/rss_aural.css"?>
```

You can offer users a choice of different stylesheets by giving each stylesheet a `title` pseudo-attribute and an `alternate="yes"` pseudo-attribute. The browser should then indicate the choices to users and allow them to pick. For example, the following set of `xml-stylesheet` processing instructions offers different stylesheets for different web browsers.

```
<?xml-stylesheet type="text/css" title="Opera" alternate="yes"
                 href="styles/rss_opera.css"?>
<?xml-stylesheet type="text/css" title="Internet Explorer"
                 alternate="yes" href="styles/rss_ie.css"?>
<?xml-stylesheet type="text/css" title="Safari" alternate="yes"
                 href="styles/rss_khtml.css"?>
<?xml-stylesheet type="text/css" title="Konqueror" alternate="yes"
                 href="styles/rss_khtml.css"?>
<?xml-stylesheet type="text/css" title="Netscape" alternate="yes"
                 href="styles/rss_gecko.css"?>
<?xml-stylesheet type="text/css" title="Mozilla" alternate="yes"
                 href="styles/rss_gecko.css"?>
```

Alternate stylesheets are not loaded by default, even if the media matches. The user has to make a choice, in which case the choice replaces the default nonalternate stylesheet. Unfortunately, this is mostly theoretical. Current browsers have limited if any support for allowing users to pick a stylesheet from a list of alternates.

Since CSS does not include a transformation step, this only works when the content in the document is already pretty close to the content you want to show the user. The content should be essentially words in a row that can be straightforwardly divided into paragraphs, lists, and tables. The structures in the document are going to have to clearly map to the presentation. This works well for narrative structures such as DocBook and even for simple record-like structures such as RSS. It doesn't work nearly as well for more complex, data-heavy applications such as RDF or the MegaBank Statement Markup Language. Of course, applications like SVG and MathML that don't describe text at all may need a specialized renderer.

It is possible to use both XSLT and CSS. An XSLT stylesheet can transform a document into a form that's closer to the finished presentation, and then CSS can describe how the individual parts of that document are styled. This works especially well when you transform into HTML+CSS because all browsers handle that at least somewhat and most current browsers handle it quite well.

Item 45   Pick the Correct MIME Media Type

XML processors, web browsers, and many other tools rely on MIME media types to dispatch XML content to the correct processor. Just a few minutes ago I got an e-mail from an annoyed reader because I'd published some SVG pictures with the MIME type text/xml instead of application/xml+svg, so his SVG viewer couldn't read them. It's not hard to set the correct MIME type in most web servers. However, most existing servers ship with incorrect or incomplete MIME types, so you probably have to fix your server's configuration before publishing.

Pure, undifferentiated XML comes in two flavors:

1. text/xml
2. application/xml

If no more specific MIME type has been registered for an application with the IANA, you'll almost always want to use application/xml. The semantics of the text MIME type require that parsers and browsers treat a text/xml document as ASCII, *even if the encoding declaration or byte order mark says something different!* Not all parsers, browsers, and applications get this right. Nonetheless, some do, and they will have trouble if you serve anything except an ASCII document with this MIME type.

The application/xml MIME type makes no assertions about the character encoding of the XML document. When a parser receives an XML document with the MIME type application/xml, it will read the XML declaration and byte order mark to determine the encoding.

You can also add a charset field to the MIME type to indicate the character encoding of the document. For example,

- text/xml; charset="iso-8859-2"
- application/xml; charset="utf-16be"

In this case, the specified charset should take precedence over whatever the encoding declaration specifies. However, in practice you can't rely on parsers or browsers paying attention to this, so it's best to choose application/xml, leave the charset unspecified, and include an encoding declaration in the document itself. This also makes it much easier to use different encodings for different documents with the same file-name extension on the same server or in the same directory.

There are two similar MIME types for external parsed entities that are not complete XML documents:

1. text/xml-external-parsed-entity
2. application/xml-external-parsed-entity

The text/xml-external-parsed-entity MIME type has the same flaw as text/xml; that is, it asserts that the content is ASCII in the face of all evidence to the contrary. Use application/xml-external-parsed-entity instead.

The application/xml-dtd MIME type has been registered for use on document type definitions and fragments thereof.

As of mid-2003, a few MIME types, including those listed below, have been registered for specific XML applications:

- application/xhtml+xml for XHTML
- text/vnd.wap.wml for the Wireless Markup Language
- application/cnrp+xml for the Common Name Resolution Protocol
- application/beep+xml for the Blocks Extensible Exchange Protocol

More are anticipated in the future, including the following:

- application/mathml+xml for MathML
- application/xslt+xml for XSLT
- application/rdf+xml for RDF
- image/svg+xml for SVG

However, these are not yet official.

One MIME nontype deserves special comment. This is the mythical text/xsl used by Microsoft Internet Explorer to identify XSLT stylesheets in `xml-stylesheet` processing instructions, as shown below.

```
<?xml-stylesheet type="text/xsl" href="book.xsl"?>
```

Microsoft made up this type without consulting the rest of the community or attempting to use the well-established procedures for registering new MIME types. text/xsl is not endorsed by the W3C, the IETF, or the IANA. Microsoft has not attempted to register this type and does not seem likely to do so in the future. Use of this alleged MIME type in software, documents, HTTP headers, or anywhere else is incorrect. Eventually, application/xslt+xml will be officially registered to identify XSLT documents. In the meantime, you should use application/xml instead.

```
<?xml-stylesheet type="application/xml" href="book.xsl"?>
```

Currently Mozilla, Galeon, and Netscape recognize this, but Internet Explorer does not. This is a bug in Internet Explorer. Most other browsers do not support XSLT at all, so for them the question is moot.

If you're using the Apache web server, you can adjust the system default MIME type mappings for various file-name extensions in the mime.types file. This customarily resides in the $SERVER_ROOT/conf directory. For example, here's a list that duplicates the suggestions in this item.

```
application/xml                          xml rdf svg
application/xml-dtd                       dtd
application/xml+xhtml                     xhtml xhtm
application/xml-external-parsed-entity    ent
text/vnd.wap.wml                          wml
```

These are not the mappings Apache uses by default, so you'll also want to delete the mappings it does use that map these types to text/xml.

If you don't have root access to your web server, you can add these mappings in an `AddType` directive in the .htaccess file in the directory where the documents reside.

```
AddType application/xml                          xml rdf svg
AddType application/xml-dtd                      dtd
AddType application/xml+xhtml                    xhtml xhtm
AddType application/xml-external-parsed-entity   ent
AddType text/vnd.wap.wml                         wml
```

If you're using the Microsoft Internet Information Services (IIS) HTTP server, the GUI can map file-name extensions to individual MIME types. The exact instructions depend on which versions of IIS and Windows you have, but generally you'll open the Properties panel for the web site (in Windows 2000 you'll find this in the Computer Management section of the Administrative Tools control panel), select the HTTP Headers tab, and click File Types to bring up the File Types dialog. After you click New Type, a dialog box pops up in which you can enter the file-name extension and the MIME type to map it to. Figure 45–1 shows the various dialogs involved.

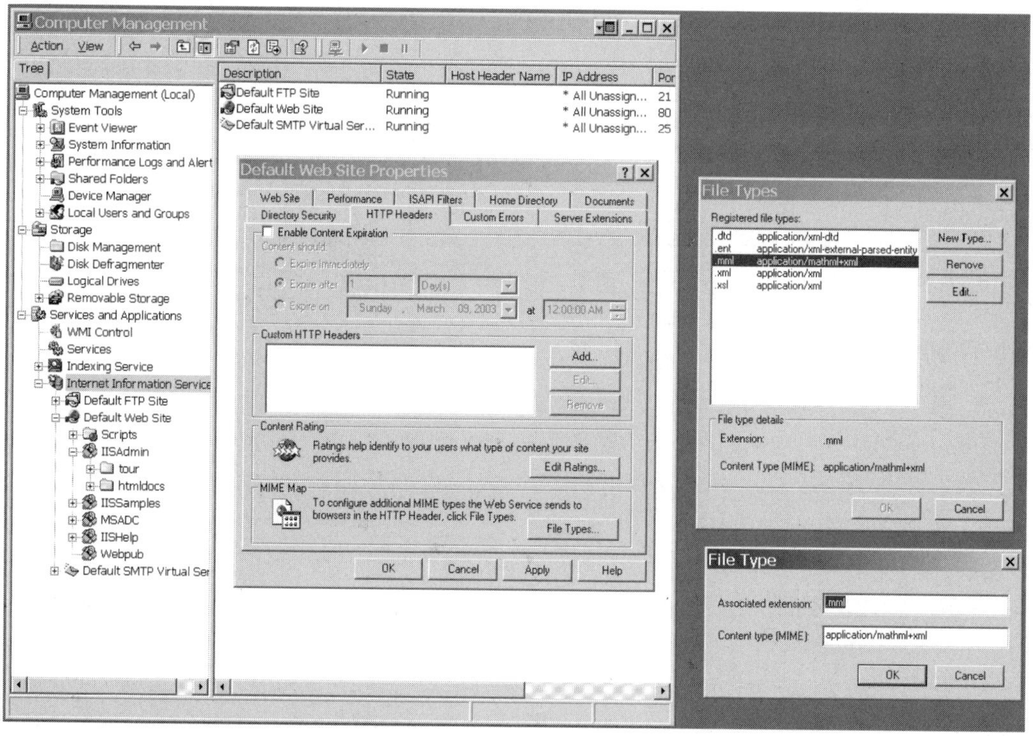

Figure 45–1 Adding a MIME Type to IIS on Windows 2000 Professional

For other web servers, consult the server documentation to determine how to change the MIME type mappings.

Whether you're using IIS, Apache, or something else, the main thing you need to remember is to reconfigure the MIME type mapping for XML as application/xml. The default is almost certainly text/xml, and this is almost never what you actually want. Using application/xml ensures that the encodings the documents declare for themselves will be respected.

Item 46   Tidy Up Your HTML

Converting HTML to XHTML often exposes and corrects bugs in web pages that you didn't realize were there, especially if you didn't test each page in several dozen browsers. It also makes it much easier to write software to search or modify the pages. And it makes it much easier to write software that processes the pages. For example, I converted my Cafe au Lait and Cafe con Leche web sites to XHTML solely so I could use a simple XSLT stylesheet to generate RSS feeds. The alternative to moving the pages to XHTML would have been installing a complicated, database-backed content management system that completely changed my workflow.

There are three steps to converting HTML to XHTML.

1. Add the appropriate document type declaration.
2. Validate the resulting document.
3. Fix any bugs the validation uncovers.

In practice, this is an iterative process that normally requires several repetitions before you finally produce valid XHTML. However, the process is worth it. I find that this almost always produces better pages and better results in web browsers.

There are three document type declarations you can use, shown below.

```
<!DOCTYPE html
      PUBLIC "-//W3C//DTD XHTML 1.0 Strict//EN"
      "http://www.w3.org/TR/xhtml1/DTD/xhtml1-strict.dtd">
<!DOCTYPE html
      PUBLIC "-//W3C//DTD XHTML 1.0 Transitional//EN"
      "http://www.w3.org/TR/xhtml1/DTD/xhtml1-transitional.dtd">
<!DOCTYPE html
```

```
PUBLIC "-//W3C//DTD XHTML 1.0 Frameset//EN"
"http://www.w3.org/TR/xhtml1/DTD/xhtml1-frameset.dtd">
```

The first DTD is appropriate for pages that do not use frames or deprecated markup. The second, transitional DTD, should be used if the page contains lots of deprecated presentational markup like `font` and `center` tags. The third, frameset DTD, should be chosen if the page uses frames. You may want to point to a local copy of the DTD instead of the main one on the W3C web server.

Besides adding the DTD, there are a number of changes you're likely to have to make when converting a web page from regular HTML to XHTML.

- Add a default namespace declaration `xmlns="http://www.w3.org/1999/xhtml"` on the root element.
- Add end tags to typically unclosed elements such as `p` and `li`.
- Rewrite empty elements such as `br` and `hr` with empty-element tags.
- Convert all tag and attribute names to lower case.
- Put quotes around all attribute values.
- Move inline elements such as `strong` and `code` from outside to inside block-level elements such as `div`, `p`, and `h1`.

MIME Type

Although I recommend using XHTML in the pages themselves, I do not yet recommend using the XHTML MIME media type, application/xhtml+xml. Instead, you should serve your pages as plain text/html. Many existing browsers, including relatively recent ones such as Internet Explorer 5.1 for Mac OS and Internet Explorer 5.2 for Mac OS X, do not recognize application/xhtml+xml. Instead of displaying the page, they attempt to download it. I am not aware of any browsers that won't accept XHTML pages identified as text/html.

HTML Tidy

Dave Raggett's HTML Tidy (http://tidy.sourceforge.net) is a wonderful open source tool for cleaning up HTML pages, including converting them to XHTML. Use it. HTML Tidy is a command line tool written in reasonably portable ANSI C that runs on most major platforms. Binaries are available for most platforms. To run it, just put the binary somewhere in your path, and use the `--output-xhtml` option to indicate you want XHTML output (instead of HTML). For example, the code below converts the file shows.html to XHTML.

```
C:/>tidy --output-xhtml shows.html
```

This dumps the converted document onto stdout, from where it can be redirected into a file in the usual way. If you prefer to convert the file in place, use the -m option.

```
C:/>tidy --output-xhtml -m shows.html
```

HTML Tidy cannot fix all the errors it finds in a typical malformed HTML document. However, it can do a very good job with most files. There will likely still be a few corrections that must be applied manually. However, HTML Tidy will fix enough problems to save you a significant amount of time.

Older Browsers

Some older browsers such as Netscape 3.0 and Internet Explorer 4.0 do have varying degrees of difficulty with XHTML constructs such as empty-element tags. For example, Netscape 3 places two horizontal lines when it sees `<hr></hr>` and none at all when it sees `<hr/>`. It is unwise to use the full panoply of XML syntax when serving XHTML to browsers. In particular, here are my suggestions.

- Include at least one space before the `/>` in an empty-element tag.
- Do not use CDATA sections.
- Do not use processing instructions such as `xml-stylesheet`, especially in the document prolog.
- Do not use character references such as `&#x111;` or `&#968;`.
- Do not use entity references that were not available in HTML 1.0 such as `&rdquo;` and `&tau;`.
- Do not include an internal DTD subset.
- Do not use an XML declaration. Encode the document in UTF-8 and use an HTML `http-equiv` meta tag to indicate that.

None of this should significantly affect what you can or cannot do in a web page. There are alternatives for all of these that work in older browsers. For instance, instead of CDATA sections, you can simply escape all literal less-than signs and ampersands as < and &, respectively.

However, if this proves too limiting for you, there is an alternative. You can author and validate your content in XHTML, then convert it to HTML before serving it. The simplest way to do this is with an XSLT stylesheet that reads XHTML and outputs plain-vanilla HTML. You can either preconvert all the documents before placing them on the web server or automatically convert them when they're requested, using one of the techniques discussed in Item 44. Example 46–1 demonstrates.

Example 46–1 A Stylesheet That Converts XHTML to HTML

```
<xsl:stylesheet
  version="1.0"
  xmlns:xsl="http://www.w3.org/1999/XSL/Transform"
  xmlns:html="http://www.w3.org/1999/xhtml">

 <xsl:output method="html"/>

  <xsl:template match="@*|node()">
    <xsl:copy>
      <xsl:apply-templates select="@*|node()"/>
    </xsl:copy>
  </xsl:template>

  <xsl:template match="html:*">
    <xsl:element name="{name(.)}">
      <xsl:apply-templates select="@*|node()"/>
    </xsl:element>
  </xsl:template>

</xsl:stylesheet>
```

This stylesheet copies all nodes that are not elements in the XHTML name-space to the output tree. Nodes that are elements in the XHTML namespace are also copied. However, they're changed to elements with the same local name that are not in any namespace. If you start with valid strict XHTML and then use this stylesheet, you're guaranteed HTML that's about as perfectly compatible with existing browsers as possible. In fact, I'd venture to say that if you find a browser that can't display what comes out of this process reasonably, there's about a 99% chance that the bug is in that browser, not your code.

Item 47   Catalog Common Resources

Many XML processes use system IDs (in practice, URLs) to locate the standard DTDs, schemas, stylesheets, and other supporting files for applications like DocBook, XHTML, and SVG. However, this can put quite a load on the central server, and it means your application may have to wait on a potentially slow remote server you don't control. You might not even be able to process your documents when the central server is down due to hardware failure, a system crash, or network outages. Alternatively, you can use XML catalogs to remap public IDs and URLs. A catalog can convert public IDs like -//OASIS//DTD DocBook XML V4.2//EN into absolute URLs like http://www.oasis-open.org/docbook/xml/4.2/docbookx. dtd. It can replace remote URLs like http://www.oasis-open.org/docbook/ xml/4.2/docbookx.dtd with local URLs like file:///home/elharo/docbook/ docbookx.dtd. This offers fast, reliable access to the DTDs and schemas without making the documents less portable across systems and networks.

Catalogs provide the extra level of indirection that makes XML processing much more flexible. They allow Uniform Resource Names (URNs) to be used just as easily as URLs. Even if you're only using URLs, catalogs allow documents to be much more easily moved between systems. For instance, when I move the text of my manuscripts from my Linux desktop to my Windows laptop, I can change the location of the DTD just by editing one catalog file. I don't have to edit every chapter document separately to tell the XML parser and the XSLT processor where to find the right DTD.

Of course, not all requests have to (or should) go through a catalog. If the catalog doesn't have an entry for a particular public ID or URL, the parser can fall back to the original remote URL. For instance, it could load the XHTML DTD from the W3C web site. However, the parser needs to make a network connection only if the resource isn't available locally. This saves both processing time and network bandwidth.

You can even use catalogs to choose different stylesheets or schemas depending on your needs. For instance, by editing the catalog, you can test several different possible schemas or stylesheets to see which one you prefer. You might even choose between a stylesheet that generates HTML and one that generates XHTML.

Catalog Syntax

A catalog is just an XML document in the syntax defined by the OASIS XML Catalogs standard (http://www.oasis-open.org/committees/entity/specs/cs-entity-xml-catalogs-1.0.html). The root element of this document is `catalog`, which is in the `urn:oasis:names:tc:entity:xmlns:xml:catalog` namespace. The `catalog` element contains `public` elements that remap public IDs and `system` elements that remap system IDs. Example 47–1 shows a simple catalog that maps the public ID for DocBook to a file in the local file system.

Example 47–1 | A Catalog Document

```
<?xml version="1.0"?>
<catalog xmlns="urn:oasis:names:tc:entity:xmlns:xml:catalog">

  <public publicId="-//OASIS//DTD DocBook XML V4.2//EN"
          uri="file:///opt/xml/docbook/docbookx.dtd"/>

</catalog>
```

The `public` element maps the public ID -//OASIS//DTD DocBook XML V4.2//EN to the local URL file:///opt/xml/docbook/docbookx.dtd. The beginning of each chapter has the following document type declaration.

```
<!DOCTYPE chapter PUBLIC "-//OASIS//DTD DocBook XML V4.2//EN"
    "http://www.oasis-open.org/docbook/xml/4.2/docbookx.dtd">
```

Its system ID points to the remote DTD on the OASIS web site. However, that won't be used. The parser looks for the public ID in the local catalog.xml file. The parser then uses the URL from the catalog (if found) instead of the one in the document itself. However, if the catalog doesn't contain a mapping for the public ID, the parser will use the URL included in the document itself.

As mentioned above, you can also remap system IDs by using the `system` element. This is useful for loading content that doesn't have a public ID, such as stylesheets referenced by an `xml-stylesheet` processing instruction or multiple source documents loaded by the `document()` function in XSLT. For example, the `system` element shown next remaps the DocBook XSL stylesheet at SourceForge to a local copy stored in /opt/xml/docbook-xsl/.

```
<system systemId=
"http://docbook.sourceforge.net/release/xsl/current/html/docbook.xsl"
    uri="file:///opt/xml/docbook-xsl/html/docbook.xsl"/>
```

The `rewriteURI` element can remap a whole set of URLs from a particular server. This is very much like the mod_rewrite module in the Apache web server. For example, the code below maps all the DocBook stylesheet URLs to a local directory on a UNIX box.

```
<rewriteURI uriStartString=
    "http://docbook.sourceforge.net/release/xsl/current/"
    rewritePrefix="file:///opt/xml/docbook-xsl/" />
```

For various technical reasons, if you're remapping the URLs in DTD system identifiers, use a `rewriteSystem` element instead of a `rewriteURI` element.

```
 <rewriteSystem systemIdStartString=
     "http://www.oasis-open.org/docbook/xml/4.2/"
     rewritePrefix="/opt/xml/docbook/" />
```

Using Catalog Files

The details of how to load a catalog file when processing a document vary from parser to parser and tool to tool. Not all XML processors support catalogs, but most of the important ones do. The Gnome Project's xslt-proc, Michael Kay's Saxon, and the XML Apache Project's Xerces-J and Xalan-J all support catalogs. Notably lacking from this list are the C++ versions of Xerces and Xalan as well as Microsoft's MSXML. Of course, it isn't hard to integrate catalog processing into your own applications with just a little bit of open source code.

libxml2

Daniel Veillard's libxml2 XML parser for C supports catalogs, as does his libxslt processor that sits on top of libxml2. libxml2 reads the catalog location from the `XML_CATALOG_FILES` environment variable, which contains a white-space-separated list of file names. This can be set in all the usual ways. For example, in bash or other Bourne shell derivatives, to specify that libxml should use the catalog file found at /opt/xml/catalog. xml you would simply type the following:

```
% XML_CATALOG_FILES=/opt/xml/catalog.xml
% export XML_CATALOG_FILES
```

In Windows, you'd set this environment variable in the System control panel.

This property can also be set to a white-space-separated list of file names to indicate that libxml should try several different catalogs in sequence. For example, the setting below requests that libxml first look in the file catalog.xml in the current working directory and then in the file /opt/xml/docbook/docbook.cat.

```
% XML_CATALOG_FILES="catalog.xml /opt/xml/docbook/docbook.cat"
% export XML_CATALOG_FILES
```

If you expect to use the same catalog file consistently, you could set XML_CATALOG_FILES in your .bashrc or .cshrc file.

Once this environment variable is set, libxml will consult the catalog for all documents it loads, whether you're calling the library from your own C++ source code, calling it from the XSLT stylesheet with the document() function, or using the command line tools xmllint and xsltproc.

If you're having trouble with the catalog, you can put libxml in debug mode by setting the XML_DEBUG_CATALOG environment variable. (No value is required. It just needs to be set.) libxml will then tell you when it recognizes a catalog entry and what it's actually loading when. I often find this useful for discovering small, nonobvious mismatches between the IDs used in the instance documents and those used in the catalog. For instance, when I was writing this item, libxml helped me uncover a mismatch between the public ID in the catalog and the documents. The catalog was using -//OASIS//DTD DocBook XML V4.2.0//EN and the source documents were using -//OASIS//DTD DocBook XML V4.2//EN. The strings really do have to match exactly—4.2 is not the same as 4.2.0 when resolving public IDs.

Saxon, Xalan, and Other Java-Based XSLT Processors

Most XML parsers and XSLT processors written in Java can use Norm Walsh's catalog library (now donated to the XML Apache Project). You can download it from http://xml.apache.org/dist/commons/. Download the file resolver-1.0.jar (the version number may have changed) and add it to your classpath. Next create a CatalogManager.properties file in a directory that is included in your classpath. The resolver will look in this file to determine the locations of the catalog files. Example 47–2 shows a properties file that loads the catalog named catalog.xml from the current working directory and the standard DocBook catalog from the absolute path /opt/xml/docbook/docbook.cat.

Example 47–2 | A CatalogManager.properties File for Norm Walsh's Catalog Resolver

```
catalogs=catalog.xml;/opt/xml/docbook/docbook.cat
relative-catalogs=true
static-catalog=yes
catalog-class-name=org.apache.xml.resolver.Resolver
verbosity=1
```

If you're having trouble, turn up the verbosity to 4 to provide more detailed error messages about exactly which files the resolver is loading when.

You tell Saxon to use the Apache Commons catalog with several command line options, as shown below.

```
% java com.icl.saxon.StyleSheet
    -x org.apache.xml.resolver.tools.ResolvingXMLReader
    -y org.apache.xml.resolver.tools.ResolvingXMLReader
    -r org.apache.xml.resolver.tools.CatalogResolver
  chapter1.xml docbook.xsl
```

Xalan is similar.

```
% java org.apache.xalan.xslt.Process
    -ENTITYRESOLVER
org.apache.xml.resolver.tools.CatalogResolver
    -URIRESOLVER org.apache.xml.resolver.tools.CatalogResolver
    -in chapter1.xml -xsl  docbook.xsl
```

jd.xslt works the same except that it uses lowercase argument names.

```
% java jd.xml.xslt.Stylesheet
    -entityresolver
org.apache.xml.resolver.tools.CatalogResolver
    -uriresolver org.apache.xml.resolver.tools.CatalogResolver
    chapter1.xml docbook.xsl
```

In all three cases, what you're really doing is telling the processor where to find an instance of the SAX `EntityResolver` interface and the TrAX `URIResolver` interface. The `org.apache.xml.resolver.tools.CatalogResolver` class can also be used for these purposes in your own SAX and TrAX programs.

TrAX

In TrAX both the `Transformer` and `TransformerFactory` classes have `setURIResolver` methods that allow you to provide a resolver that's used to look up URIs used by the document function and the `xsl:import` and `xsl:include` elements. Setting the `URIResolver` for a `Transformer` just changes that one `Transformer` object. Setting the `URIResolver` for a `TransformerFactory` sets the default resolver for all `Transformer` objects created by that factory.

To use catalogs, just pass in an instance of the `org.apache.xml.resolver.tools.CatalogResolver` class.

```
URIResolver resolver = new CatalogResolver();
TransformerFactory factory = TransformerFactory.newInstance();
factory.setURIResolver(resolver);
```

The location of the catalog file is determined by a CatalogManager. properties file as shown in Example 47–2.

You will of course need to add the resolver.jar file to your classpath to make this work.

SAX

SAX programs access catalogs through the `EntityResolver` interface, which, conveniently, `org.apache.xml.resolver.tools.CatalogResolver` also implements. To add catalog support to your own application just pass an instance of this class to the `setEntityResolver` method of the `XMLReader` class before beginning to parse a document.

```
EntityResolver resolver = new CatalogResolver();
XMLReader parser = XMLReaderFactory.createXMLReader();
parser.setEntityResolver(resolver);
```

That's all there is to it. From here on, you just parse the XML as usual. Whenever the `XMLReader` loads a DTD fragment from either a system or a public ID it will first consult the catalogs identified by the Catalog Manager.properties file.

Item 48   Verify Documents with XML Digital Signatures

XML documents are used on Wall Street for financial transactions totaling hundreds of millions of dollars per day. Worldwide, the figure's even larger. There's significant incentive for criminals to modify XML documents moving from one system to another. XML digital signatures can help ensure that XML documents have not been tampered with in transit. Not all documents need to be digitally signed, but those that do need to be signed need it badly.

The basic process of signing something digitally involves a keyed hash function. A hash function converts documents into numbers, generally smaller than the document itself. Feed a document into the hash function; get a 128-byte number out. A very simple hash function might count up the number of 1 bits in the document and take the remainder when dividing by 256. This would give 256 possible different hash codes between 0 and 255. Essentially this is a one-byte hash function. Real-world hash functions used for signatures are much larger, much more complex, and much more secure.

To be useful for digital signatures, the hash function is keyed. One key is used to sign the document, and a separate, related key is used to compare the document against its signature and verify that they match. The signing key is kept private while the verification key is published. Since only the holder of the signing key can create a hash code for a document, if you receive a signed document whose signature matches when computed with Alice's public key, you have a fair amount of confidence that Alice signed the document.

For purposes of security, it's important that the hash codes generated by the signing process be widely dispersed. That is, changing even one bit of the document should result in a completely different hash code when the document is signed. Otherwise, it would be possible for a forger to make small changes to the document until he or she got a verifiable signature.

Most algorithms for digital signatures are based around signing an entire file, which is treated as just a sequence of bytes. However, XML signatures are a little more complicated than that. XML allows you to sign only certain elements or document fragments, rather than entire documents. Furthermore, the signatures can be embedded in the documents they sign. And finally, not all details of XML are necessarily relevant to the signature. For instance, it doesn't matter whether a check approval is written as `<approved authority="Winston Sherlock" transaction="P87RET"/>` or `<approved transaction = 'P87RET' authority= 'Winston Sherlock' />`; but it's very important that it not be changed to `<approved transaction = "P88RET" authority= "Winston Sherlock" />`. XML digital signatures generally sign a fragment of a document that is identified by an XPath expression. The actual data to be signed is calculated by canonicalizing that part of the XML document before signing its bytes.

Digital Signature Syntax

I'm going to give you just a brief overview of what a digitally signed XML document looks like. The arithmetic is far too complex for most humans to do by hand (even programmers). It's virtually certain that you'll use some software application or library to sign and verify your documents. XML documents aren't signed by hand.

There are three basic kinds of signatures.

1. An *enveloping signature* contains the data it signs.
2. An *enveloped signature* is contained inside the document it signs.
3. A *detached signature* signs data external to the document identified by a URL.

Before any XML document can be signed, it needs to be transformed into a canonical form that normalizes syntactically irrelevant details like attribute order and the amount of white space inside tags. For example, let us suppose we have a document that represents order and payment information, as shown in Example 48–1.

Example 48–1 An Order Document

```
<?xml version="1.0"?>
<Order>
```

```
<Item type="BackIssue">
  <Title>Fables</Title>
  <Issue>2</Issue>
  <Publisher>DC</Publisher>
</Item>
<Item type="BackIssue">
  <Title>Gen 13</Title>
  <Issue>46</Issue>
  <Publisher>Wildstorm</Publisher>
</Item>
<CreditCard type="VISA">
  <Name>Elliotte Rusty Harold</Name>
  <Number>5555 3142 2718 2998</Number>
  <Expires>
    <Month>06</Month>
    <Year>2006</Year>
  </Expires>
</CreditCard>
</Order>
```

Suppose the comic shop wants to verify that I actually sent this order before charging my credit card. The store could require that I sign the document with my private key, which they would then verify with my public key.

The most common way to do this is with an enveloping signature. This includes the document being signed inside the signature. Example 48–2 demonstrates, using the order document from Example 48–1. The root element is now `Signature` instead of `Order`. However, the last child element of the `Signature` element is a `dsig:Object` element that contains the root `Order` element of the original document. This is what has been signed. After verifying the signature, you can extract the original element using any of the usual techniques. A tree-based API such as JDOM, XOM, or DOM is probably the simplest approach here.

Example 48–2 | An Enveloping Signature

```
<Signature xmlns="http://www.w3.org/2000/09/xmldsig#">
  <SignedInfo>
    <CanonicalizationMethod Algorithm=
      "http://www.w3.org/TR/2001/REC-xml-c14n-20010315"/>
```

```
<SignatureMethod Algorithm=
    "http://www.w3.org/2000/09/xmldsig#dsa-sha1"/>
<Reference URI="#Res0">
  <Transforms>
    <Transform Algorithm=
       "http://www.w3.org/TR/2001/REC-xml-c14n-20010315"/>
  </Transforms>
  <DigestMethod Algorithm=
     "http://www.w3.org/2000/09/xmldsig#sha1"/>
  <DigestValue>tRJGGSB544BQ1CVyj9UdR3+8/PE=</DigestValue>
</Reference>
</SignedInfo>
<SignatureValue>
  GzgtyIj1DYTBX1idqH0wjae7U2lUBCXaAkuvBKeVIUWkwWyGHqBXqQ==
</SignatureValue>
<KeyInfo>
  <KeyValue>
    <DSAKeyValue>
      <P>
        /X9TgR11EilS30qcLuzk5/YRt1I870QAwx4/gLZRJmlFXUAiUftZPY
        1Y+r/F9bow9subVWzXgTuAHTRv8mZgt2uZUKWkn5/oBHsQIsJPu6nX
        /rfGG/g7V+fGqKYVDwT7g/bTxR7DAjVUE1oWkTL2dfOuK2HXKu/yIg
        MZndFIAcc=
      </P>
      <Q>l2BQjxUjC8yykrmCouuEC/BYHPU=</Q>
      <G>
        9+GghdabPd7LvKtcNrhXuXmUr7v6OuqC+VdMCz0HgmdRWVeOutRZT+
        ZxBxCBgLRJFnEj6EwoFhO3zwkyjMim4TwWeotUfI0o4KOuHiuzpnWR
        bqN/C/ohNWLx+2J6ASQ7zKTxvqhRkImog9/hWuWfBpKLZl6Ae1UlZA
        FMO/7PSSo=
      </G>
      <Y>
        7bQ9Utz1cuAXbXGPwSC/v29fxGDiqXMO3nnyp3qvCzS351MWvYC3pf
        zW4KAqxEUdMeBzSpysBAhBW4IwEYSTRZ3RFtJUf2hjHhxo93oakMKZ
        /pfeg4MTPLM1rAQuTZ7tRI8jvXu/snhJknhhnGPGWGt1ZOePT24Mlx
        f+1hTGRck=
      </Y>
    </DSAKeyValue>
  </KeyValue>
  <X509Data>
```

```
    <X509IssuerSerial>
      <X509IssuerName>
        CN=Elliotte Harold,OU=Metrotech,O=Polytechnic,
        L=Brooklyn, ST=New York,C=US</X509IssuerName>
      <X509SerialNumber>1046543415</X509SerialNumber>
    </X509IssuerSerial>
    <X509SubjectName>
      CN=Elliotte Harold,OU=Metrotech,O=Polytechnic,
      L=Brooklyn,ST=New York,C=US</X509SubjectName>
    <X509Certificate>
MIIDJDCCAuECBD5g/DcwCwYHKoZIzjgEAwUAMHcxCzAJBgNVBAYTAlVTMREwDwYD
VQQIEwhOZXcgWW9yazERMA8GA1UEBxMIQnJvb2tseW4xFDASBgNVBAoTC1BvbHl0
ZWNobmljMRIwEAYDVQQLEwlNZXRyb3RlY2gxGDAWBgNVBAMTD0VsbGlvdHRlIEhh
cm9sZDAeFw0wMzAzMDExODMwMTVaFw0wMzA1MzAxODMwMTVaMHcxCzAJBgNVBAYT
AlVTMREwDwYDVQQIEwhOZXcgWW9yazERMA8GA1UEBxMIQnJvb2tseW4xFDASBgNV
BAoTC1BvbHl0ZWNobmljMRIwEAYDVQQLEwlNZXRyb3RlY2gxGDAWBgNVBAMTD0Vs
bGlvdHRlIEhhcm9sZDCCAbgwggEsBgcqhkjOOAQBMIIBHwKBgQD9f1OBHXUSKVLf
Spwu7OTn9hG3UjzvRADDHj+AtlEmaUVdQCJR+1k9jVj6v8X1ujD2y5tVbNeBO4Ad
NG/yZmC3a5lQpaSfn+gEexAiwk+7qdf+t8Yb+DtX58aophUPBPuD9tPFHsMCNVQT
WhaRMvZ1864rYdcq7/IiAxmd0UgBxwIVAJdgUI8VIwvMspK5gqLrhAvwWBz1AoGB
APfhoIXWmz3ey7yrXDa4V7l51K+7+jrqgvlXTAs9B4JnUVlXjrrUWU/mcQcQgYC0
SRZxI+hMKBYTt88JMozIpuE8FnqLVHyNKOCjrh4rs6Z1kW6jfwv6ITVi8ftiegEk
O8yk8b6oUZCJqIPf4VrlnwaSi2ZegHtVJWQBTDv+z0kqA4GFAAKBgQDttD1S3PVy
4BdtcY/BIL+/b1/EYOKpcw7eefKneq8LNLfnUxa9gLel/NbgoCrERR0x4HNKnKwE
CEFbgjARhJNFndEW0lR/aGMeHGj3ehqQwpn+l96DgxM8szWsBC5Nnu1EjyO9e7+y
eEmSeGGcY8ZYa3Vk549PbgyXF/7WFMZFyTALBgcqhkjOOAQDBQADMAAwLQIVAIQs
71E6P19ImxGIwBQfmB9ov0HTAhRtlgIWB6YUqt7ilNcSxfbHWOMKLA==
    </X509Certificate>
  </X509Data>
</KeyInfo>
<dsig:Object xmlns:dsig="http://www.w3.org/2000/09/xmldsig#"
             xmlns="" Id="Res0"><Order>
<Item type="BackIssue">
  <Title>Fables</Title>
  <Issue>2</Issue>
  <Publisher>DC</Publisher>
</Item>
<Item type="BackIssue">
  <Title>Gen 13</Title>
  <Issue>46</Issue>
```

```
      <Publisher>Wildstorm</Publisher>
   </Item>
   <CreditCard type="VISA">
     <Name>Elliotte Rusty Harold</Name>
     <Number>5555 3142 2718 2998</Number>
     <Expires>
        <Month>06</Month>
        <Year>2006</Year>
     </Expires>
   </CreditCard>
</Order></dsig:Object>
</Signature>
```

Do not concern yourself excessively with the detailed syntax of this example. Even if the XML structure is intelligible to a person, the mathematics required to produce the Base64-encoded signature really aren't. I suppose it's theoretically possible that an arithmetical savant could do this by hand, but in practice it's always done by computer. You don't need to worry about the details unless you're writing the software to generate and verify digital signatures. Most programmers just use a library written by somebody else such as XML-Security from the XML Apache Project (http://xml.apache.org/security/) or XSS4J from IBM (http://www.alphaworks.ibm.com/tech/xmlsecuritysuite).

You should also not worry about the size. Since the original example was quite small, the signature markup forms a large part of the signed document. However, the size of the signature markup is almost constant. You could sign a multimegabyte document with the same number of bytes used here. The size of the signature is independent of the document signed and only lightly coupled to the size of the key or the algorithm used.

Sometimes it may be more convenient to keep the same root element but add the Signature element inside that document. This is a little tricky because verification needs to be careful to verify the document without considering the signature to be part of it. Still, although this caused a little extra work for the designers of the XML digital signature specification, the details are now encapsulated in the different libraries you might use, so it's not really any extra work for your code. Example 48–3 shows a version of Example 48–1 that contains an enveloped signature.

Example 48–3 | An Enveloped Signature

```
<Order>
  <Item type="BackIssue">
    <Title>Fables</Title>
    <Issue>2</Issue>
    <Publisher>DC</Publisher>
  </Item>
  <Item type="BackIssue">
    <Title>Gen 13</Title>
    <Issue>46</Issue>
    <Publisher>Wildstorm</Publisher>
  </Item>
  <CreditCard type="VISA">
    <Name>Elliotte Rusty Harold</Name>
    <Number>5555 3142 2718 2998</Number>
    <Expires>
      <Month>06</Month>
      <Year>2006</Year>
    </Expires>
  </CreditCard>
  <Signature xmlns="http://www.w3.org/2000/09/xmldsig#">
    <SignedInfo>
      <CanonicalizationMethod Algorithm=
        "http://www.w3.org/TR/2001/REC-xml-c14n-20010315"/>
      <SignatureMethod Algorithm=
        "http://www.w3.org/2000/09/xmldsig#dsa-sha1"/>
      <Reference URI="">
        <Transforms>
          <Transform Algorithm=
         "http://www.w3.org/2000/09/xmldsig#enveloped-signature"
          />
        </Transforms>
        <DigestMethod Algorithm=
            "http://www.w3.org/2000/09/xmldsig#sha1"/>
        <DigestValue>pCD81qloCPf9UBbJ1CnTwMh+Wo4=</DigestValue>
      </Reference>
    </SignedInfo>
    <SignatureValue>
        dguuK7RO1THsftPd/yHJK+1ImHYd8dAy8mGk7GzAH/vVFxFkysJplQ==
```

```
        </SignatureValue>
    <KeyInfo>
      <KeyValue>
        <DSAKeyValue>
          <P>
            /X9TgR11EilS30qcLuzk5/YRt1I870QAwx4/gLZRJmlFXUAiUftZPY
            1Y+r/F9bow9subVWzXgTuAHTRv8mZgt2uZUKWkn5/oBHsQIsJPu6nX
            /rfGG/g7V+fGqKYVDwT7g/bTxR7DAjVUE1oWkTL2dfOuK2HXKu/yIg
            MZndFIAcc=
          </P>
          <Q>l2BQjxUjC8yykrmCouuEC/BYHPU=</Q>
          <G>
            9+GghdabPd7LvKtcNrhXuXmUr7v6OuqC+VdMCz0HgmdRWVeOutRZT+
            ZxBxCBgLRJFnEj6EwoFhO3zwkyjMim4TwWeotUfI0o4KOuHiuzpnWR
            bqN/C/ohNWLx+2J6ASQ7zKTxvqhRkImog9/hWuWfBpKLZl6Ae1UlZA
            FMO/7PSSo=
          </G>
          <Y>
            7bQ9Utz1cuAXbXGPwSC/v29fxGDiqXMO3nnyp3qvCzS351MWvYC3pf
            zW4KAqxEUdMeBzSpysBAhBW4IwEYSTRZ3RFtJUf2hjHhxo93oakMKZ
            /pfeg4MTPLM1rAQuTZ7tRI8jvXu/snhJknhhnGPGWGt1ZOePT24Mlx
            f+1hTGRck=
          </Y>
        </DSAKeyValue>
      </KeyValue>
    <X509Data>
      <X509IssuerSerial>
        <X509IssuerName>
         CN=Elliotte Harold,OU=Metrotech,O=Polytechnic,
         L=Brooklyn,ST=New York,C=US
        </X509IssuerName>
        <X509SerialNumber>1046543415</X509SerialNumber>
      </X509IssuerSerial>
      <X509SubjectName>
       CN=Elliotte Harold,OU=Metrotech,O=Polytechnic,
       L=Brooklyn,ST=New York,C=US</X509SubjectName>
      <X509Certificate>
MIIDJDCCAuECBD5g/DcwCwYHKoZIzjgEAwUAMHcxCzAJBgNVBAYTAlVTMREwDwYD
VQQIEwhOZXcgWW9yazERMA8GA1UEBxMIQnJvb2tseW4xFDASBgNVBAoTC1BvbHl0
ZWNobljMRIwEAYDVQQLEwlNZXRyb3RlY2gxGDAWBgNVBAMTD0VsbGlvdHRlIEhh
```

```
cm9sZDAeFw0wMzAzMDExODMwMTVaFw0wMzA1MzAxODMwMTVaMHcxCzAJBgNVBAYT
AlVTMREwDwYDVQQIEwhOZXcgWW9yazERMA8GA1UEBxMIQnJvb2tseW4xFDASBgNV
BAoTC1BvbHl0ZWNobmljMRIwEAYDVQQLEwlNZXRyb3RlY2gxGDAWBgNVBAMTD0Vs
bGlvdHRlIEhhcm9sZDCCAbgwggEsBgcqhkjOOAQBMIIBHwKBgQD9f1OBHXUSKVLf
Spwu7OTn9hG3UjzvRADDHj+AtlEmaUVdQCJR+1k9jVj6v8X1ujD2y5tVbNeBO4Ad
NG/yZmC3a5lQpaSfn+gEexAiwk+7qdf+t8Yb+DtX58aophUPBPuD9tPFHsMCNVQT
WhaRMvZ1864rYdcq7/IiAxmd0UgBxwIVAJdgUI8VIwvMspK5gqLrhAvwWBz1AoGB
APfhoIXWmz3ey7yrXDa4V7l5lK+7+jrqgvlXTAs9B4JnUVlXjrrUWU/mcQcQgYC0
SRZxI+hMKBYTt88JMozIpuE8FnqLVHyNKOCjrh4rs6Z1kW6jfwv6ITVi8ftiegEk
O8yk8b6oUZCJqIPf4VrlnwaSi2ZegHtVJWQBTDv+z0kqA4GFAAKBgQDttD1S3PVy
4BdtcY/BIL+/b1/EYOKpcw7eefKneq8LNLfnUxa9gLel/NbgoCrERR0x4HNKnKwE
CEFbgjARhJNFndEWOlR/aGMeHGj3ehqQwpn+l96DgxM8szWsBC5Nnu1EjyO9e7+y
eEmSeGGcY8ZYa3Vk549PbgyXF/7WFMZFyTALBgcqhkjOOAQDBQADMAAwLQIVAIQs
71E6P19ImxGIwBQfmB9ov0HTAhRtlgIWB6YUqt7ilNcSxfbHWOMKLA==
```
```
        </X509Certificate>
      </X509Data>
    </KeyInfo>
  </Signature>
</Order>
```

A detached signature neither contains nor is contained in the document it signs. Instead it points to the document being signed with a URI. This allows it to sign things besides XML documents such as JPEG images and Microsoft Word files. The object signed is identified by the URI attribute of a Reference element. Example 48–4 is a detached signature for the order document shown in Example 48–1.

Example 48–4 | A Detached Signature

```
<Signature xmlns="http://www.w3.org/2000/09/xmldsig#">
  <SignedInfo>
    <CanonicalizationMethod Algorithm=
       "http://www.w3.org/TR/2001/REC-xml-c14n-20010315"/>
    <SignatureMethod Algorithm=
       "http://www.w3.org/2000/09/xmldsig#dsa-sha1"/>
    <Reference URI=
     "file:///home/elharo/books/effectivexml/examples/order.xml"
    >
      <DigestMethod Algorithm=
         "http://www.w3.org/2000/09/xmldsig#sha1"/>
      <DigestValue>J4qs6XERp3S9frY9Je3IiZL2yvs=</DigestValue>
```

```xml
        </Reference>
      </SignedInfo>
      <SignatureValue>
        TIptdglMXBgmHWFm1jOygQiMr4JJGGPAMW8XR65mGpjNeV469EiieQ==
      </SignatureValue>
      <KeyInfo>
        <KeyValue>
          <DSAKeyValue>
            <P>
              /X9TgR11EilS30qcLuzk5/YRt1I870QAwx4/gLZRJmlFXUAiUftZPY
              1Y+r/F9bow9subVWzXgTuAHTRv8mZgt2uZUKWkn5/oBHsQIsJPu6nX
              /rfGG/g7V+fGqKYVDwT7g/bTxR7DAjVUE1oWkTL2dfOuK2HXKu/yIg
              MZndFIAcc=
            </P>
            <Q>l2BQjxUjC8yykrmCouuEC/BYHPU=</Q>
            <G>
              9+GghdabPd7LvKtcNrhXuXmUr7v6OuqC+VdMCz0HgmdRWVeOutRZT+
              ZxBxCBgLRJFnEj6EwoFhO3zwkyjMim4TwWeotUfI0o4KOuHiuzpnWR
              bqN/C/ohNWLx+2J6ASQ7zKTxvqhRkImog9/hWuWfBpKLZl6Ae1UlZA
              FMO/7PSSo=
            </G>
            <Y>
              7bQ9Utz1cuAXbXGPwSC/v29fxGDiqXMO3nnyp3qvCzS351MWvYC3pf
              zW4KAqxEUdMeBzSpysBAhBW4IwEYSTRZ3RFtJUf2hjHhxo93oakMKZ
              /pfeg4MTPLM1rAQuTZ7tRI8jvXu/snhJknhhnGPGWGt1ZOePT24Mlx
              f+1hTGRck=
            </Y>
          </DSAKeyValue>
        </KeyValue>
        <X509Data>
          <X509IssuerSerial>
            <X509IssuerName>
              CN=Elliotte Harold,OU=Metrotech,O=Polytechnic,
              L=Brooklyn,ST=New York,C=US</X509IssuerName>
            <X509SerialNumber>1046543415</X509SerialNumber>
          </X509IssuerSerial>
          <X509SubjectName>
            CN=Elliotte Harold,OU=Metrotech,O=Polytechnic,
            L=Brooklyn,ST=New York,C=US</X509SubjectName>
          <X509Certificate>
```

```
MIIDJDCCAuECBD5g/DcwCwYHKoZIzjgEAwUAMHcxCzAJBgNVBAYTAlVTMREwDwYD
VQQIEwhOZXcgWW9yazERMA8GA1UEBxMIQnJvb2tseW4xFDASBgNVBAoTC1BvbHl0
ZWNobmljMRIwEAYDVQQLEwlNZXRyb3RlY2gxGDAWBgNVBAMTD0VsbGlvdHRlIEhh
cm9sZDAeFw0wMzAzMDExODMwMTVaFw0wMzA1MzAxODMwMTVaMHcxCzAJBgNVBAYT
AlVTMREwDwYDVQQIEwhOZXcgWW9yazERMA8GA1UEBxMIQnJvb2tseW4xFDASBgNV
BAoTC1BvbHl0ZWNobmljMRIwEAYDVQQLEwlNZXRyb3RlY2gxGDAWBgNVBAMTD0Vs
bGlvdHRlIEhhcm9sZDCCAbgwggEsBgcqhkjOOAQBMIIBHwKBgQD9f1OBHXUSKVLf
Spwu7OTn9hG3UjzvRADDHj+AtlEmaUVdQCJR+1k9jVj6v8X1ujD2y5tVbNeBO4Ad
NG/yZmC3a5lQpaSfn+gEexAiwk+7qdf+t8Yb+DtX58aophUPBPuD9tPFHsMCNVQT
WhaRMvZ1864rYdcq7/IiAxmd0UgBxwIVAJdgUI8VIwvMspK5gqLrhAvwWBz1AoGB
APfhoIXWmz3ey7yrXDa4V7l5lK+7+jrqgvlXTAs9B4JnUVlXjrrUWU/mcQcQgYC0
SRZxI+hMKBYTt88JMozIpuE8FnqLVHyNKOCjrh4rs6Z1kW6jfwv6ITVi8ftiegEk
O8yk8b6oUZCJqIPf4VrlnwaSi2ZegHtVJWQBTDv+z0kqA4GFAAKBgQDttD1S3PVy
4BdtcY/BIL+/b1/EYOKpcw7eefKneq8LNLfnUxa9gLel/NbgoCrERROx4HNKnKwE
CEFbgjARhJNFndEW0lR/aGMeHGj3ehqQwpn+l96DgxM8szWsBC5Nnu1EjyO9e7+y
eEmSeGGcY8ZYa3Vk549PbgyXF/7WFMZFyTALBgcqhkjOOAQDBQADMAAwLQIVAIQs
71E6P19ImxGIwBQfmB9ov0HTAhRtlgIWB6YUqt7ilNcSxfbHWOMKLA==
```

```
        </X509Certificate>
      </X509Data>
    </KeyInfo>
</Signature>
```

If you're signing non-XML data, you must use a detached signature. If you're signing XML data, you should use either an enveloped or enveloping signature because they ignore XML-insignificant details like white space in tags and whether empty elements are represented with one tag or two. Whether you use enveloped or enveloping signatures depends mainly on which seems simpler to you. Most tools and class libraries for generating and verifying signatures work equally well with either.

Digital Signature Tools

I'm not aware that digital signature software is restricted or forbidden by law anywhere. However, the mathematics and basic algorithms for digital signatures are essentially the same as those used for some forms of cryptography. The most common signature algorithms are essentially public key cryptography algorithms run in reverse; that is, signatures are encrypted with private keys and decrypted with public keys. Consequently, the software is less available than it should be and often excessively difficult to install or configure. Vendors have to jump through hoops to be allowed to publish, sell, and export their products. The exact number of hoops varies a lot from one jurisdiction to the next. Thus, unfortunately, XML digital signature tools and libraries are somewhat sparser than they otherwise would be.

Possibly the most advanced open source library at the time of this writing is XML-Security from the Apache XML Project. This is a Java class library that runs on top of Java 1.3.1 and later.[1] It relies on Sun's Java Cryptography Extension for its mathematics. The preferred implementation of this API is from the Legion of the Bouncy Castle which, being based in Australia, doesn't have to submit to U.S. export laws. The Apache XML project can't legally ship the Bouncy Castle JCE with their software, but you can grab it yourself from http://www.bouncycastle.org/.

XML-Security also depends on Xalan and Xerces. These products also need to be installed in your classpath. Sun ships a buggy, beta version of Xalan with Java 1.4, so if you're using Java 1.4 you'll need to put the Xalan jar archive in your jre/lib/endorsed directory rather than the jre/lib/ext directory.[2] Otherwise XML-Security will fail with strange error messages. Once you've done that, using this package to digitally sign DOM documents is not too difficult. Numerous samples are included with the package. However, the user interface is nonexistent.

Slightly less advanced in the API department but slightly more advanced when it comes to user interface is IBM's XSS4J. This includes a couple of sample command line applications for signing documents. First you'll need to use the keytool bundled with the JDK to create a key based on a password.

```
C:> keytool -genkey -dname "CN=Elliotte Harold, OU=Metrotech,
 O=Polytechnic, L=Brooklyn, S=New York, C=US"
 -alias elharo -storepass mystorepassword -keypass mykeypassword
```

(For various technical reasons the password can't be used as the key directly. It needs to be transformed into a more random sequence of bits.)

---

1. It may run on earlier versions, but the lead developer wasn't sure if it did when I asked him. Even if you can get the current version to run on a pre-1.3 VM, there's no guarantee future releases will.

2. Shortly before we went to press Sun posted a beta of Java 1.4.2 that includes a much more current version of Xalan. If you're using Java 1.4.2 or later, you're good to go.

Next you can run the program `dsig.SampleSign2` across the document to sign it.

```
C:\> java dsig.SampleSign2 elharo mystorepassword mykeypassword
  -ext file:///home/elharo/books/effectivexml/examples/order.xml
   > signed_order.xml
Key store:  file:///home/elharo/.keystore
  Sign: 703ms
```

This is how I produced the enveloping and detached examples earlier in this chapter. (XSS4J does not yet support enveloped signatures.) However, more commonly you'll want to integrate digital signatures into your own application, and XML-Security has a comprehensive API that allows you to do this.

There are also several commercial offerings for Java. The first is Baltimore Technologies' KeyTools XML (http://www.baltimore.com/keytools/xml/index.asp). Phaos has released a commercial XML Security Suite for Java (http://phaos.com/products/category/xml.html) that supports XML encryption and XML digital signatures. Both of these products rely on the JCE to do the math.

Beyond Java, the pickings are very slim at this time. The only C/C++ library I've been able to locate is Infomosaic's payware SecureXML (http://www.infomosaic.net/). The System.Security.Cryptography.XML package in the .NET framework provides complete support for signing and verifying XML digital signatures. I haven't seen any libraries or tools in Perl, Python, or other languages. But this is all still pretty bleeding-edge stuff; 2004 should see many more options developed and released.

Item 49 Hide Confidential Data with XML Encryption

As web services based on SOAP, REST, and XML-RPC explode in popularity, more and more sensitive data is passed around the Internet as XML documents. This includes data thieves might want to use for illicit financial gain, such as credit card numbers, social security numbers, account numbers, and more. It includes data governments might want to use to attack opponents, such as names, addresses, political beliefs, donor lists, and so forth. It includes data users might simply wish to keep private for its own sake, such as medical records and sexual preferences. There are large incentives for bad people to try to read XML documents moving from one system to another. XML encryption can help prevent this. Not all documents need to be encrypted, but those that do need encryption need it badly.

To some extent, standard encryption technologies like PGP and HTTPS can render some assistance. These protocols, programs, and algorithms are for the most part format-neutral. They can encrypt any sequence of bytes into another sequence of bytes. Naturally, they can encrypt an XML file just as easily as an HTML file, a Word document, a JPEG image, or any other computer data; and sometimes this suffices. However, none of these generic encryption tools retain any of the advantages of the XML nature of the original file. The documents they produce are binary, not text. They cannot be processed with standard XML tools.

XML encryption is a technology more geared to the specific needs of encrypting XML documents. It allows some parts of a document to be encrypted while other parts are left in plain text. It can encrypt different parts of a document in different ways. For example, a customer can submit an order to a merchant in which the product ordered and the shipping address are encrypted with the merchant's public key, but the credit card information is encrypted with the credit card company's public key. The merchant can easily extract the information needed and forward the rest to the credit card company for approval or rejection. The merchant has no way of knowing or storing the user's credit card data and thus could not at a later time charge the customer for products he or she hadn't ordered nor expose the data to hackers.

Encryption Syntax

I'm going to give you just a brief overview of what an encrypted XML document looks like. As with digital signatures (which use a lot of the same math), the arithmetic is far too complex for most humans to do by hand. You'll always use a software application or library to encrypt documents. Encrypted XML isn't intended to be authored by a text editor like normal XML.

When a document or portion of a document is encrypted, that part is replaced by an `EncryptedData` element like the one that follows.

```
<EncryptedData xmlns="http://www.w3.org/2001/04/xmlenc#"
  Type="URI" MimeType="MIME type" Encoding="URI">
    <EncryptionMethod Algorithm="URI"/>
    <ds:KeyInfo xmlns:ds="http://www.w3.org/2000/09/xmldsig#">
      <EncryptedKey>
        Base64-encoded, encrypted key value
      </EncryptedKey>
      <ds:KeyName>
        Name of the key used to encrypt this data
      </ds:KeyName>
      <ds:RetrievalMethod>
        Where to find the key
      </ds:RetrievalMethod>
    </ds:KeyInfo>
    <CipherData>
      <CipherValue>Base64-encoded, encrypted data</CipherValue>
        or
      <CipherReference
        URI="http://www.example.com/encrypteddata.dat"/>
    </CipherData>
</EncryptedData>
```

Each `EncryptedData` element represents one chunk of encrypted XML. This can decrypt to plain text, to a single element, to several elements, or to mixed content. The result of this replacement must be well-formed. That is, you cannot encrypt an attribute alone, or the start-tag of an element but not the end-tag. This is all sensible. It just means that structures you encrypt are the structures found in the XML document. The `Type` attribute indicates what was encrypted. It can have the following values.

- `http://www.w3.org/2001/04/xmlenc#Element`: A single element was encrypted.
- `http://www.w3.org/2001/04/xmlenc#Content`: A sequence of XML nodes was encrypted, potentially including any number of elements, text nodes, comments, and processing instructions in any order and combination.

At a minimum, the `EncryptedData` element has a `CipherData` child element. This contains either a `CipherValue` or a `CipherReference`. A `CipherValue` contains the encrypted data encoded in Base64. A `Cipher`

Reference points to the encrypted data using its URI attribute. The data is not included with the document. For example, consider the comic book order from Item 48, which is repeated in Example 49–1.

Example 49–1 | An Order Document

```xml
<?xml version="1.0"?>
<Order>
  <Item type="BackIssue">
    <Title>Fables</Title>
    <Issue>2</Issue>
    <Publisher>DC</Publisher>
  </Item>
  <Item type="BackIssue">
    <Title>Gen 13</Title>
    <Issue>46</Issue>
    <Publisher>Wildstorm</Publisher>
  </Item>
  <CreditCard type="VISA">
    <Name>Elliotte Rusty Harold</Name>
    <Number>5555 3142 2718 2998</Number>
    <Expires>
      <Month>06</Month>
      <Year>2006</Year>
    </Expires>
  </CreditCard>
</Order>
```

If I encrypted the content of the CreditCard element, the result would look something like Example 49–2 (depending on the choice of key and algorithm, of course).

Example 49–2 | Encrypting the Content of an Element

```xml
<?xml version="1.0"?>
<Order>
  <Item type="BackIssue">
    <Title>Fables</Title>
    <Issue>2</Issue>
    <Publisher>DC</Publisher>
  </Item>
  <Item type="BackIssue">
```

```
      <Title>Gen 13</Title>
      <Issue>46</Issue>
      <Publisher>Wildstorm</Publisher>
    </Item>
    <CreditCard type="VISA"><EncryptedData
      Id="ed1" Type="http://www.w3.org/2001/04/xmlenc#Content"
      xmlns="http://www.w3.org/2001/04/xmlenc#">
    <EncryptionMethod
      Algorithm="http://www.w3.org/2001/04/xmlenc#tripledes-cbc"/>
    <CipherData>
      <CipherValue>ZPbIV3QYoAK/m1c81yu+37mylmmvFocDas7BxR94FA0qjm/
6u0GY59lluoclaLiq/fGHXS8P69YShwIaehDGG2n56JS8B0/h3m1AHf5Ozm9zUop
gyqn7k8HcXAkB7oAFLiKvHc/R+ZjU8XpVJdCFfTjaJ3Jy4bQNR3TWrbmCTPK5//C
WedrnLuebpq2r88/y</CipherValue>
    </CipherData>
    </EncryptedData>
    </CreditCard>
</Order>
```

This would allow a process that did not have the key to know that the encrypted data is credit card information for a VISA card. However, it would not know the card number, the expiration date, or the cardholder's name.

If I encrypted the entire `CreditCard` element, the result would look like Example 49–3. Now you don't know for sure that the encrypted data is credit card information unless you know the decryption key.

Example 49–3 | Encrypting a Single Element

```
<?xml version="1.0"?>
<Order>
  <Item type="BackIssue">
    <Title>Fables</Title>
    <Issue>2</Issue>
    <Publisher>DC</Publisher>
  </Item>
  <Item type="BackIssue">
    <Title>Gen 13</Title>
    <Issue>46</Issue>
    <Publisher>Wildstorm</Publisher>
```

```
      </Item>
      <EncryptedData
        Id="ed1" Type="http://www.w3.org/2001/04/xmlenc#Element"
        xmlns="http://www.w3.org/2001/04/xmlenc#">
        <EncryptionMethod
          Algorithm="http://www.w3.org/2001/04/xmlenc#
          tripledes-cbc"/>
        <CipherData>
        <CipherValue>ZPbIV3QYoAK/m1c81yu+37mylmmvFocDas7BxR94FA0qjm/
6uOGY59lluoclaLiq/fGHXS8P69YShwIaehDGG2n56JS8B0/h3m1AHf5Ozm9zUop
gyqn7k8HcXAkB7oAFLiKvHc/R+ZjU8XpVJdCFfTjaJ3Jy4bQNR3TWrbmCTPK5//C
WedrnLuebpq2r88/y</CipherValue>
        </CipherData>
      </EncryptedData>
    </Order>
```

In some cases, it may be useful to include additional information beyond the encrypted data itself. An empty `EncryptionMethod` element specifies the algorithm that was used to encrypt the data so that it can more easily be decrypted. The `Algorithm` attribute contains a URI identifying the algorithm. There's no exhaustive list of these because new algorithms continue to be invented, but some common ones include the following:

- Triple DES: http://www.w3.org/2001/04/xmlenc#tripledes-cbc
- AES 128 bit: http://www.w3.org/2001/04/xmlenc#aes128-cbc
- AES 256 bit: http://www.w3.org/2001/04/xmlenc#aes256-cbc
- AES 192 bit: http://www.w3.org/2001/04/xmlenc#aes192-cbc

Depending on the algorithm, it may be useful to include either the actual key used or the name of the key. If the name of the key is included, presumably the recipient knows how to find the value of that key in some central repository. The actual value of the encryption key may be included for public key/private key systems since knowing the encryption key doesn't help you decrypt the message. Alternately, because public key cryptography is relatively slow, the actual message may be encoded using a symmetric cipher such as DES using a randomly chosen key. The random key is then encoded using the recipient's public key and stored in the key info. None of this information is required for XML encryption. All of it is allowed if you find it useful.

If present, such information is stored in a `KeyInfo` element in the `http://www.w3.org/2000/09/xmldsig#` namespace. As the URI suggests, this is the same `KeyInfo` element used in XML digital signatures. (See Item 48.) It can provide keys by name, reference, or value. Example 49–4 includes the RSA (public) key used to encrypt the data encoded by both name and value. If you have the private key that matches this public key, you can decrypt the information. Nobody else should be able to, at least not easily.

Example 49–4 | Bundling Key Info with the Encrypted Data

```xml
<?xml version="1.0"?>
<Order>
  <Item type="BackIssue">
    <Title>Fables</Title>
    <Issue>2</Issue>
    <Publisher>DC</Publisher>
  </Item>
  <Item type="BackIssue">
    <Title>Gen 13</Title>
    <Issue>46</Issue>
    <Publisher>Wildstorm</Publisher>
  </Item>
  <EncryptedData
    Id="ed1" Type="http://www.w3.org/2001/04/xmlenc#Element"
    xmlns="http://www.w3.org/2001/04/xmlenc#">
    <EncryptionMethod
       Algorithm="http://www.w3.org/2001/04/xmlenc#rsa-1_5"/>
    <KeyInfo xmlns="http://www.w3.org/2000/09/xmldsig#">
      <KeyName>Bob</KeyName>
      <KeyValue>
        <RSAKeyValue>
          <Modulus>
              V5foK5hhmbktQhyNdy/6LpQRhDUDsTvK+g9Ucj47es9AQJ3U
              xA7SEU+e0yQH5rm9kbCDN9o3aPIo7HbP7tX6WOocLZAtNfyx
              SZDU16ksL6WjubafOqNEpcwR3RdFsT7bCqnXPBe5ELh5u4VE
              y19MzxkXRgrMvavzyBpVRgBUwUl=
          </Modulus>
          <Exponent>AQAB</Exponent>
        </RSAKeyValue>
      </KeyValue>
    </KeyInfo>
```

```
<CipherData>
  <CipherValue>
    ZPbIV3QYoAK/m1c81yu+37mylmmvFocDas7BxR94FA0qjm/6u0GY59l
    luoclaLiq/fGHXS8P69YShwIaehDGG2n56JS8B0/h3m1AHf5Ozm9zUo
    vHc/R+ZjU8XpVJdCFfTjaJ3Jy4bQNR3TWrbmCTPK5//CWedrnLuebpq
    2r88/y
  </CipherValue>
</CipherData>
  </EncryptedData>
</Order>
```

For a symmetric key, you'd normally just use the name you had previously agreed on for the key with the recipient. Exactly how keys are named is beyond the scope of the XML Encryption specification.

Encryption Tools

Encryption software, whether for XML or otherwise, is restricted by law in many jurisdictions, including the United States. Consequently, encryption software is less available than it should be, and it is often excessively difficult to install or configure. Vendors have to jump through hoops to be allowed to publish, sell, and export their products. The exact number of hoops varies a lot from one jurisdiction to the next. Thus, unfortunately, XML encryption tools and libraries are less advanced than they otherwise would be.

Almost all implementations of XML encryption at the current time seem to be Java class libraries, although that's likely to change in the future. The only non-Java library I've found so far is Aleksey Sanin's XMLSec (http://www.aleksey.com/xmlsec), an open source implementation of XML Encryption for C and C++ that sits on top of the Gnome project's libxml and libxslt.

Moving into the Java realm, there are a lot more choices. Baltimore Technologies' KeyTools XML (http://www.baltimore.com/keytools/xml/index. asp) is a commercial offering written in Java that supports both XML encryption and digital signatures on top of the Java Cryptography Extension (JCE). Phaos has released a commercial XML Security Suite (http:// phaos.com/products/category/xml.html) for Java that also supports encryption and digital signatures.

Possibly the most advanced open source offering at the time of this writing is XML-Security (http://xml.apache.org/security/) from the Apache XML Project. This is the same library discussed in Item 48 for producing digital signatures. It is a Java class library that runs on top of Java 1.3.1 and later. It relies on Sun's Java Cryptography Extension to perform the necessary math. The preferred implementation of this API is from the Legion of the Bouncy Castle, which, being based in Australia, doesn't have to submit to U.S. export laws. The Apache XML project can't legally ship the Bouncy Castle JCE with its software, but the Ant build file will download it for you automatically.

IBM's XSS4J also implements various XML encryption algorithms and has a slightly better user interface than XML-Security (that is, it has a user interface). It was used to encrypt the examples shown in this chapter. XSS4J prefers different implementations of the JCE. It can run with Sun's own JCE, but it wants the IBM (http://www7b.boulder.ibm.com/wsdd/wspvtdevkit-info.html) or IAIK (http://jce.iaik.tugraz.at/products/01_jce/) implementations, especially if you want to use RSA encryption or key exchange.

The complexity of the JCE has made most implementations noninteroperable at the API level. However, at the XML document level, matters are much better. Encrypted XML produced by one tool can be read by different tools, provided they support the same algorithms. If you stick to the required algorithms (basically AES and Triple DES for encryption, RSA for key exchange, SHA-1 for message digest, and Base64 for encoding), your documents should be able to be easily encrypted and decrypted by anyone who knows the right key.

Item 50 Compress if Space Is a Problem

Verbosity is a common criticism of XML. However, in practice, most developers' intuitions about the verbosity of XML are wrong. XML documents are almost always smaller than the equivalent binary file format. The sad truth is that most modern software pays little to no attention to optimizing documents for space. However, if your XML documents are so big or your available space so small that size is a real issue, you can simply gzip (or zip or bzip or compress) the XML documents.

For example, consider Microsoft Word. A 70-page chapter including about a dozen screen shots and diagrams from one of my previous books occupied 6.7MB. Opening that document in OpenOffice 1.0 and immediately resaving it into OpenOffice's native compressed XML format reduced the file's size to 522K, a savings of more than 90%. I unzipped the OpenOffice document into its component parts, and the resulting directory was also 6.7MB, almost exactly the same size as the original binary file format. Most of that space was taken up by the pictures.

For another example, consider a typical database. One of the fundamental principles of a modern DBMS is that the physical storage is decoupled from the logical representation. This allows the database to optimize performance by carefully deciding where to place which fields on the disk. Holes are left in the files to allow for insertion of additional data in the future. Indexes are created across the data. Some data may even be duplicated in multiple places if that helps optimize performance. But one thing that is not optimized is storage space. A typical relational database uses several times to several dozen times the space that would be required purely to store the data without worrying about optimization.

As an experiment, I took a small FileMaker Pro 6 database containing information about 650 books and exported it to XML. The original database was 1.5MB. The exported XML document was only 1.0MB, a savings of 33%. This is actually on the small side of the savings you can expect by moving to XML, mostly because FileMaker does a better than average job of cramming data into limited space. It's not uncommon to produce XML documents that are as small as 10% of the size of the original database.

Information theory tells us that given a perfectly efficient compression algorithm, two documents containing the same information will compress to the same final size, regardless of format. Reasonably fast compression algorithms like gzip and bzip2 aren't perfectly efficient. Nonetheless, in actual tests when I've compared gzipped XML documents to the gzipped binary equivalents, most files were within 10% of each other in size. Whether the gzipped binary file is 10% smaller or 10% larger than the gzipped XML equivalent seems unpredictable. Sometimes it's one way, sometimes the other; but at this point the details are too small to care about.

Java includes built-in support for zip, gzip, and inflate/deflate algorithms in the java.util.zip package. These are all implemented as filter streams, so it's straightforward to hook one up to your original source of data and then pass it to a parser that reads from or writes to the stream as normal. For example, suppose you've built up a DOM `Document` object named `doc` in memory and you want to serialize it into a file named `data.xml.gz` in the current working directory. The data in the file will be gzipped. First open a `FileOutputStream` to the file, chain this to a `GZipOutputStream`, and then write the document onto the `Output Stream` as normal. For example, the following code uses Xerces's `XMLSerializer` class to write a DOM `Document` object into a compressed file.

```
Document doc;
// load the document...
try {
  OutputStream fout    = new FileOutputStream("data.xml.gz");
  OutputStream out     = new GZipOutputStream(fout);
  OutputFormat format  = new OutputFormat(document);
  XMLSerializer output = new XMLSerializer(out, format);
  output.serialize(doc);
}
catch (IOException ex) {
  System.err.println(ex);
}
```

From this point forward you neither need to know nor care that the data is compressed. It's all done behind the scenes automatically.

Input is equally easy. For example, suppose later you want to read `data.xml.gz` back into your program. Decompression adds just one line of code to hook up the `GZipInputStream`.

```
InputStream fin = new FileInputStream("data.xml.gz");
InputStream in  = new GZipInputStream(fin);
DocumentBuilderFactory factory
   = DocumentBuilderFactory.newInstance();
DocumentBuilder parser = factory.newDocumentBuilder();
Document doc = parser.parse(in);
// work with the document...
```

Of course, the same techniques work if you need to read or write from the network instead of a file. You'll just hook up the filter streams to network streams rather than file streams.

Similar techniques are available for C and C++. Although compression is not a standard part of the C or C++ libraries, Greg Roelofs, Mark Adler, and Jean-loup Gailly's zlib library (http://www.gzip.org/zlib/) should satisfy most needs. zlib is available in source and binary forms for pretty much all modern platforms. Indeed, the java.util.zip package is just a wrapper around calls to this library. Python includes the `GzipFile` class for convenient access to this library. The Compress::Zlib module available from CPAN performs the same task for Perl. .NET aficionados can use Mike Krueger's open source #ziplib (http://www.icsharpcode.net /OpenSource/SharpZipLib/) instead.

Finally, if you're serving data over the Web, modern web servers and browsers have built-in support for compression. They can transparently compress and decompress documents as necessary before transmitting them. Since bandwidth tends to be a lot more expensive and limited on both ends than CPU speed, this is normally a win-win proposition.

By no means should you let fear of fatness stop you from using XML file formats. Most of the time the fear is unfounded. Even in those rare cases where it isn't, standard compression algorithms neatly solve the problem.

Recommended Reading

Bray, Tim (ed.). *Internet Media Type registration, consistency of use.* World Wide Web Consortium, September 4, 2002. Available online at http://www.w3.org/2001/tag/2002/0129-mime.

Dürst, Martin, and Asmus Freytag. *Unicode in XML and Other Markup Languages.* Unicode Consortium and World Wide Web Consortium, February 2002. Available online at http://www.w3.org/TR/unicode-xml/.

Dürst, Martin, Asmus Freytag, Richard Ishida, Tex Texin, Misha Wolf, and François Yergeau (eds.). *Character Model for the World Wide Web 1.0.* World Wide Web Consortium, April 2002. Available online at http://www.w3.org/TR/charmod/.

Hollenbeck, Scott, Larry Masinter, and Marshall Rose. *Guidelines for the Use of Extensible Markup Language (XML) within IETF Protocols.* Internet Engineering Task Force, January 2003. Available online at http://www.ietf.org/rfc/rfc3470.txt.

Jelliffe, Rick. *The XML and SGML Cookbook.* Upper Saddle River, NJ: Prentice Hall, 1999.

Kohn, Dan, Murata Makoto, Simon St. Laurent, and E. Whitehead. *XML Media Types.* Internet Engineering Task Force, January 2001. Available online at http://www.ietf.org/rfc/rfc3023.txt.

Megginson, David. *Structuring XML Documents.* Upper Saddle River, NJ: Prentice Hall, 1998.

The MITRE Corporation and Members of the xml-dev Mailing List. *XML Schemas: Best Practices.* Available online at http://www.xfront.com/BestPracticesHomepage.html.

Spencer, Paul (ed.). *e-Government Schema Guidelines for XML.* December 2002. Available online at http://www.e-envoy.gov.uk/oee/oee.nsf/sections/guidelines-top/$file/guidelines_index.htm.

The Unicode Consortium. *The Unicode Standard, Version 3.0.* Boston, MA: Addison-Wesley, 2000.

Walsh, Norman (ed.). *Using Qualified Names (QNames) as Identifiers in Content.* World Wide Web Consortium, July 25, 2002. Available online at http://www.w3.org/2001/tag/doc/qnameids.html.

Index

A

Absolute namespace URI, 114
AccountInfo element, 128
Adams, Douglas, 242
AddClosingBalance entity, 40–41
Address vocabulary, 144–145
AddType directive, 251
Adler, Mark, 286
AElfred, 90
AES 128 bit algorithm, 280
AES 192 bit algorithm, 280
AES 256 bit algorithm, 280
Algorithm attribute, 280
α entity reference, 108
alternate pseudo attribute, 248
Amount element, 60
& entity reference, xviii
Ancillary documents, identifying version, 146–147
Apache ASP module, 245
Apache Commons catalog, 261
Apache Tomcat, 245
Apache web server, 244–245, 251
Apache XML Project, 274, 283
APIs
  character references, xix
  entity references, xix
  exposing information in XML declaration, xxvi
  hiding XML behind, 229
  reporting entities or entity references, xviii
  shielding developers from raw XML, 227

standard, 229
  XML declarations, 2
' entity reference, xviii
Application domain, semantics of, 79
application/beep+xml MIME type, 250
application/cnrp+xml MIME type, 250
application/mathml+xml MIME type, 251
application/rdf+xml MIME type, 251
Applications
  accessing all data in document, 184
  common prefixes, 118–119
  conditional sections, 46
  defining appropriate semantics, 80
  defining separate modules, 46
  fitting document structures loosely, 196
  identifying version in ancillary documents, 146–147
  including and not including modules, 46–47
  libraries performing best for, 170–171
  modified copy of DTD, 191
  navigating backward and up in tree, 184
  portable across languages, 184
  public ID, 145–146
  restricting syntax, 82
  significance of white space, 53

speed, 178–183
  tree-oriented API, 181–182
application/xhtml+xml MIME type, 250, 254
application/xml MIME type, 249–250, 253
application/xml-external-parsed-entity MIME type, 250
application/xslt+xml MIME type, 251
ASCII
  encoding text, 109–111
  marking up with, 5–10
  markup, 214
  UTF-8 is strict superset of, 215
ASCII character set and namespace URIs, 116
Attr object, 184
Attribute value, xvii
Attributes, xvii
  adding content, 74
  child elements instead of, xvii
  crucial, 187
  dividing citations into, 72–73
  housekeeping information, 71
  name of, xvii
  namespace prefixes in values, 121–123
  normalizing values, 55–56
  not supporting structure, 62
  order of, xvii
  overabbreviated, unclear names, 227
  parameterizing, 35

289

ELLIOTTE RUSTY HAROLD

PROCESSING XML WITH JAVA™

A Guide to SAX, DOM, JDOM, JAXP, and TrAX

© 2003, PAPER, 1120 PAGES,
0-201-77186-1, $54.99

Written for Java programmers who want to integrate XML into their systems, this practical, comprehensive guide and reference shows how to process XML documents with the Java programming language. It leads experienced Java developers beyond the basics of XML, allowing them to design sophisticated XML applications and parse complicated documents.

Processing XML with Java™ provides a brief review of XML fundamentals, including XML syntax; DTDs, schemas, and validity; stylesheets; and the XML protocols XML-RPC, SOAP, and RSS. The core of the book comprises in-depth discussions on the key XML APIs Java programmers must use to create and manipulate XML files with Java. These include the Simple API for XML (SAX), the Document Object Model (DOM), and JDOM (a Java native API). In addition, the book covers many useful supplements to these core APIs, including XPath, XSLT, TrAX, and JAXP.

Practical in focus, *Processing XML with Java™* is filled with over two hundred examples that demonstrate how to accomplish various important tasks related to file formats, data exchange, document transformation, and database integration. You will learn how to read and write XML documents with Java code, convert legacy flat files into XML documents, communicate with network servers that send and receive XML data, and much more. Readers will find detailed coverage of the following:

- How to choose the right API for the job
- Reading documents with SAX
- SAX filters
- Validation in several schema languages
- DOM implementations for Java
- The DOM Traversal Module
- Output from DOM
- Reading and writing XML documents with JDOM
- Searching XML documents with XPath
- Combining XSLT transforms with Java code
- TrAX, the Transformations API for XML
- JAXP, the Java API for XML Processing

In addition, the book includes a convenient quick reference that summarizes the major elements of all the XML APIs discussed. A related Web site, located at http://www.cafeconleche.org/books/xmljava/, contains the entire book in electronic format, as well as updates and links referenced in the book.

With thorough coverage of the key XML APIs and a practical, task-oriented approach, *Processing XML with Java™* is a valuable resource for all Java programmers who need to work with XML.

Elliotte Rusty Harold is an internationally respected writer, programmer, and educator. He is an Adjunct Professor of Computer Science at Polytechnic University in Brooklyn, where he lectures on Java and object-oriented programming. His Cafe con Leche Web site has become one of the most popular sites for information on XML. In addition, he is the author and coauthor of numerous books, the most recent of which are *The XML Bible* (John Wiley & Sons, 2001) and *XML in a Nutshell* (O'Reilly, 2002).

Addison
Wesley